FLOWERS IN
WATERCOLOUR

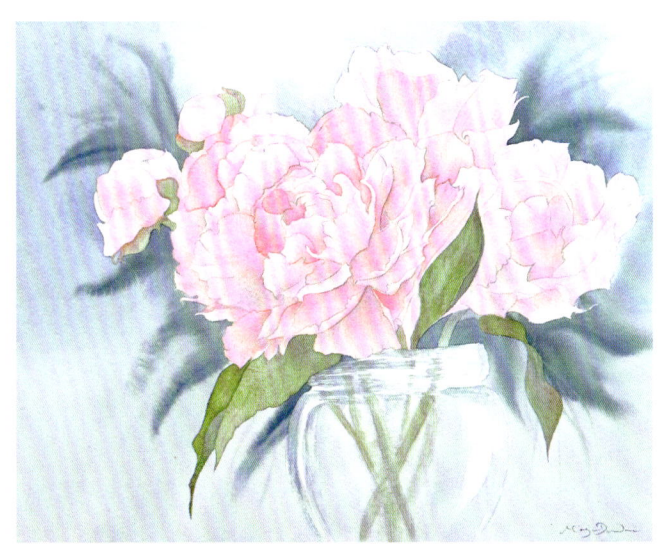

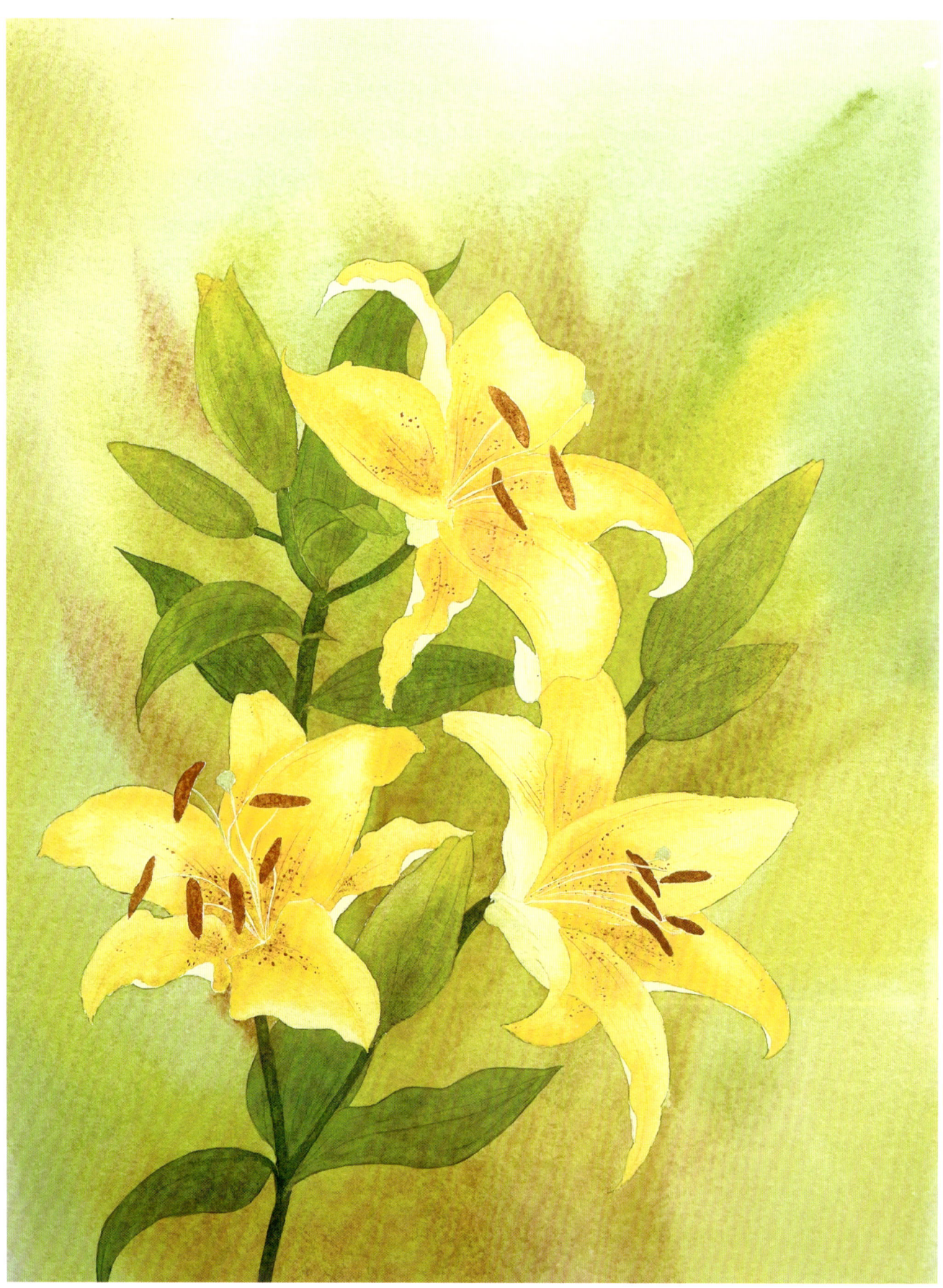

FLOWERS IN WATERCOLOUR

TECHNIQUES AND TUTORIALS
FOR THE COMPLETE BEGINNER

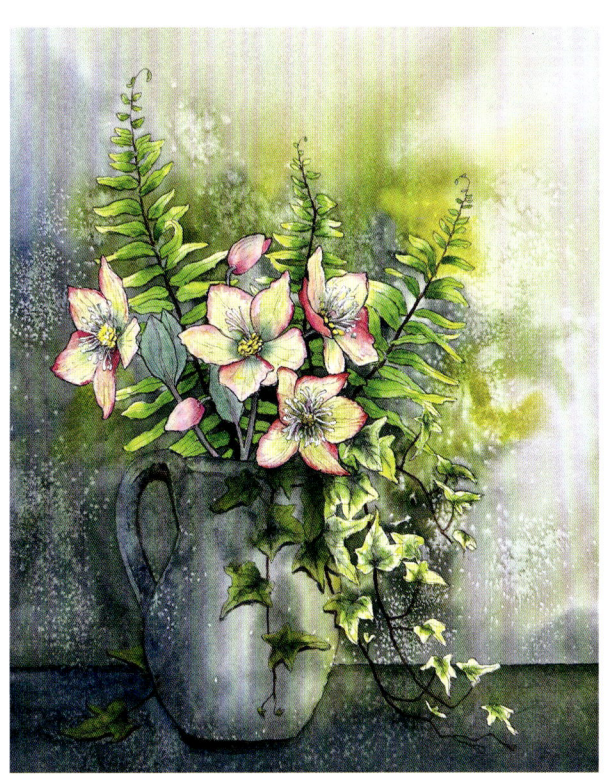

LOIS DAVIDSON AND MORGAINE DAVIDSON

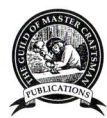

First published 2025 by
Guild of Master Craftsman Publications Ltd
Castle Place, 166 High Street, Lewes,
East Sussex, BN7 1XU, UK
www.gmcbooks.com

ISBN 978 1 78494 713 2

The EEA authorised representative is Authorised Rep Compliance Ltd.
Ground Floor, 71 Baggot Street Lower, Dublin, DO2 P593, Ireland
www.arccompliance.com

A catalogue record for this book is available from the British Library.

PUBLISHER **Jonathan Bailey**
PRODUCTION MANAGER **Jim Bulley**
MANAGING ART EDITOR **Robin Shields**
SENIOR PROJECT EDITOR **Tom Kitch**
DESIGNER **Ellie Smith**
EDITOR **Theresa Bebbington**
PHOTOGRAPHY **Morgaine Davidson and Lois Davidson**

The publisher would like to thank Belinka/Shutterstock (page 19, bottom) and
Yulcha/Shutterstock (page 45, top) for permission to reproduce copyright material.

Set in Baskerville
Colour origination by GMC Reprographics
Printed and bound in China

Dedicated to the
memory of Chya,
the studio cat;
beloved companion
and friend.

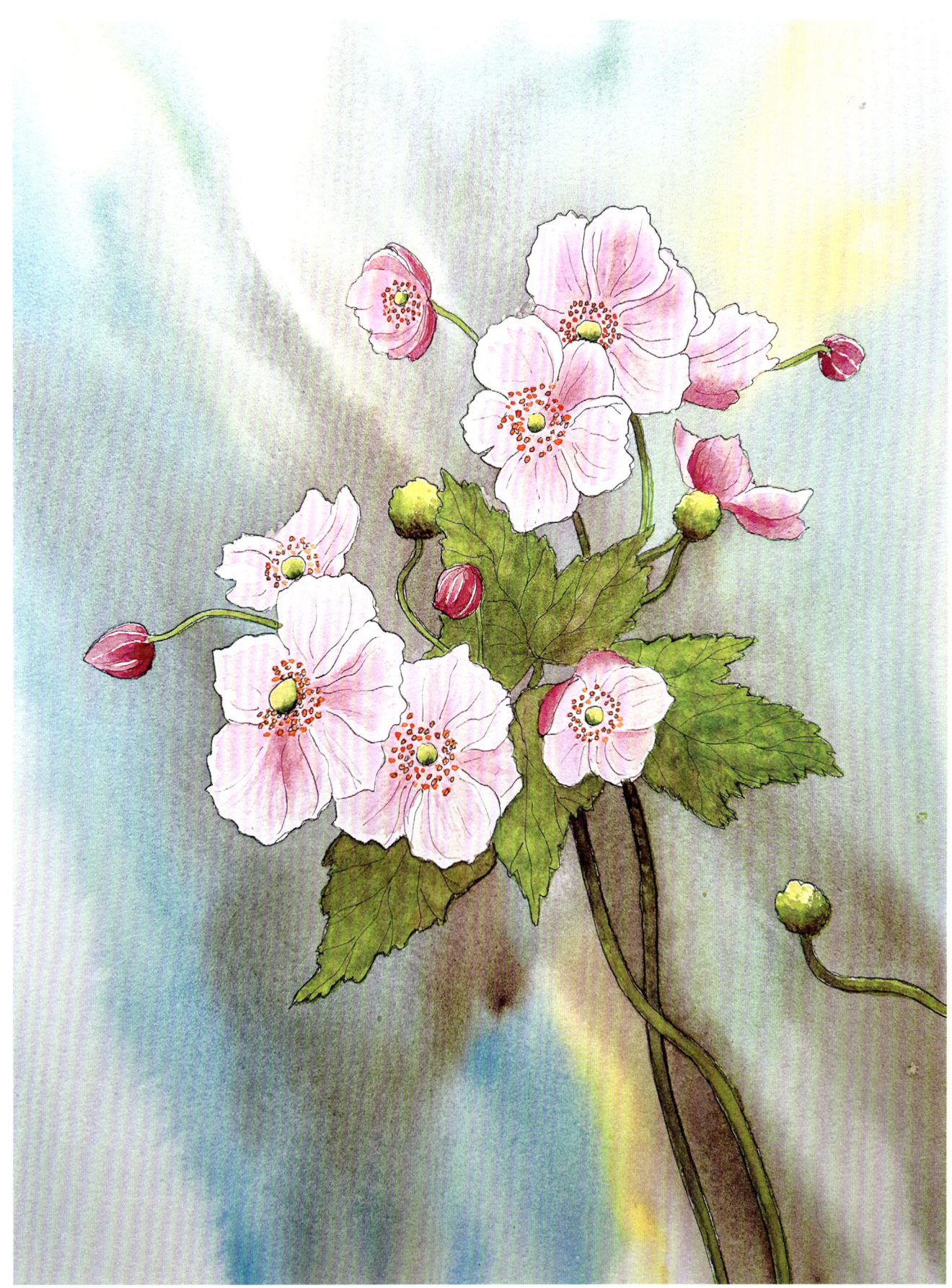

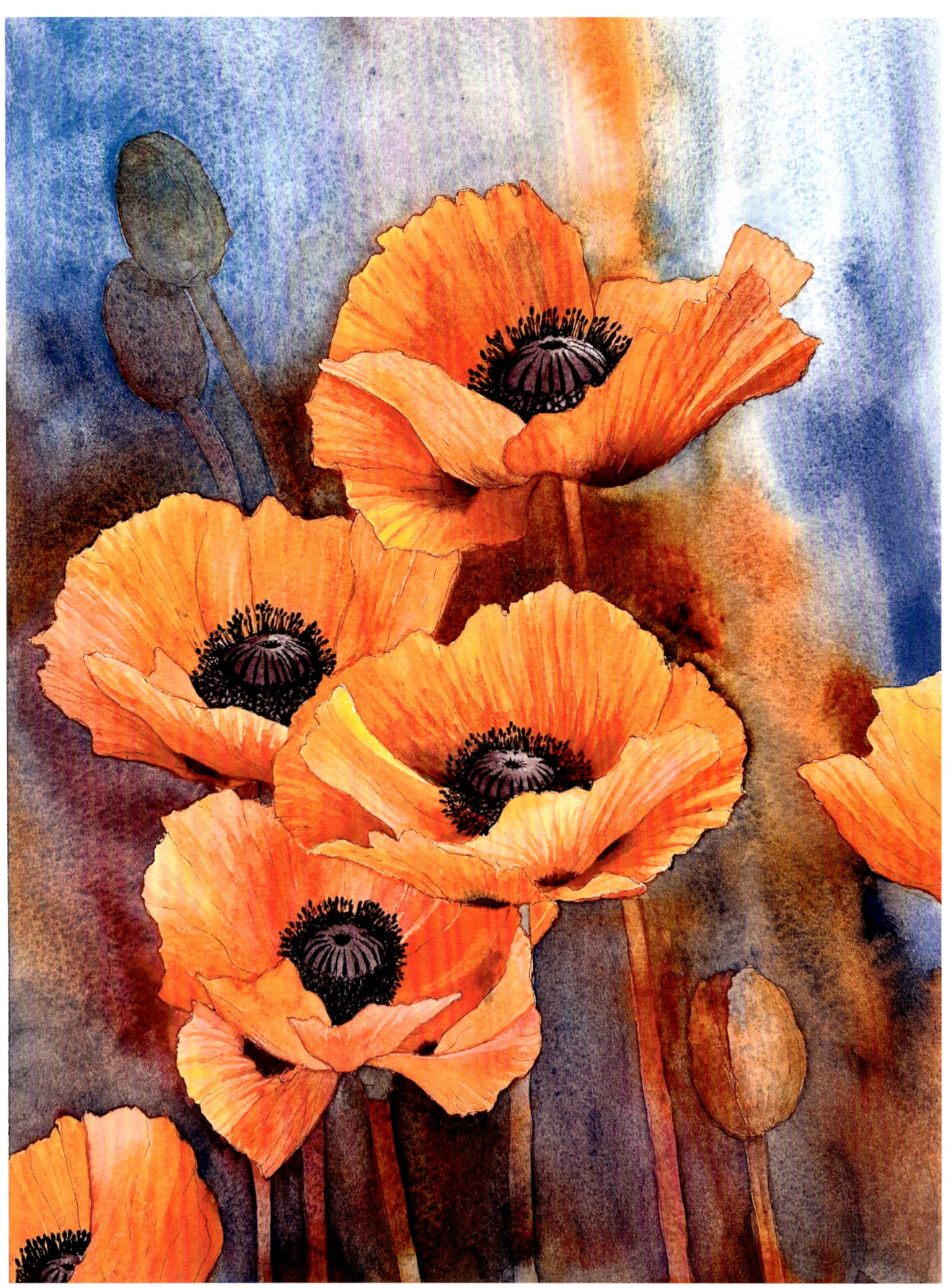

Contents

Introduction

From the tiniest to the largest, from the humble, cheerful daisy to the graceful calla lily, flowers have long been a source of inspiration for all manner of artists across time, whether they be poets, playwrights or painters. Today, we are fortunate to have access to a myriad of astonishing blooms from across our entire planet, providing an enormous range of inspiration for all artists. While there are, of course, more species of flowering plants than could possibly be covered in a single volume, this comprehensive beginner's reference to painting flowers in watercolour is designed to offer the right tools, guidance and inspiration needed to get started.

As a medium, watercolour is ideally suited for capturing flowers. The paint's transparent nature lends the colours a unique luminosity, a quality often seen in many flowers: for instance, in the translucent, diaphanous petals of the classic red poppy, or the sheer brilliance of colour in a flamboyant bouquet of parrot tulips. While this book is designed to act as a guide to flower painting, it also provides an introduction to watercolour painting in general, offering information on basic equipment, useful techniques and sketchbook practice. In addition, you'll find ten step-by-step unique tutorials to give you the tools and guidance to tackle a wide variety of flower paintings.

Together, we have carefully composed this book in a way that is designed to help a fledgling painter approach what can, admittedly, be an intimidating and fiddly subject matter. Even the seemingly simplest flowers, once you take a closer look, can be remarkably complex in their construction; however, by breaking our paintings down into easy-to-follow steps, and offering a variety of templates to use as painting guides, this book will help you learn the skills to approach any flower painting with confidence: from delicate wild flowers to garden favourites and exotic beauties. Most importantly, remember to enjoy the sheer beauty and magnificence of our subject matter: flowers are, after all, one of the most astonishingly lovely things in the entire world, and successfully bringing them to life using paint and paper is a joy.

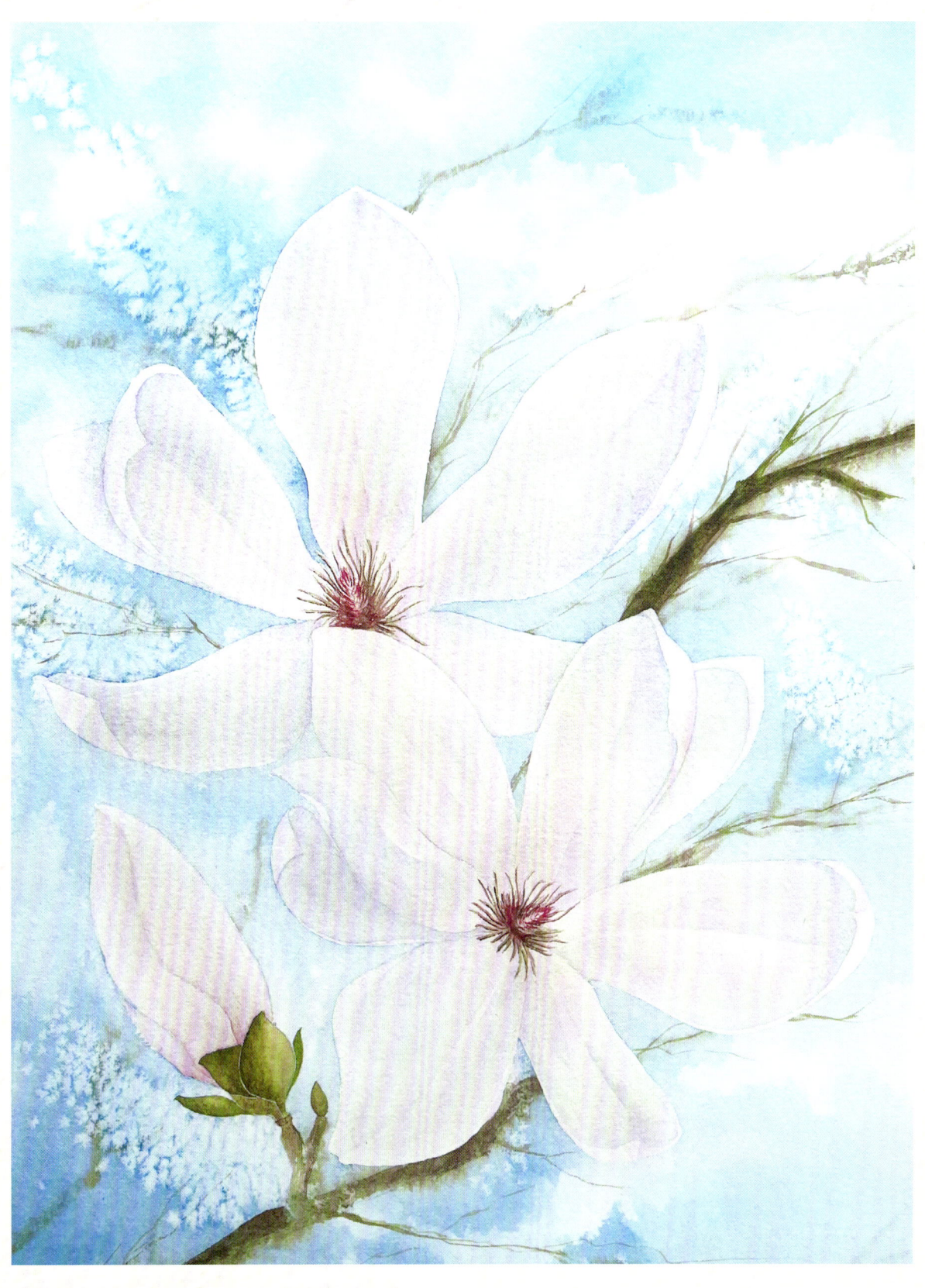

Equipment and Materials

You don't need a huge array of materials and equipment for painting flowers in watercolour, but it can be a little confusing when confronted by the immense range of art materials available. In this section, we'll share a little about what we use for all the projects to help you get started.

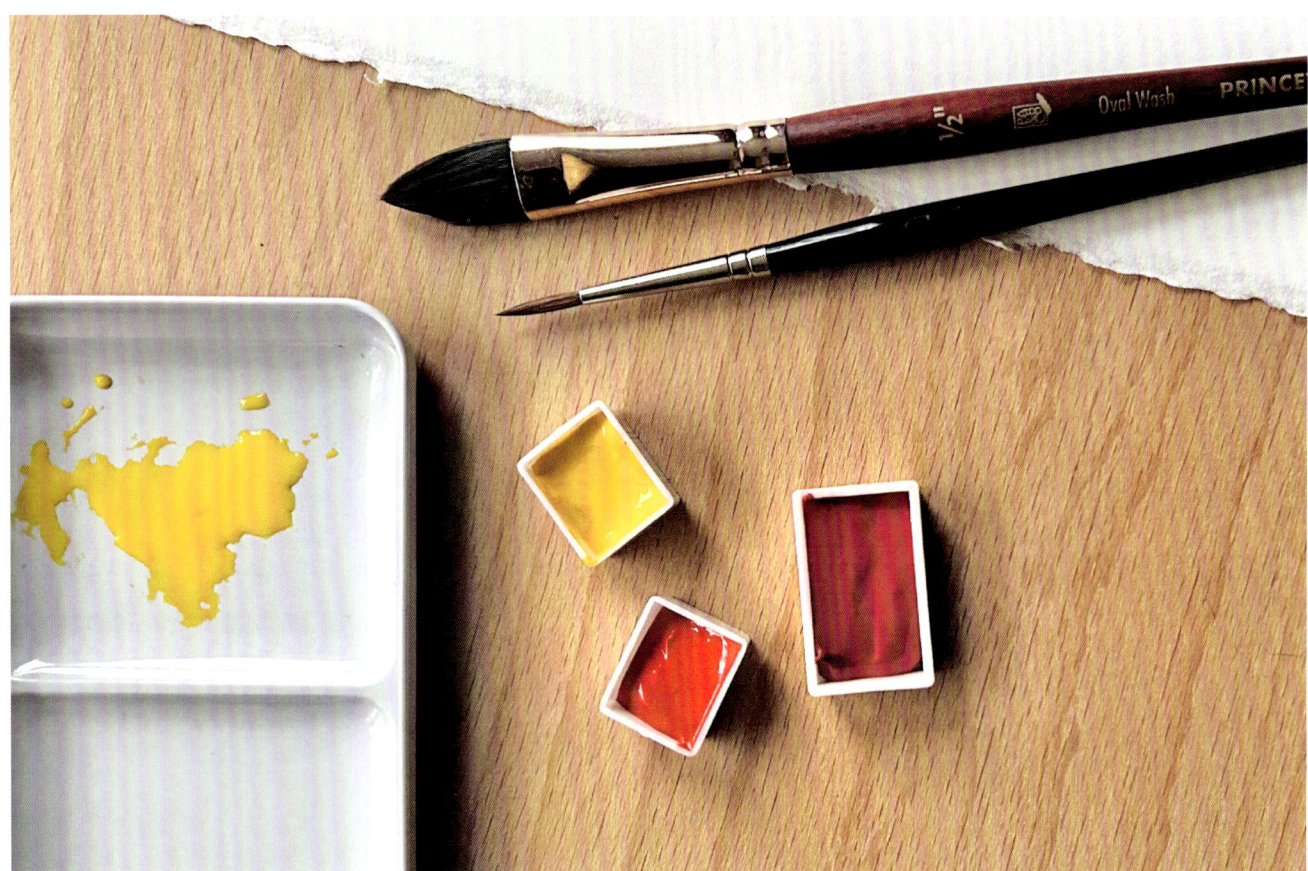

Paint and palettes

Watercolour paints can be found as tubes of paint or in dried pans/half pans; either type is suitable. Tube paints are fresh and ready to go with the addition of a little water, whereas pans need to be activated, either by brushing water over the surface of the pan or spritzing with a water misting spray to re-wet the dried pigments.

Watercolour paint comes in two distinct grades: artist quality or student quality. Artist-quality paints contain purer pigment loads but are quite expensive; however, a little goes a long way, so even a small pan will last a long time. Student-quality paints are comparatively inexpensive and come in the full range of colours. Because they are cheaper, there's less worry about waste as you practise and develop your skills.

Our colours

Along with a veritable rainbow of vibrant colours, we have selected a few pre-mixed greens and some subtle, earthy colours to complement the brighter hues. Don't worry if you don't have all these colours – you can use anything similar.

You will often find there can be subtle variation in tone and hue between paints bought from different brands or manufacturers, despite the colours having the same names. A handy way to combat this is to pay attention to the pigment numbers of your chosen paints, which can be found on the packaging. Single pigment colours tend to be more useful for creating your own colour mixes, as they're less likely to turn 'muddy' – for example, the Transparent Yellow we use is a single pigment paint, made with pigment PY150.

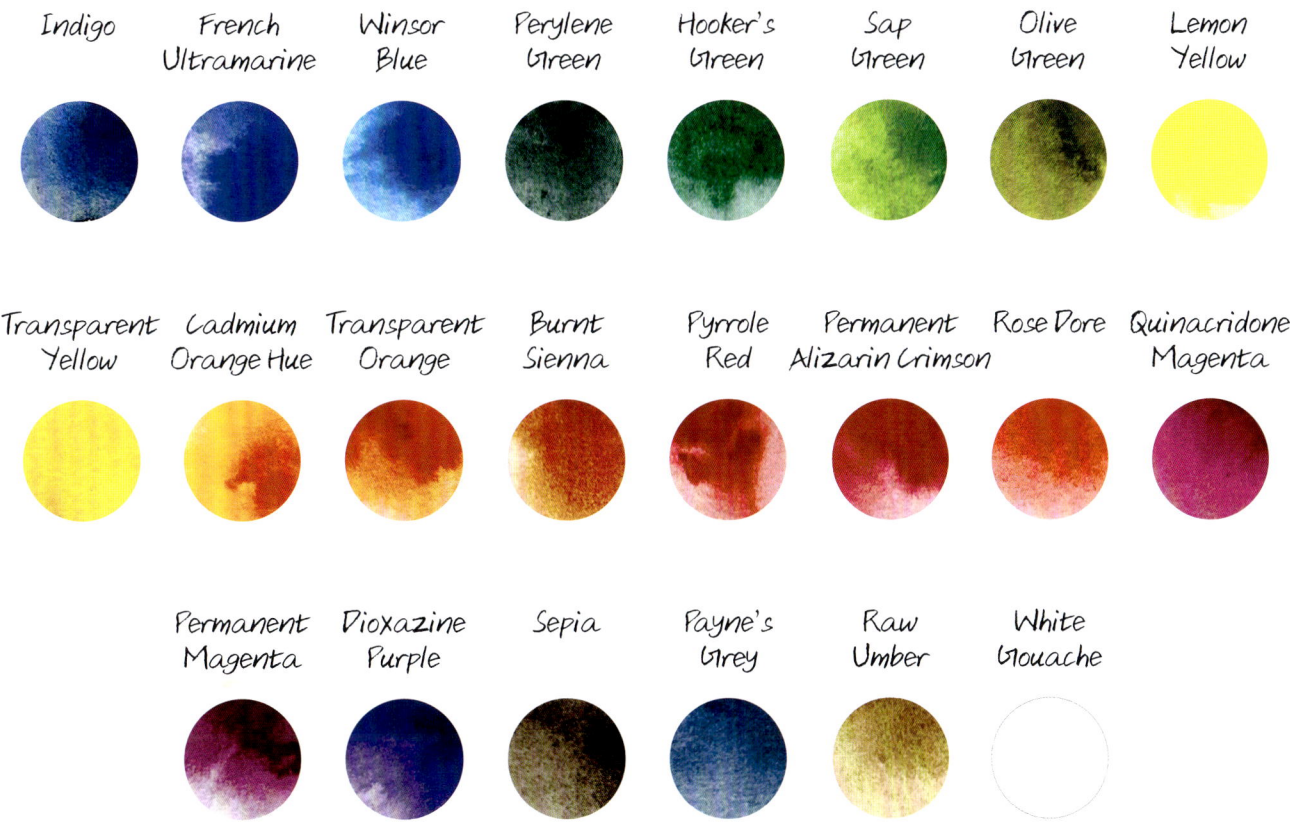

Indigo · French Ultramarine · Winsor Blue · Perylene Green · Hooker's Green · Sap Green · Olive Green · Lemon Yellow

Transparent Yellow · Cadmium Orange Hue · Transparent Orange · Burnt Sienna · Pyrrole Red · Permanent Alizarin Crimson · Rose Dore · Quinacridone Magenta

Permanent Magenta · Dioxazine Purple · Sepia · Payne's Grey · Raw Umber · White Gouache

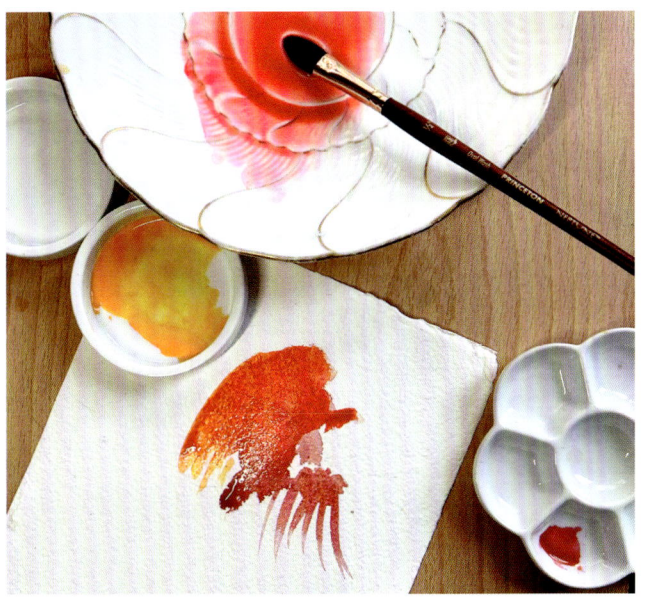

Paint palettes

We recommend a palette with a variety of sizes of mixing wells for the projects: large wells for mixing background washes and smaller ones for petal and leaf mixes.

Plates and saucers can be used as palettes, as long as the mixing area is white, as this allows you to judge the true qualities of the colours and blends as you mix.

Be mindful of the quantity of water you use while mixing colours. Too much, and the mix will end up pale and watery; too little, and the paint will remain thick and unworkable. For those just beginning their watercolour journey, we recommend using a palette with larger mixing wells, as this will make it easier to test and adjust the consistency of your colour mixes. If you do feel uncertain about the consistency or tone of a particular mix, check it first by doing a couple of quick swatches in your sketchbook.

Watercolour paper

Watercolour paper is designed especially for wet media, to allow the paint to flow on the surface as well as sink into the pores of the paper, giving the transparent luminosity and flow of colour that is characteristic of watercolour painting.

It comes in a choice of weights or thicknesses, and three different surface textures: smooth hot pressed, medium-textured cold pressed (also called NOT), and rough, which is heavily textured. It can be made from cotton, cellulose pulp or a mixture of the two.

We will be using 140lb (300gsm) weight hot-pressed watercolour paper for the projects. We find that the smooth surface works well for creating luminous and interesting background washes, as well as for soft blends and crisper detail where needed. However, you can use cold pressed paper if you prefer a little texture.

All the projects are painted on 11 x 15in (28 x 38cm) paper, but feel free to use whatever size you prefer.

Watercolour paper can be pre-stretched to avoid the buckling associated with watercolour painting, but we find that 140lb/300gsm weight paper works well un-stretched: it buckles a little when wet but then usually dries flat.

Tip

To pre-stretch watercolour paper, evenly soak both sides with clean water, remove any excess water from the edges with a damp sponge, and tape the paper to a clean board with brown gummed paper tape (you can obtain this tape from art suppliers). Once dry, the paper will remain flat as you paint on it.

Sketchbooks

Sketchbooks are an invaluable tool for practising and planning, and they come in a wide variety of shapes and sizes.

If you want to take one out and about with you, then something small and portable is ideal, but indoor sketchbooks can be any size that you find useful. Sketchbooks come with a wide range of different papers such as drawing paper, watercolour paper and mixed media paper. We suggest you use watercolour or mixed media paper because they can be used with wet media as well as dry media such as pencils and fine-liner pens.

Cold press (NOT) paper is most commonly found in watercolour sketchbooks, but they also come with hot press (smooth) or rough textured paper as well. For flower painting or botanical-style illustrations, we recommend a smoother-textured paper, such as hot press.

Paintbrushes

You don't need every paintbrush available, but having a small selection will allow you to achieve a mixture of results. We use the larger paintbrushes for pre-wetting the paper, painting background washes and softening transitions between colour or tone. The smaller paintbrushes are perfect for creating petal shapes, leaves, and adding colour and tone to aspects of a painting, while the size 0 detail brush is perfect for finishing touches, fine details and neatening up edges.

The brushes you will need for the projects are:

1 Size 20 mop brush

2 Small oval wash brush

3 Small sword liner brush

4 Size 2 quill brush

5 Size 3 round brush

6 Size 0 round detail brush

7 Size 2 fan brush

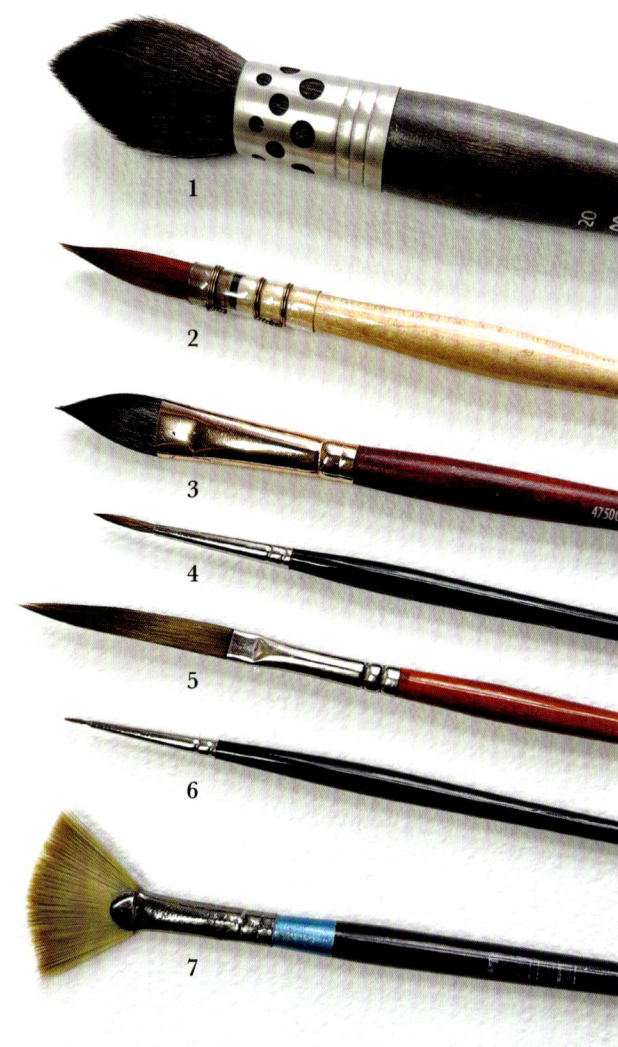

SIZE 20 MOP BRUSH

This is a large, round, soft brush which is perfect for holding enough paint and water to quickly cover a large area of paper. It's particularly useful for adding swathes of textural background colour, as its pointed tip makes the mop a versatile tool for creating shape and pattern.

SMALL OVAL WASH BRUSH

This particular shape of brush is much favoured by botanical artists, and is also sometimes called a cats-tongue brush. The oval shape, combined with a pointed tip, is designed to mimic the graceful curves of petals and leaves, and allows such shapes to be painted in a single stroke.

SMALL SWORD LINER BRUSH

This slender, shapely brush is designed for painting long, unbroken lines. By varying the pressure of the brushstroke, a painter may vary the width and curve of the stroke, to produce a variety of unbroken flourishes and calligraphic marks.

SIZE 2 QUILL BRUSH

This is a wonderful all-round workhorse of a brush, which combines decent water-holding qualities with a nice fine point, allowing you to work from large to small without having to constantly switch brushes.

SIZE 3 ROUND BRUSH

This is a small and versatile brush, with a fine, rounded point. It is perfect for painting small, delicate flower shapes such as petals and stems.

SIZE 0 ROUND DETAIL BRUSH

Use this tiny brush to create fine lines in areas that are too small to wield the sword liner brush, such as the delicate veining across small petals and leaves. It also works beautifully to drop small amounts of colour into a specific area when painting wet-in-wet (see page 22).

SIZE 2 FAN BRUSH

This is a handy little techniques brush with wide-splayed bristles. This makes it perfect for adding spatter detail into paintings, as the wide spread of bristles allows for a delicate droplet pattern that appears pleasingly random and non-directional. To create delicate spatter detail, fill the fan brush with paint that is roughly the consistency of ink, then tap it against your finger (or the handle of another brush) to release a small spray of tiny droplets.

Masking equipment

The projects use masking fluid to preserve white areas in the paper, allowing you to paint freely over these protected areas and create all sorts of beautiful background effects.

Keep a small old brush with a good point for applying the masking fluid, as it can ruin brushes if it dries in the hairs. To help protect the brush, rub a little brush soap or hand soap into the hairs before dipping into the masking fluid, and wash brushes immediately after use with a little more soap.

While dry masking fluid can be rubbed away with a clean finger, we recommend using an adhesive eraser (also known as a rubber cement pickup) as it removes the dried fluid more cleanly, with less chance of damaging the paper.

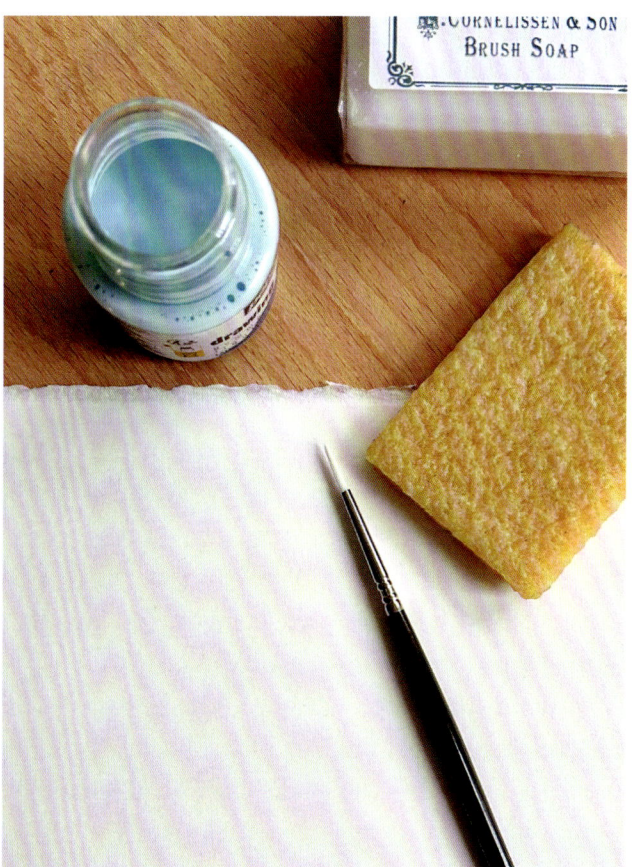

Tip

It is very important to test whether your watercolour paper is compatible with masking fluid before you start painting. Apply a little of the fluid to your paper, allow it to dry, then paint over it and leave to dry overnight. The next day, remove the mask by rubbing gently with the corner of the adhesive eraser. If the removal process causes the paper to tear or become damaged, that paper isn't suitable for using with masking fluid.

Other equipment

PENCILS AND FINE-LINER PENS

A couple of different grades of pencil are useful for sketching and preliminary drawings: a softish grade such as a 2B is suitable for sketching and for the transfer process, and a slightly harder grade HB pencil is good for creating lightly drawn outlines. Four projects use the 'ink and watercolour' technique, so you'll need waterproof black fine-liner pens in sizes 0.1mm and 0.3mm.

ERASERS

No doubt you'll want to make a change or two to a pencil sketch, in which case you'll find an eraser is helpful. A soft putty eraser won't damage the soft surface of the watercolour paper, but an ordinary eraser can be used – remember to brush away the crumbs left behind before painting.

TRACING PAPER

Translucent tracing paper can be an invaluable tool for transferring your finished sketches to your watercolour paper (see page 21), to avoid over-using erasers and potentially damaging the softer surface of the paper.

PAINTING BOARD AND MASKING TAPE

Each project starts by taping a sheet of watercolour paper to a painting board using decorator's masking tape. You can buy boards from art suppliers or simply use a piece of MDF that is slightly larger than your paper.

COTTON BUDS

Cotton buds, sometimes called cotton swabs, are helpful: they can be used to wipe paint from the latex surface of masking fluid to avoid unwanted smudging when the fluid is removed.

WATER POTS

It is vital to keep your colours pure and clean. Using two water pots helps with this goal: one to rinse brushes between colours, and a second filled with clean water to add to paint mixes. Changing the water regularly is also advised! You could use a couple of drinking glasses or recycled jars, or you can buy purpose-made water pots from art suppliers.

MARK-MAKING TOOLS

We like to use a fan brush where we want to create paint spatter effects, and a palette knife and sharpened wooden stick are useful to make marks in damp paint. An old wooden chopstick or the end of an old wooden paintbrush can be sharpened in a pencil sharpener and are perfect for this purpose!

ABSORBENT KITCHEN PAPER

Absorbent kitchen paper is a versatile addition to the list: not only is it useful for mopping up splashes and spills, it can also be used to dab off or 'lift out' paint, to remove excess water from brushes or to create interesting textures when dabbed lightly into damp paint.

HAIRDRYER

While it is preferable to allow washes to dry naturally to achieve maximum diffusion of the paint, a hairdryer can be used on a low to medium setting to speed up the drying time if needed, and to control salt effects. Avoid using it directly on masking fluid as this can make it difficult to remove.

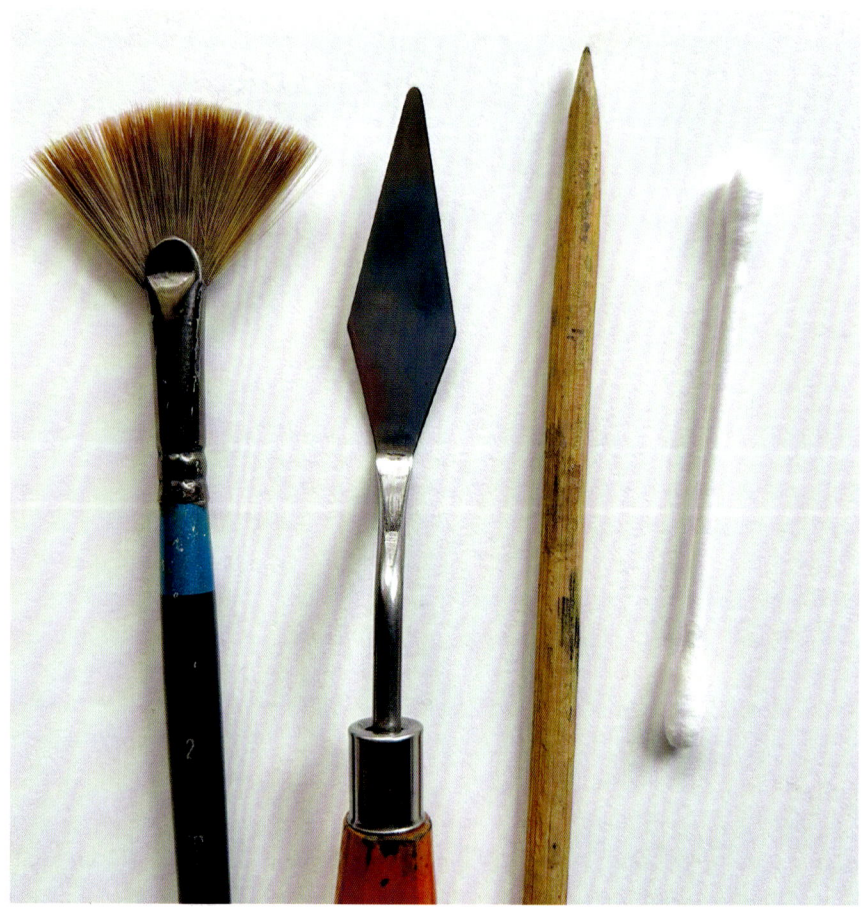

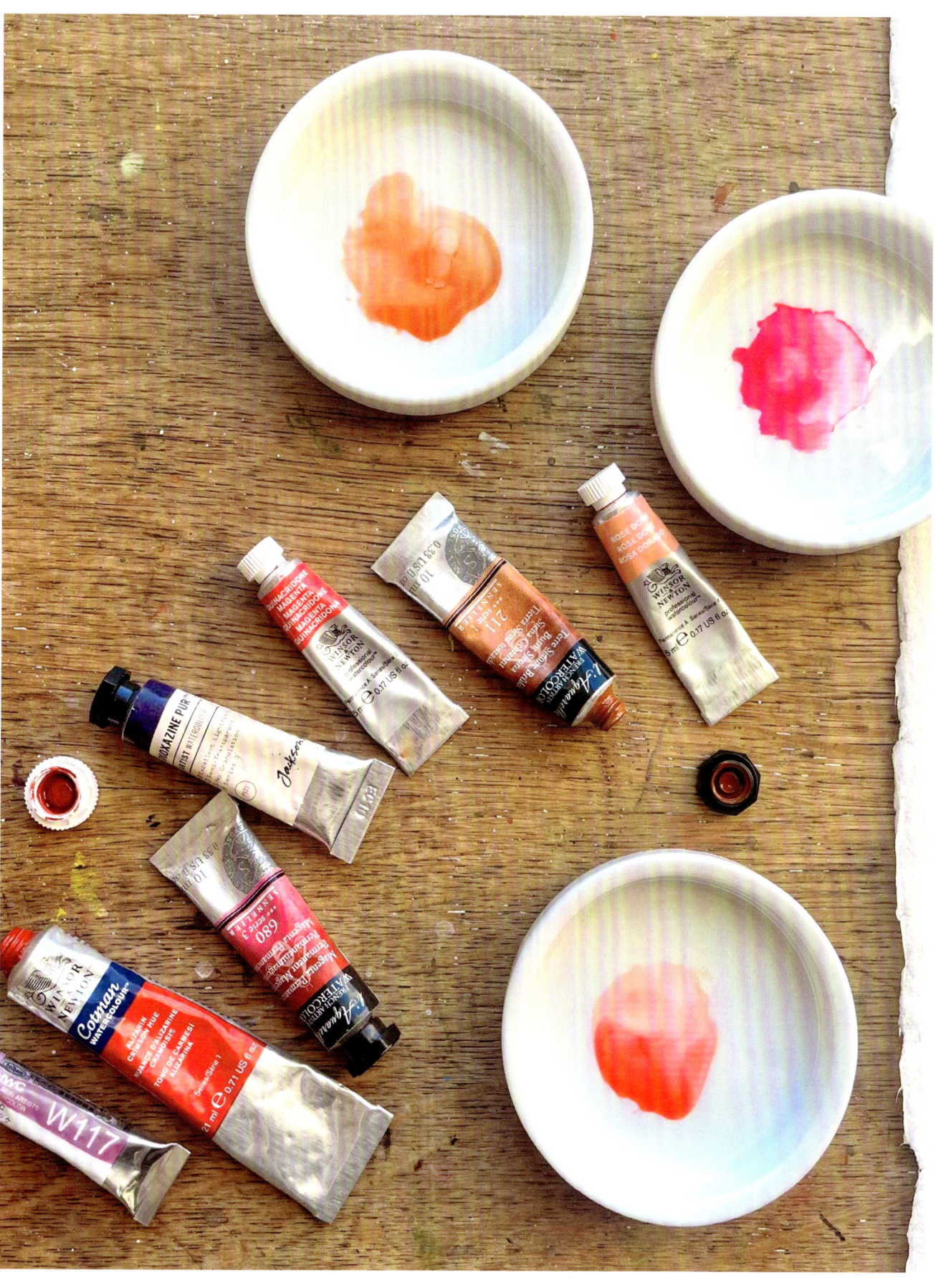

Colour and Tone

From sombre blues to sunny yellows, colour is the biggest factor for determining the mood of your painting, and how your audience reacts to it. But equally as important is tonal value, which can bring excitement and contrast into the composition.

Basic colour theory

Ever since the first colour wheel was designed by Sir Issac Newton in 1666, there have been numerous variations on its design. At its core, a colour wheel simply displays a balanced progression of colour. Red, blue and yellow are known as the primary colours: it is from these three primaries that all other shades can be mixed. Green, orange and purple are known as the secondary colours: these can be created by combining two of the three primaries.

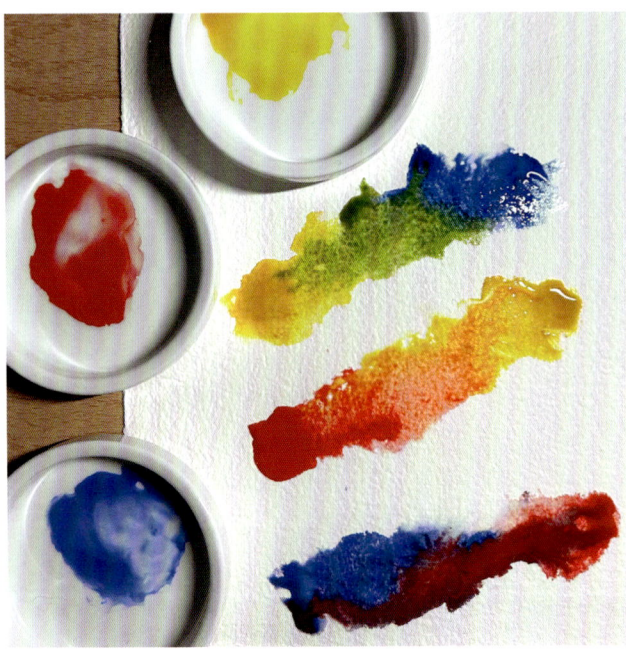

When combined, yellow and blue create a variety of greens. Likewise, blue and red can be mixed for different mauve and violet shades, and red and yellow together create orange tones.

Complementary colours

Juxtapositions of colour are great ways to draw a viewer's eye in a painting. The simplest way to do this is by using complementary colours: those that are opposite one another on the colour wheel. The main complementary pairings are blue with orange, red with green, and yellow with purple. For example, in a mostly green-hued painting, an artist may wish to draw attention to a certain area by adding shades of orange and crimson.

These kinds of colour contrasts lend themselves particularly well to floral paintings, as flowers come in every imaginable colour on the spectrum. Knowing the basics of colour theory can help you decide how best to showcase your chosen subjects, but the use of complementary colours doesn't always have to be glaringly obvious. For example, in a painting composed mostly of yellow flowers, adding hints of mauve or deep violet into the leaves can add delightful subtle contrast, as well as serve to intensify the yellows.

Warm colours versus cool colours

All colours tend to lean towards being either warm or cool in temperature. Classically, yellow, orange and red are classed as warm colours, while blue, green and purple are classed as cool. However, when working with paint, you will find there is more nuance in colour temperature than initially appears. Not all yellows, reds and oranges are warm, and not all blues, greens and violets are cool; the subtleties lie in whether the colour has a hint of blue or red in them. For example, Cadmium Red is considered warm, as it leans more towards the orange side of the colour spectrum and mixes well with other warm colours; in contrast, Permanent Alizarin Crimson is considered a cool red, as it contains underlying blueish tones.

It's worth noting that you can achieve clearer, brighter colour mixes by combining like with like, for example warm with warm, and cool with cool. A green mixed from two cool colours such as Cerulean Blue and Lemon Yellow will produce a cleaner, more vibrant shade than the grungier colour made by mixing Lemon Yellow (cool) with French Ultramarine (warm).

Tip

Creating a swatch chart in your sketchbook can help to identify which of your paints is cool and which is warm, making it a very useful reference tool.

Bear in mind that colour temperature can affect more than a colour mix. Cool colours tend to recede, while warm colours come forward, so using cooler tones in the background of your painting and warmer tones in the foreground can help improve the sense of depth and distance in your composition. Colour temperature can also assist with the overall feel of your painting. For example, when composing a winter scene, using primarily cool colours will harmonize with this composition. Likewise, using warm toned paints for a summery scene will help to convey the warmth and brightness of summer sunlight.

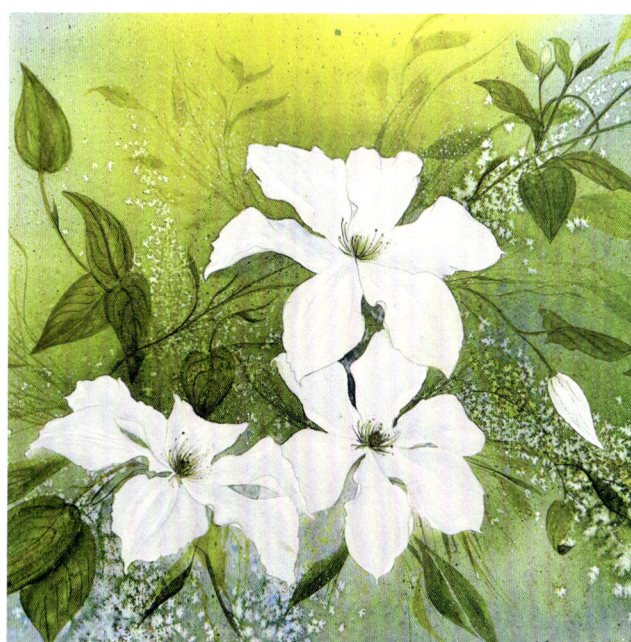

Here, warm Transparent Yellow paint adds a soft bloom of summer sunlight into this white clematis painting.

The importance of tonal value

Without sufficient tonal contrast, paintings can appear flat and lifeless. Tone is not the same as colour: the tonal value of a colour refers to how dark or pale a paint appears. Often, this is dictated by how much water is added to your paint on the palette; more water will result in a paler, light-value colour, while adding the bare minimum of water will result in a richer, dark-value colour. Getting these tones right can be a matter of trial and error, as different watercolour paints will often require varying quantities of water to achieve the same values.

Tonal studies

It's often useful to do a few rough tonal studies of a subject in your sketchbook before committing colour to your work. These can be done with simple pencil, pen and ink, or a single

rich colour of paint such as Indigo. It is not necessary to make these studies neat or pretty – their purpose is to figure out the best tonal composition for your painting, to help you to identify where the lights and darks need to go.

Bear in mind that the human eye is naturally drawn to areas of light, so this will often be your focal point. You can enhance this by placing a dark tonal value beside it, which will emphasize the light. For example, painting a swathe of dark green leaves around a single white bloom offers tonal contrast as well as colour contrast, immediately drawing the viewer's gaze.

When painting flowers from outdoors or from photographs, it may occasionally be necessary to enhance the tonal values already present, to create an exceptional painting. This can be done by exaggerating the dark values provided by foliage, cast shadows, deep-coloured skies or any dark areas provided in the backdrop such as vases or containers.

Don't be afraid of using strong tones! The temptation with watercolour is to steer away from the richer, deeper colours, often in favour of gentle, watered-down washes and pale neutrals. While these do certainly have their place, they can be enhanced a thousandfold by the addition of bold colour and strong tone. After all, we are painting flowers here: one of the most dazzlingly bright and beautiful things in the natural world!

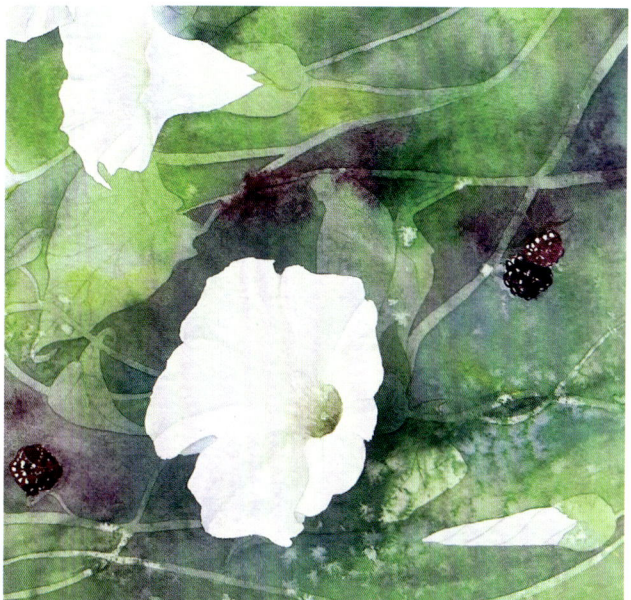

Tip

Try photographing a flower and converting the picture to black and white. This will make it easier to identify the light, mid- and dark value tones.

Composition

Working out what to include, as well as how and where to position the elements of your painting, can be a little daunting to start with, but there are a few simple guidelines that can help get you started with planning your own compositions.

Rule of thirds

When planning a painting, it can be helpful to consider the visual principles known as the rule of thirds and the rule of odds. For the rule of thirds, imagine your idea on a grid of nine equal rectangles or squares. Choose an area where a pair of the grid lines intersect, or somewhere nearby, as a good place to position a point of interest – in our case the dominant flower or flowers in a composition. If the focus is a flower group or bouquet, this can be positioned slightly to the right or left of centre.

Rule of odds

This principle considers that an odd number of elements will create a more balanced arrangement than an even number. For example, one or three flowers can be more effectively arranged on the picture plane than two or four: three flowers will lead the eye around the painting, whereas two or four flowers tend to divide the picture plane into separate blocks.

While both of these principals are helpful to get you started, don't forget they are simply guidelines, so do feel free to break them fom time to time, too!

Contrast

As the eye is always drawn to strong contrasts, incorporating different types of contrasts in your composition can help your painting. Pale flowers will stand out against a dark background; likewise, dark leaves will look striking against a pale background.

Think about using colour theory as you plan the composition: using complementary colours such as green with red together will boost the intensity of both yet still look balanced, and echoing these colours of the flowers in the props you use will add harmony.

Geometric elements such as stripes and blocks can be juxtaposed with organic, more flowing natural forms of flowers, leaves and stems.

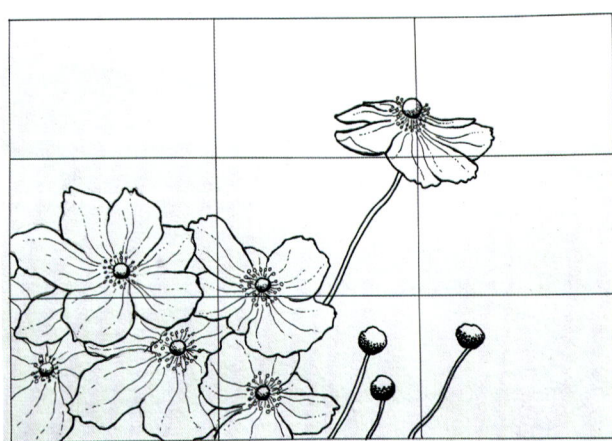

The single flower placed near one of the intersections stands out from the group, drawing the viewer's eye.

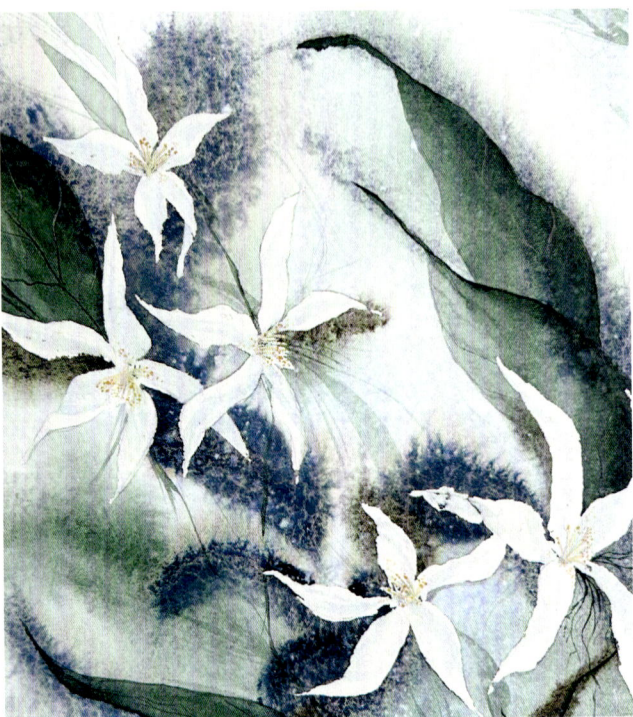

The star clematis petals contrast beautifully with the rich dark colours in the soft-focus background.

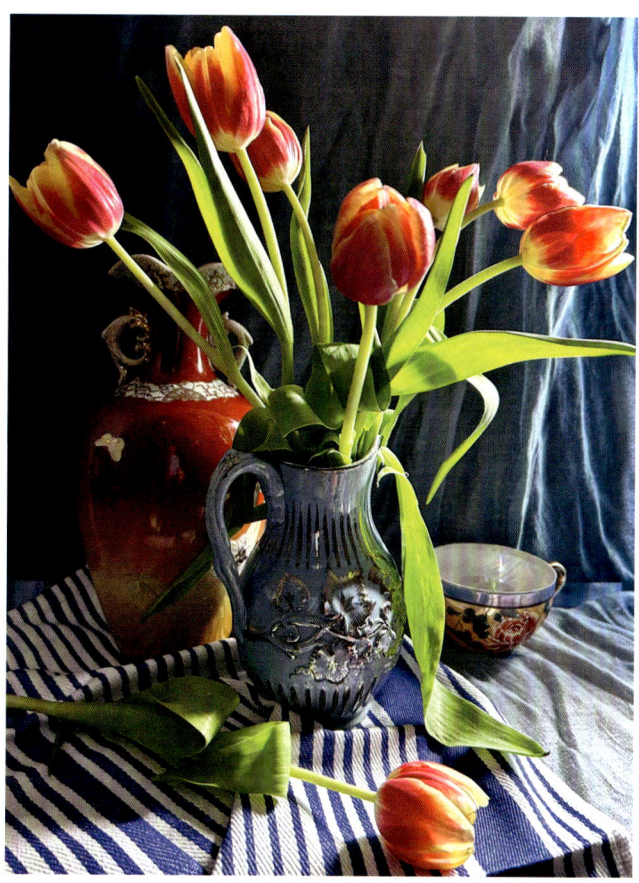

The props in the background echo the colours of the flowers and cloths, while the geometric stripes contrast well with the natural flower forms.

Test different ideas

When planning a composition, instead of copying a reference exactly, try out a few different versions in your sketchbook; zoom in and out, honing in on a particular part of your subject. Maybe try positioning the group on the left or right of the picture plane, and see how things look in a horizontal landscape format compared to a vertical portrait format, or even in a square format if you prefer.

Plan ahead by trying out different colour studies: this will help you to work out which colour combinations you like and what type of techniques you will need to use before starting to paint.

Don't be afraid to experiment with different colours and techniques – this is the stage where you can explore endless different creative possibilities!

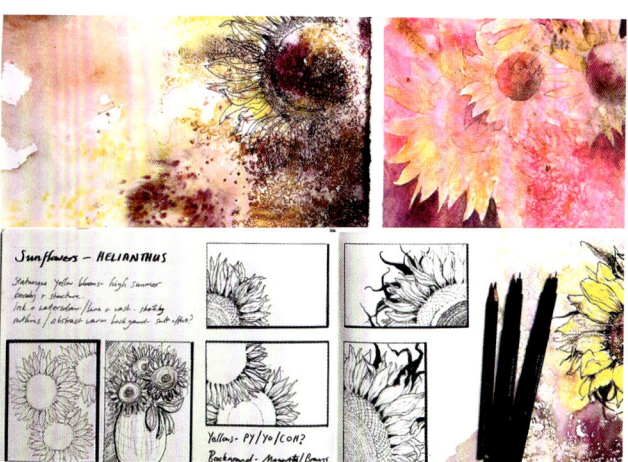

Sometimes a close-cropped flower can make a much more interesting composition than a whole vase of flowers, so try out different views of the same subject.

Use your creative licence

When planning a painting from a reference, whether a photo or live flowers, you can use your creative licence to produce a unique painting. For example, you can rearrange the scene, try different backgrounds, add or omit elements, or change their colours and size.

When people first start to paint, all too often they feel that they can't make these changes, but it's good to remind yourself that you are painting your own interpretation of the scene and not a slavish copy of a reference.

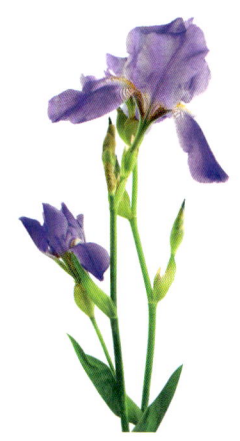
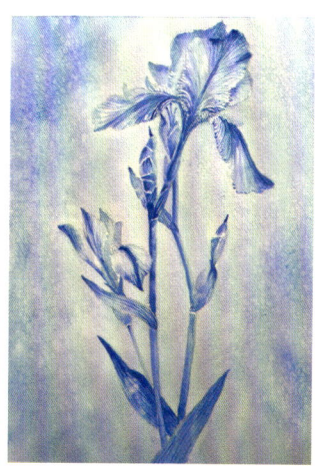

I have used creative licence to paint the iris in shades of blue instead of using the colours in the reference photo.

Sketching and Drawing

Sketching and drawing are fundamental skills for painting, but when using a sketchbook, there's no need to create perfect drawings; it is where you can practise shapes and refine your sketches. The refined ideas can then be transferred as clean outlines to watercolour paper, ready for painting.

Keeping a sketchbook

The huge variety of shapes of flowers and leaves can be quite overwhelming to start with, but this is where a sketchbook comes into its own. Whether it's trying out different compositions, refining a particularly tricky flower or leaf shape, or testing colour combinations, a sketchbook is the perfect place to practise, plan and explore ideas.

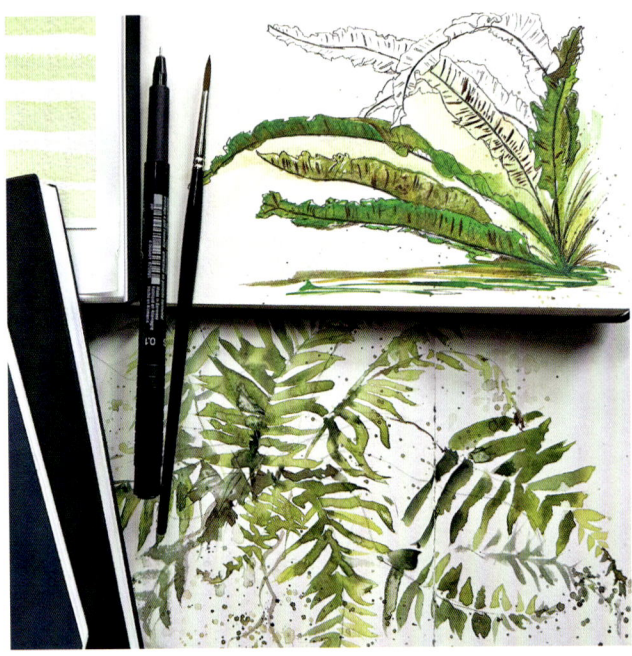

Simplifying flower shapes

It can be helpful to think of flowers in terms of their simplified shapes, whether they are discs or spheres, bells, bowls or trumpets, or even multi-headed groups of florets in one of those shapes. Construction lines can help you to create these basic shapes, and you can also use them to keep flower shapes symmetrical.

Start by drawing a simple three-dimensional shape loosely in pencil, then use that shape to help you sketch the flower so that it has shape and form.

Creating depth and distance

Leaf and flower shapes look very different depending on the angle at which they are viewed. For example, an anemone flower will appear disc-shaped when seen front on, but from the side, will be the shape of a shallow cup. Likewise, a leaf will look completely different when viewed at different angles. This visual effect is called foreshortening.

Depth and distance can also be created by using colour theory. Warmer colours attract the most attention and tend to come forward in a composition, while cooler colours recede and don't distract from the main event (see 'Warm colours versus cool colours', pages 16–17).

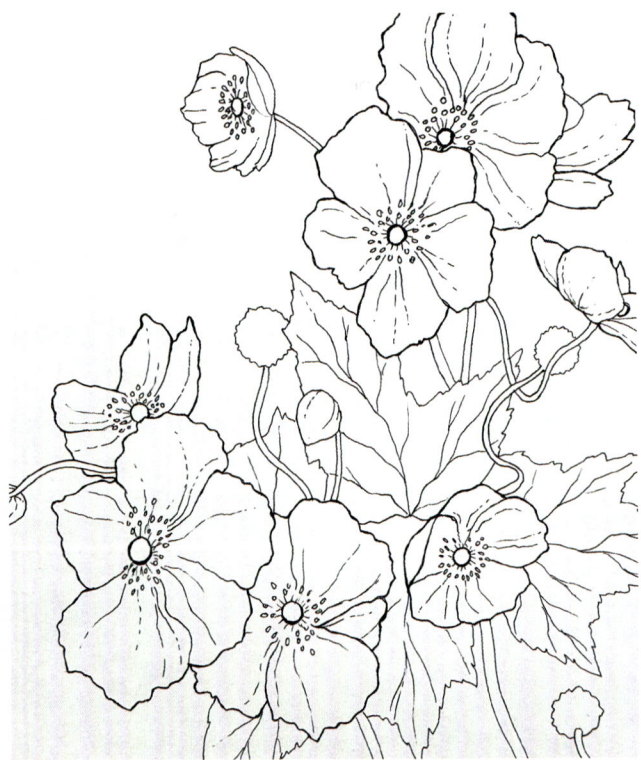

Note the different shapes of these Japanese anemones and how they depend on the angle at which they are placed.

Transferring sketches to watercolour paper

Each one of the projects in this book will start in a similar way: by using a pencil to sketch out the template provided at the beginning of the project in your sketchbook to create a preliminary drawing. When you are happy with this sketch, transfer it to watercolour paper using tracing paper. (However, note that four of the projects have inked outlines: for these, go over the pencil outline with waterproof fine-liner pens.) Lay a piece of tracing paper over the sketch, using a couple of small pieces of decorator's masking tape to hold it in place. Carefully trace over the refined lines with an HB pencil, ignoring any construction lines.

When the tracing is finished, turn the tracing paper over so the reverse side is upper-most. Place on a clean piece of scrap paper, and lightly shade over the outline on the back of the tracing with a 2B pencil to cover the reverse of the sketch with a layer of soft graphite.

Turn the paper the right way up, position it on the watercolour paper, secure it with a couple of pieces of decorator's masking tape and trace over your outline lightly with the HB pencil to transfer the graphite sketch to the watercolour paper.

Remove the tracing paper. If any traced lines are a bit faint, go over them with the HB pencil so that you can clearly see the outline, taking care not to press too hard and indent the paper.

For the pure watercolour paintings, the outline is now ready to attach to the painting board. However, for those with inked outlines, go over the outline carefully with a waterproof fine-liner pen before attaching it to the painting board.

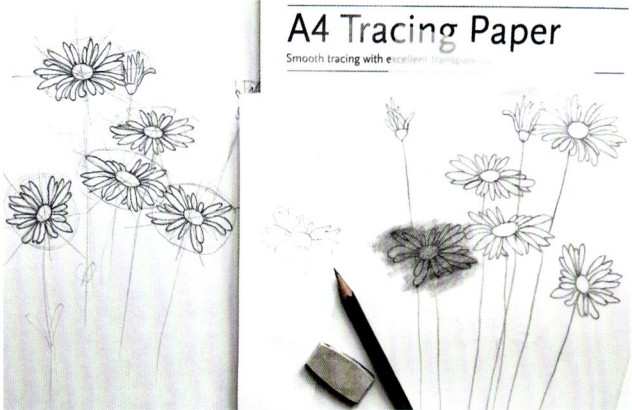

The construction lines used to sketch the disc-shaped daisies have been omitted from the refined outline.

Tip
You can purchase graphite transfer paper from art suppliers. This has a layer of graphite on the reverse, and can be used instead of tracing paper, following the instructions provided with the product.

Build a regular sketchbook practice
As well as a place to sketch and refine outlines at the start of a project, a sketchbook is the perfect place to practise your drawing and painting skills, and to explore ideas for paintings.

You can use sketchbooks like a scrapbook to save things that inspire you such as photos from magazines, items you find online, and sketches and notes on scraps of paper that you have jotted down when inspiration struck but your sketchbook wasn't handy! Used regularly, your sketchbook can become a unique and inspirational repository of ideas: somewhere to refer back to when bringing together ideas for future paintings. Sketchbooks come in a huge variety of sizes, weights and formats, so it's worth taking the time to choose one that works for you.

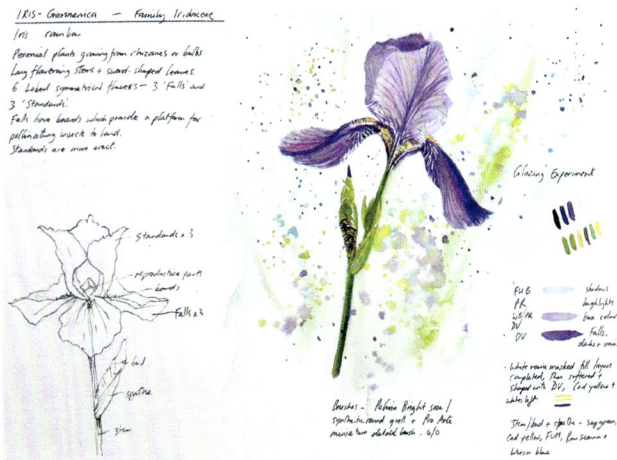

Don't limit yourself to pencils and pens in your sketchbook: you can sketch in watercolour to test colour combinations and ideas before committing to a finished painting.

Tip
Choose a selection of leaves and flowers and try sketching them from different angles to familiarize yourself with these foreshortened shapes.

Basic Watercolour Techniques

Watercolour is an astonishingly versatile medium, and as such there is a veritable ocean of techniques that are worth trying out. We've selected ones to help you ease your way into the complicated business of flower painting, and they will become the foundation for your future waterpainting practice.

Watercolour washes

Washes are a core part of painting with watercolours. These are thin layers of paint that can be applied either wet-on-dry, such as wet paint onto dry paper, or wet-in-wet, by adding colour to paper that is already damp, causing the brushstrokes to soften as the paint dries. These can be done using a single colour to create a flat or graduated wash, or with multiple colours applied together to create a variegated wash.

GRADED/GRADUATED WASH

This is a simple layer of colour that varies in tone from light to dark, or vice versa. The simplest way to achieve this is to gradually add colour to an area you have already wetted with clean water. Another method is to load your brush with a limited amount of your chosen colour, then paint into the area, allowing the colour to slowly run out as you go to create this transitional effect.

VARIEGATED WASH: WORKING INTO WET PAPER

This is a fun variation on the previous technique, which can produce more unpredictable, but still beautiful results. It relies on wetting an area with clean water first, then adding different colours of paint into the damp paper and allowing them to blend. Bear in mind that the initial layer of water will dilute the intensity of your colour, and washes created in this manner tend to dry lighter than they first appear on the page. This technique works well for flowers that naturally produce multiple colours in a single petal, such as pansies, poppies and tulips, or to produce delicately hued autumnal foliage.

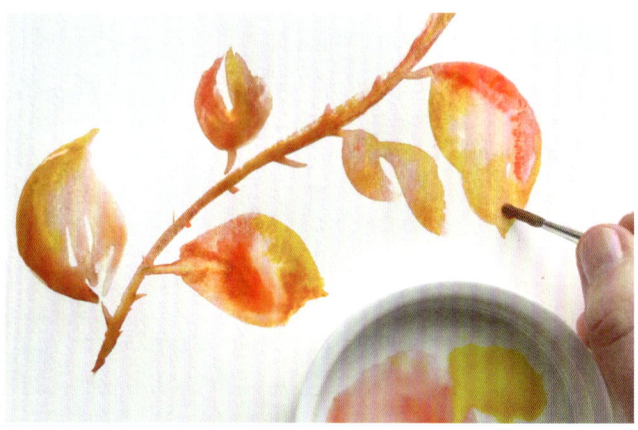

VARIEGATED WASH: WET-IN-WET COLOUR

This is a more complex wash that combines two or more paints. Begin by fully painting your chosen area using a single colour, then drop your other colour into the wet paint. Use as few brushstrokes as you can for a cleaner application; and do try to resist the urge to fiddle with it afterwards, as this can cause unsightly runbacks or streaky marks. This is a great way to achieve simple tonal variation in leaf and flower shapes.

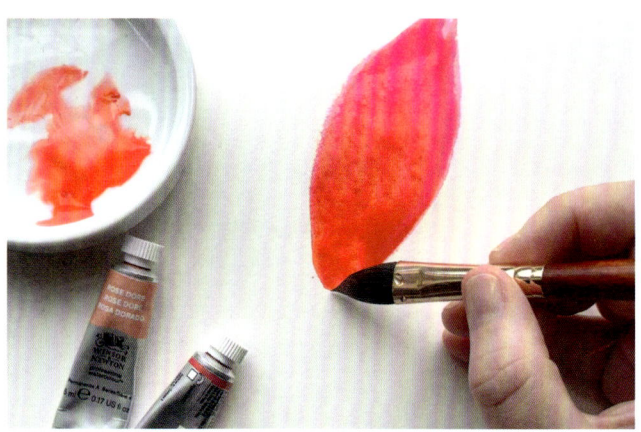

SOFT-FOCUS BACKGROUND WASHES

Each project in this book uses this technique to create a striking and beautiful backdrop for each flower painting. It relies on adding colour to paper that is already wet, so that the brushstrokes soften, with the colours blurring together as though imitating the blurred background of a photograph. Creating a backdrop of mostly soft edges serves two purposes: one, it creates a pleasing contrast with the subject, which is then painted using crisp, clean lines; and two, it provides a simple, yet effective way to add a variety of colour and tone to a flower painting, without the need to spend hours painting every single detail.

An example of this technique can be seen in the Signs of Spring project (see pages 80–85), in which the soft-focus background is a wash of simple blue, with a few strokes of brown added into the wet paint. This creates a delicate impression of bare magnolia branches reaching into a bright spring sky, without having to spend a long time adding too much detail of twigs and branches into the background, allowing the flowers themselves to be the stars of the show.

Salt techniques

A little ordinary table salt sprinkled into wet watercolour washes is a magical thing. The grains of salt draw in the water and absorb it – along with any colour it may be carrying – creating small, delicate flower or frost-like shapes, as well as larger areas of 'bloom' as the water evaporates and dries. Salt can add texture, pattern, light and movement to a soft-focus background wash. This is a technique that can take some time to master, so it's well worth practising in your sketchbook. Make a note of how things like sun exposure, warmth and humidity affect the marks that are created. Several projects in this book use salt techniques, and for this we recommend finely ground table salt, but do feel free to experiment with larger salt grains, and see what wonderful effects you can achieve.

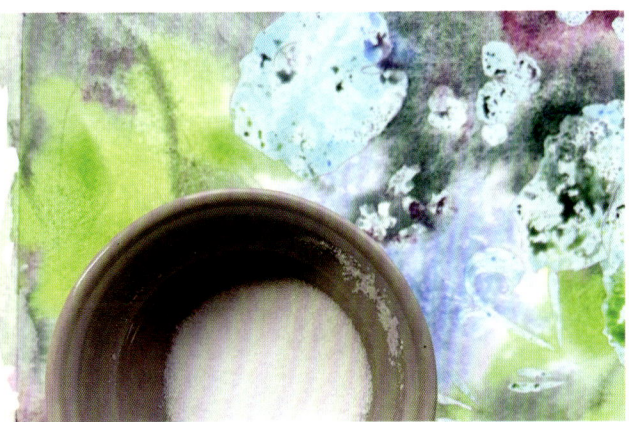

CONTROLLING SALT IN A WET WASH

If you inadvertently add salt to a very wet wash, quickly use a hairdryer on a low to medium setting to gently dry the wash, which will help control the spread of the effects. Avoid using too high a heat, as this can fuse the salt grains to the paper. It is also worth noting that the humidity in your studio can potentially affect the patterns created with salt, so choose a well-ventilated area when you leave your wash to dry.

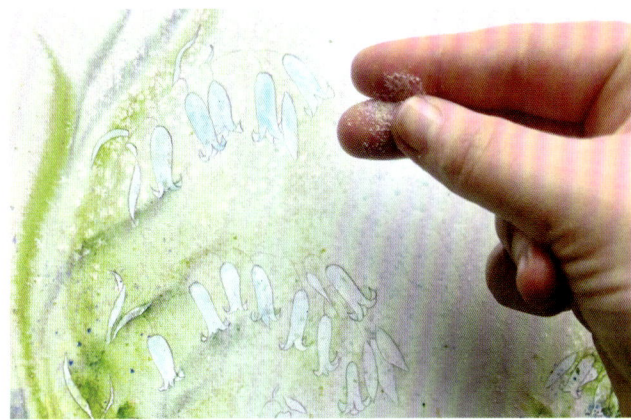

GETTING THE TIMING RIGHT

Salt reacts to the water in a watercolour wash, not the pigment, so adding it at the right stage of wetness is critical. For the effects in this book, salt is best applied to the wash just before it dries, when the shine has almost disappeared from the wet paint. You won't need much: a small sprinkle can create lovely patterns and textures. Scatter it lightly across your chosen area of paper, as you don't want the grains all clumping together. When the painting is fully dry, brush away any salt grains that haven't dissolved with a clean dry brush.

Note that if the wash is too wet, then the salt won't form delicate blooms; instead, it will simply dissolve into the wash without creating the desired pattern and possibly leaving blotchy, unwanted marks.

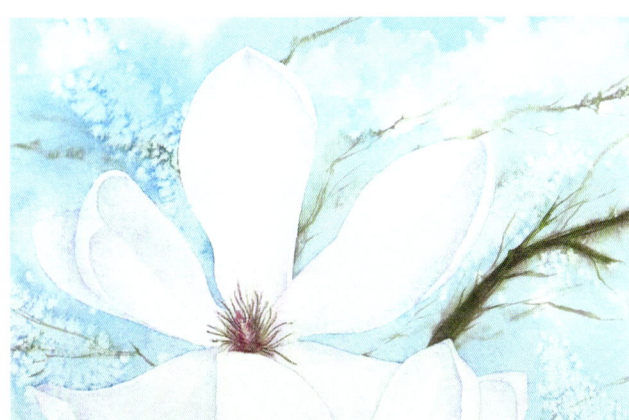

Brush marks

There is more to painting than simply picking up a brush and splashing paint around. It's worth learning some basic brushstrokes and practising them before you begin.

BRUSH PRESSURE

By applying different amounts of pressure to your brush while painting, it's easy to create a wide variety of marks in different shapes. Certain brushes are particularly good for this, such as round brushes or mop brushes that taper to a fine point while simultaneously holding a decent quantity of water and paint.

Using pressure alone, you can paint a petal in a single stroke: begin with light pressure to create a thin line, then apply heavier pressure to broaden the stroke as you go, flattening the bristles to the paper. You can then release the pressure to bring your mark back to a fine, tapered point.

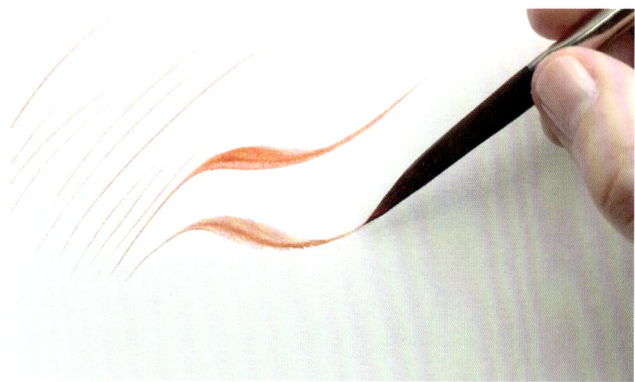

FINE LINES

These are essential for flower painting, for example, to illustrate the thin veins that appear on both leaves and petals. The sword liner brush is particularly suited to this task, as it has long, soft hairs that taper to a fine point. The taper allows you to produce thinner or thicker lines in a single stroke. It can be difficult to control, but it is capable of producing a wide variety of delicate and expressive marks.

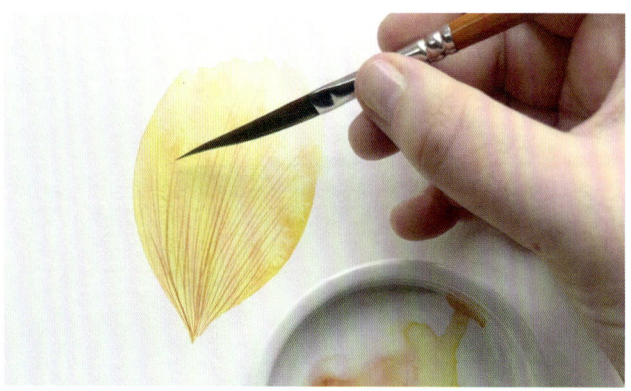

SINGLE-STROKE PETALS

For a loose approach to painting flowers, try creating a simple bloom using only a single stroke of the brush for each petal! The oval wash brush (or cat's tongue brush as it's sometimes known) is particularly prized for this technique, and is beloved by many botanical artists. Practising these kinds of bold, calligraphic brushstrokes in your sketchbook can be a great way to loosen up before approaching a larger work.

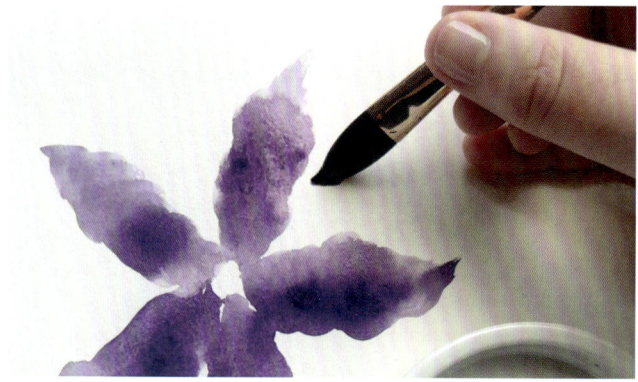

SOFTENING EDGES

There are several ways to soften the edges of your brushstrokes. The simplest is to run a clean, damp brush along the edge you wish to soften – before the paint dries. Another is to gently dab the desired area before it fully dries with something absorbent, such as a clean, damp sponge or some kitchen paper.

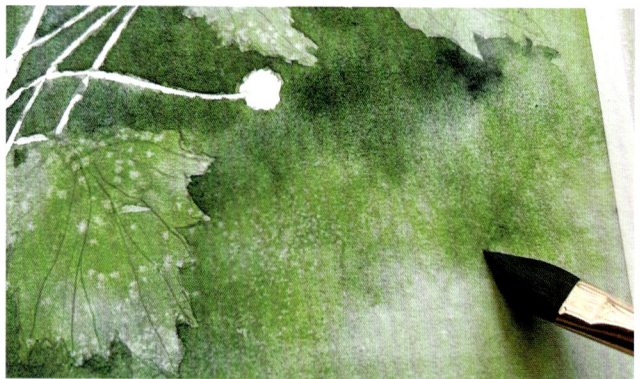

Glazing

Glazing is a technique that relies on the transparent nature of watercolour to add additional colour or tone to the marks already made on the paper. A glaze is simply a light value – in other words, very watery – mix of paint and water, applied quickly and carefully over dried paint. Glazing can only be done on a surface that is absolutely bone dry, so it doesn't lift the layer of pigment below: always check before you begin!

Negative painting

Negative painting sounds more complicated than it is. In its essence, this is a technique where the area around your subject is painted dark, allowing the pale subject matter to become the focus of the design. This is particularly handy for painting white or pale-coloured flowers, and often combines well with glazing (see above) to 'pull' pale details out of a background wash.

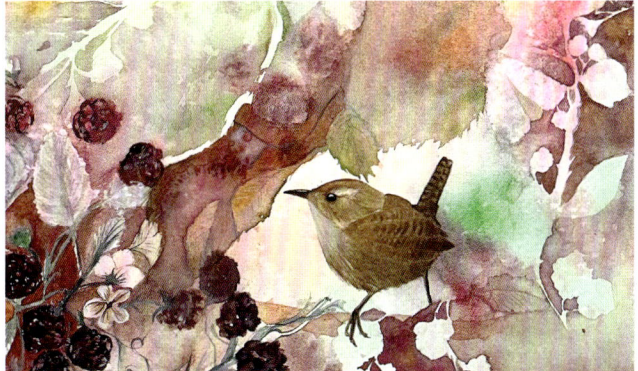

Runbacks, blooms and bleeds

Runbacks and blooms, or 'cauliflower marks', commonly occur when painting wet-in-wet, and while some artists welcome them, others do not. Runbacks generally occur when wetter paint is introduced into an area that has already begun to dry, disturbing the pigment with extra water and causing it to move, or 'bloom', into a small, textural mark. When painting wet-in-wet, try to avoid adding colour that is wetter – in other words, more diluted with water – to the paint that is already on your paper. Another great way to keep cauliflowers at bay is to use a sponge or a wad of absorbent kitchen paper to regularly remove excess water from your brushes.

When working on overlapping petals, leaving a fine white line between areas of colour will allow you to move on from one to another without the frustrating need for drying time in between each petal.

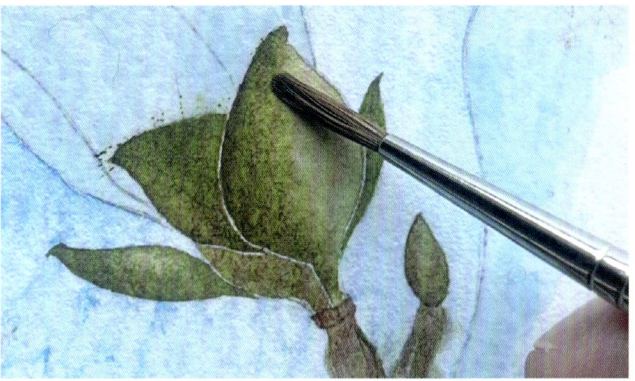

Scraping in marks

This technique, also known as sgraffito, can be done with a palette knife, the end of a paintbrush or a pointed stick. The commonest method in watercolour is to use something sharp to scrape into the dry paint, revealing the white of the paper. However, this may also be done on still-damp paint to create delicate lines or pale marks that still retain a hint of original colour. Timing is key with this variation on the technique, as the paint must not be so wet that it simply floods back into the lines and erases them; or so dry as to refuse to lift altogether.

Areas of white

There are times when we need to preserve areas of white on the paper, and masking fluid is a useful tool for this (see page 13), particularly in smaller areas. For larger areas of white you can carefully paint around them, which is a method that gives a delightfully loose effect, and this can add to the sense of life and movement within a painting.

Sometimes, however, losing areas of white paper is inevitable. Fortunately, there is a way to add pale highlights back in using a little white gouache paint. While watercolour is transparent, gouache is opaque, so tiny touches of white gouache can be painted over darker patches of watercolour. Bleed-proof white ink can also be used in a similar manner; however, gouache can be re-wetted, lifted and blended even after it has dried, using a little clean water, while white ink cannot.

Lifting colour

To remove unwanted pigment or to create some interesting effects, we can 'lift out' areas of wet colour, using a clean, damp brush, a clean sponge or absorbent kitchen paper (crumple the paper lightly, and dab gently). To lift colour from an area that has already dried, gently wet the area with a clean brush before dabbing it with clean kitchen paper. Use crisp, concise motions, and lift upwards to remove the colour, rather than scrubbing sideways, which avoids smearing.

Moon-Daisy Meadow

A meadow filled with ox-eye daisies nodding in the gentle breeze is a glorious sight on balmy summer evenings. These large daisies appear to glow in the evening light, and for this reason they are also known as moon daisies, moon pennies and marguerites.

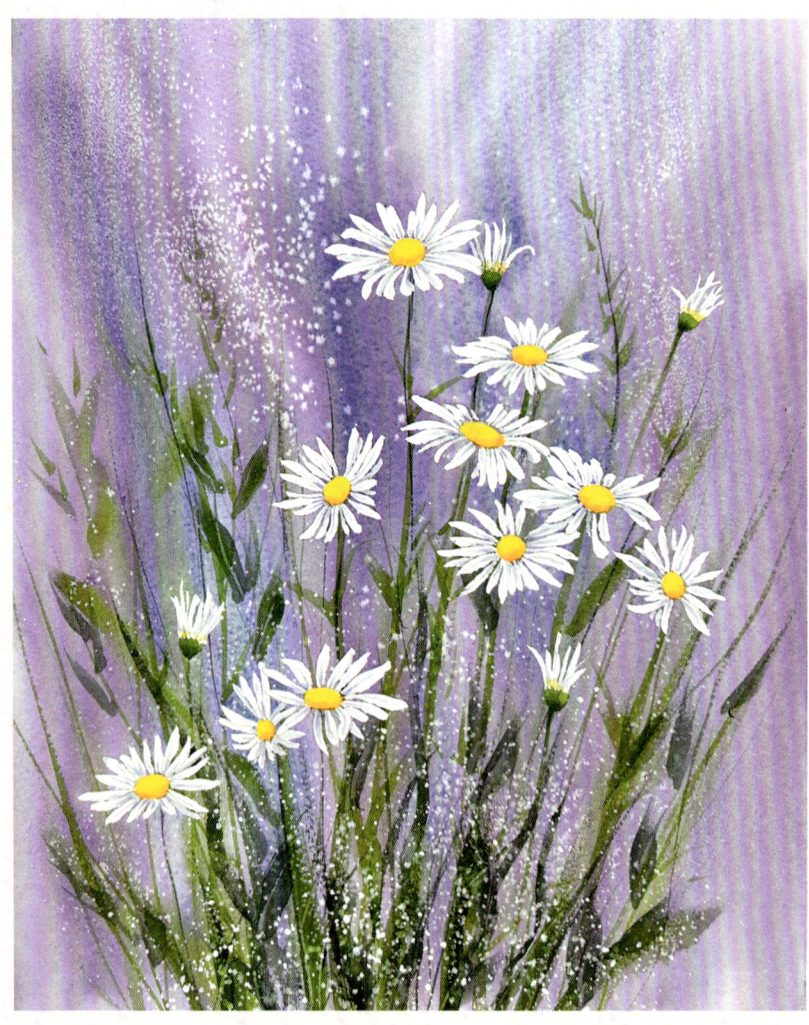

COLOURS NEEDED

Dioxazine Purple	French Ultramarine	Sap Green	Perylene Green	White gouache	Transparent Yellow	Cadmium Orange Hue
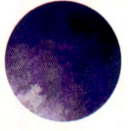	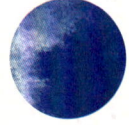	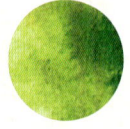	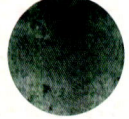			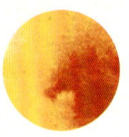

We've chosen cool violets and blues combined with warmer greens for the background in order to contrast with and complement the bright yellow daisy 'eyes'. Hints of French Ultramarine in the background are echoed in the pale shadows that add shape and form to the delicate petals.

There are almost endless possibilities for creating different versions of a painting by simply making a few small changes to the composition. For example, changing the background colours can create a dramatic difference. You could create a sunny yellow soft-focus background by using a combination of Transparent Yellow, Sap Green, Perylene Green and touches of Quinacridone Magenta. The overall effect would be to evoke the energy and heat of a hot summer afternoon instead of the cool summer evening vibe created with the blue and violet hues used for the project.

Alternatively, change the type and colour of the flowers. Delicate mauve Michaelmas daisies will evoke autumn; or black-eyed Susans, summer.

Setting up

Begin by transferring the outline from the template onto hot-pressed watercolour paper, using the method outlined on page 21. Next, using an old, small pointed brush, mask out the daisies with masking fluid, using the method outlined on page 13. Tape the pencil outline onto your board and lay it flat, ready to begin.

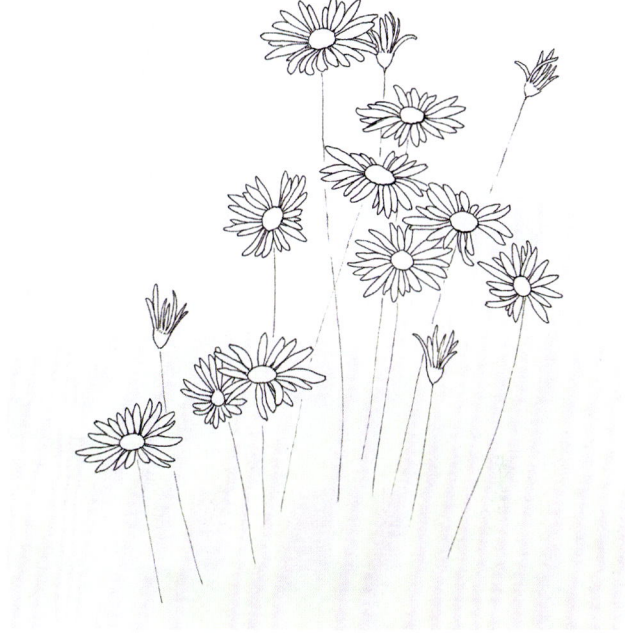

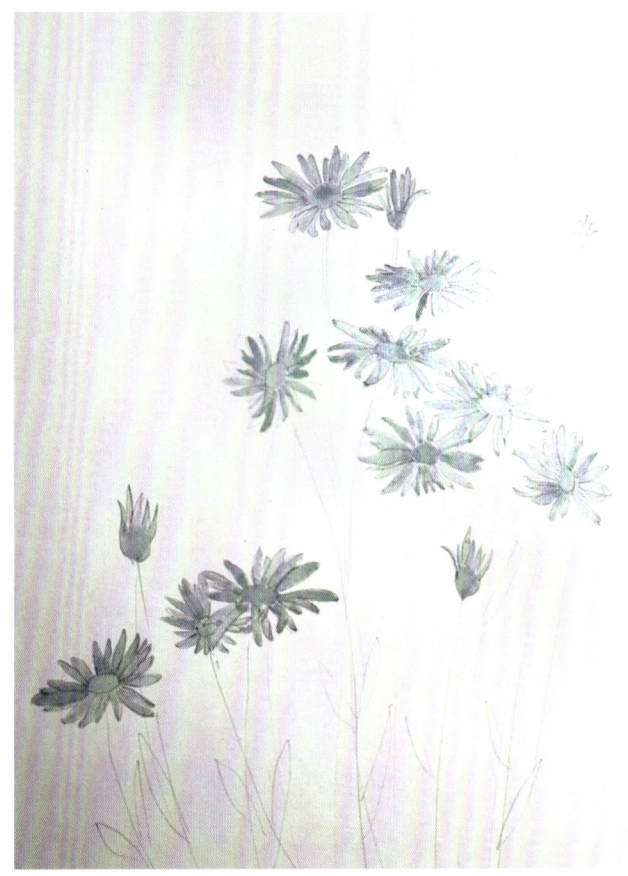

YOU WILL NEED

- 140lb (300gsm) hot-pressed watercolour paper
- Sketchbook or sketching paper
- Tracing paper
- HB pencil and eraser
- Masking fluid and a small, old pointed brush
- Painting board and decorator's masking tape
- Absorbent kitchen paper
- Adhesive eraser
- Palette with several mixing wells
- Water misting spray
- Palette knife
- Fine table salt
- Clean dry brush (for removing salt)
- Size 20 mop brush
- Size 2 quill brush
- Sword liner brush
- Fan brush
- Size 0 round detail brush
- Size 3 round brush

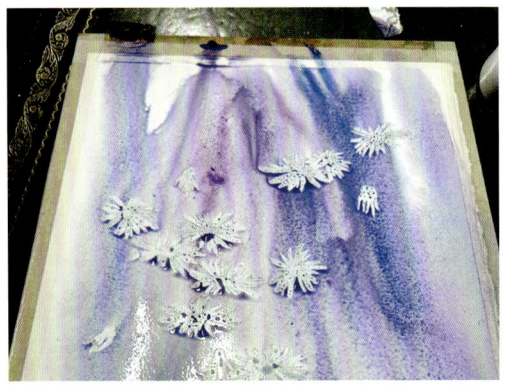

The wash should be wet enough to gently flow across the paper when the board is tilted.

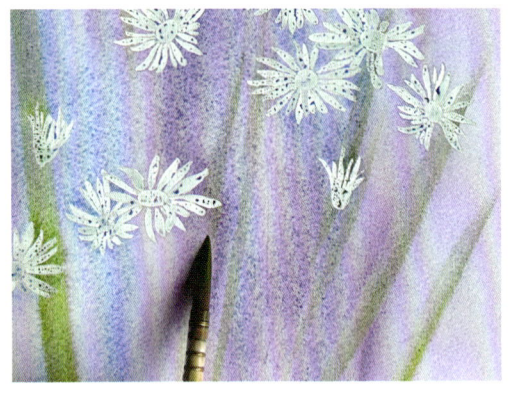

Dab the quill brush onto kitchen paper to remove excess water before painting the grasses and leaves.

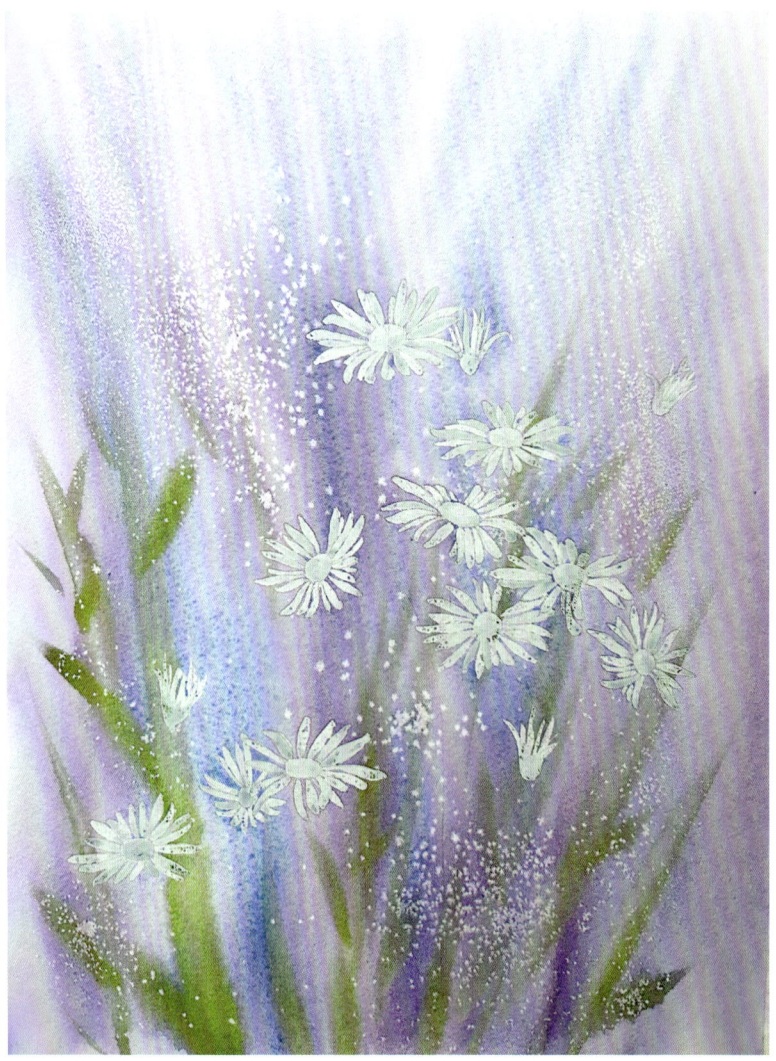

STAGE 1

Mix three large wells of mid-value colour: Dioxazine Purple, French Ultramarine and Sap Green. Wet the background with clean water with the size 20 mop brush and leave to soak for 30 seconds. Dip the mop brush into the purple mix and sweep it upwards, starting from the bottom of the paper and fanning out the brushstrokes as they reach the top, leaving unpainted gaps between brushstrokes. Without rinsing the brush, dip it into the ultramarine mix and fill in the gaps with the same sweeping brushstrokes.

Spray with the water misting spray, then tilt the board so the washes flow from top to bottom. Place the board flat, gently dabbing away any excess water pooling on the paper with kitchen paper. Wait for the shine to start to disappear, then paint some loose stem and leaf shapes with Sap Green and the size 2 quill brush. Sprinkle a little salt around the edges of the background to create texture (see page 23). Scrape a few light suggestions of stems through the damp wash with a palette knife (see page 25). Leave to dry.

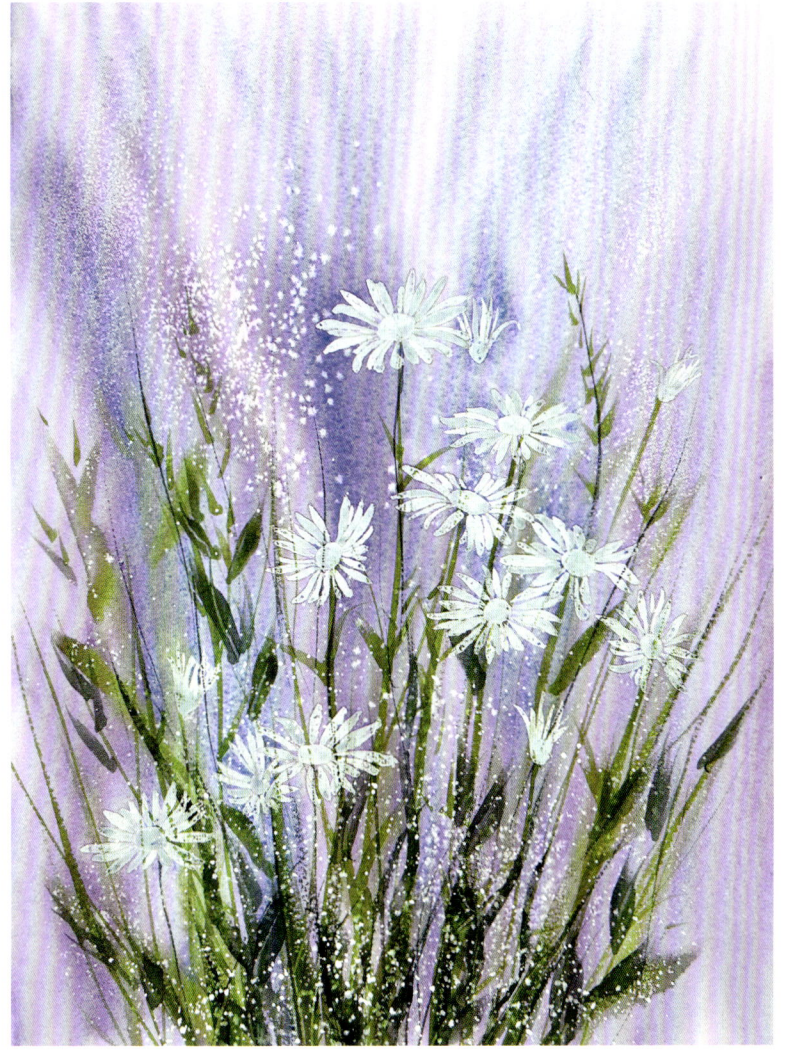

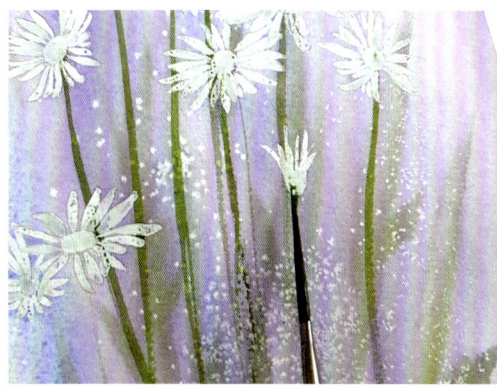

Hold the sword liner brush at a shallow angle to the paper as you paint the daisy stems for greater control.

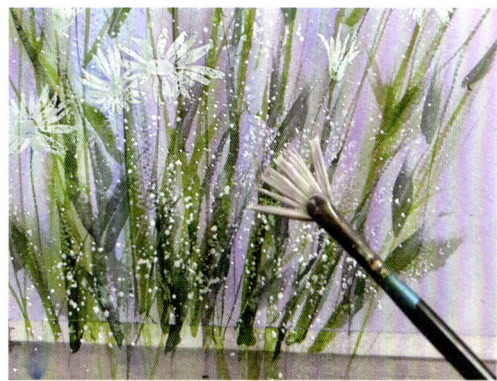

Hold the fan brush over the painting and tap the handle to release the spatter droplets.

STAGE 2

Brush away any remaining salt residue from the painting using the clean dry brush.

Mix two small wells of mid-value colour: Sap Green and Perylene Green. Paint the daisy stems with the sword liner brush: start the brushstroke just below the middle of the flower and paint vertical, slightly curved stems.

Add more grasses with the two greens, sweeping the brush upwards and out, allowing the long flexible sword liner to produce expressive marks. Paint more small leaf shapes around the stems with the size 2 quill brush and Sap Green.

Mix a small well of inky consistency white gouache, and spatter drops of it across the lower half of the painting using the fan brush. Once dry, repeat if the white speckles look a little pale. Leave to dry completely.

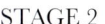

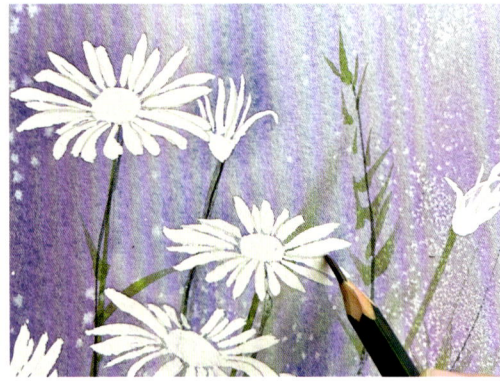

Only use light pressure when reinstating the pencil marks, so as not to indent the soft watercolour paper.

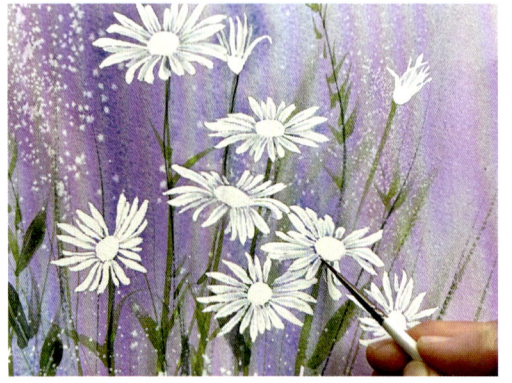

The pale shadows will add the suggestion of shape and form to the white petals.

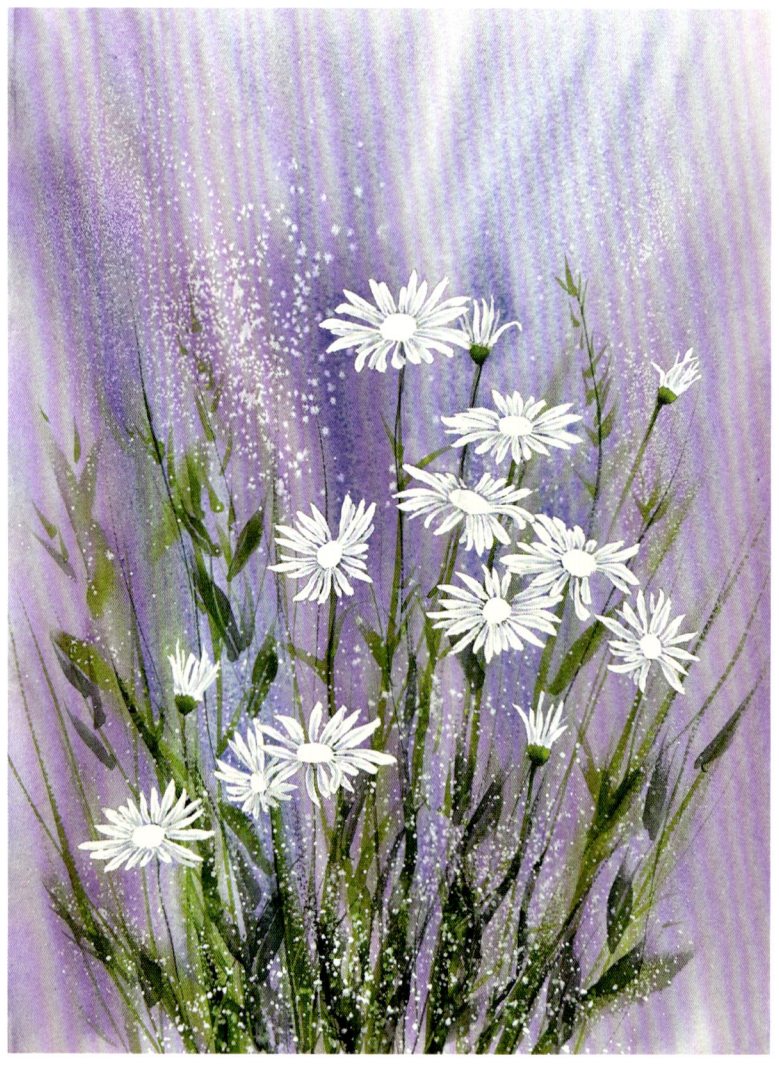

STAGE 3

Remove the masking fluid with the adhesive eraser. Lightly re-draw in any pencil lines that were lost when removing the mask so that you can clearly see the differentiation between the petals.

Mix a very light-value well of French Ultramarine and test it on a scrap of paper: it should be just pale enough to lightly tint the paper to suggest shadows on some of the white daisy petals.

Using the size 0 round detail brush, paint fine veins down the centre of the more prominent petals, and also paint shadows on any petals that sit behind others. Use a fairly dry mix of paint for this: after loading the brush with paint, dab it lightly on a piece of kitchen paper to remove any excess water before painting the delicate shadows.

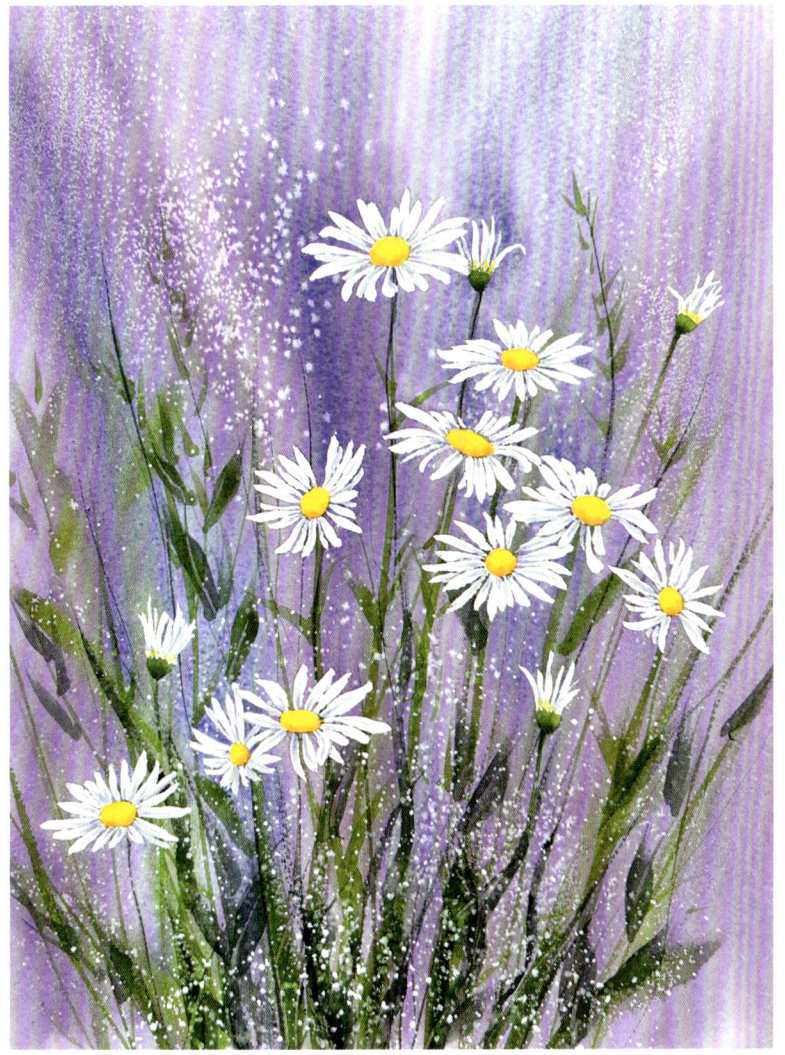

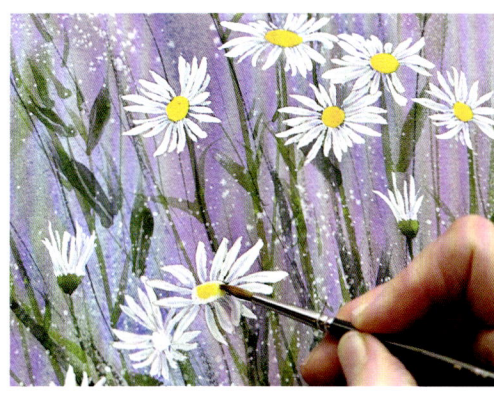

Using bright Transparent Yellow to colour the daisy centres will help them pop against the contrasting violet background.

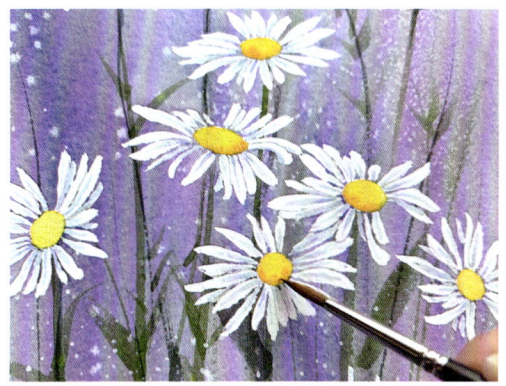

STAGE 4

Mix two mid-value wells of colour: one of Transparent Yellow and one of Cadmium Orange Hue.

Using the size 3 round brush, paint the daisy centres with the yellow mix. While the paint is still damp, dab a little orange into the base of the centre with the size 3 brush (or size 0 detail bush if you prefer) to deepen the hue.

Repeat for all the flower centres. Leave to dry.

Watercolour dries about 30% lighter in tone, so if the flower centres dry a little pale, you can glaze over them with the yellow, adding a little more orange to the base to deepen the colour.

Sweet Sunshine Lily

Lilies are strikingly beautiful plants, with their tapered, elegant leaves and array of colourful blooms. These gloriously bright yellow specimens have been painted against a simple, soft-focus backdrop, allowing their colour and natural elegance to shine.

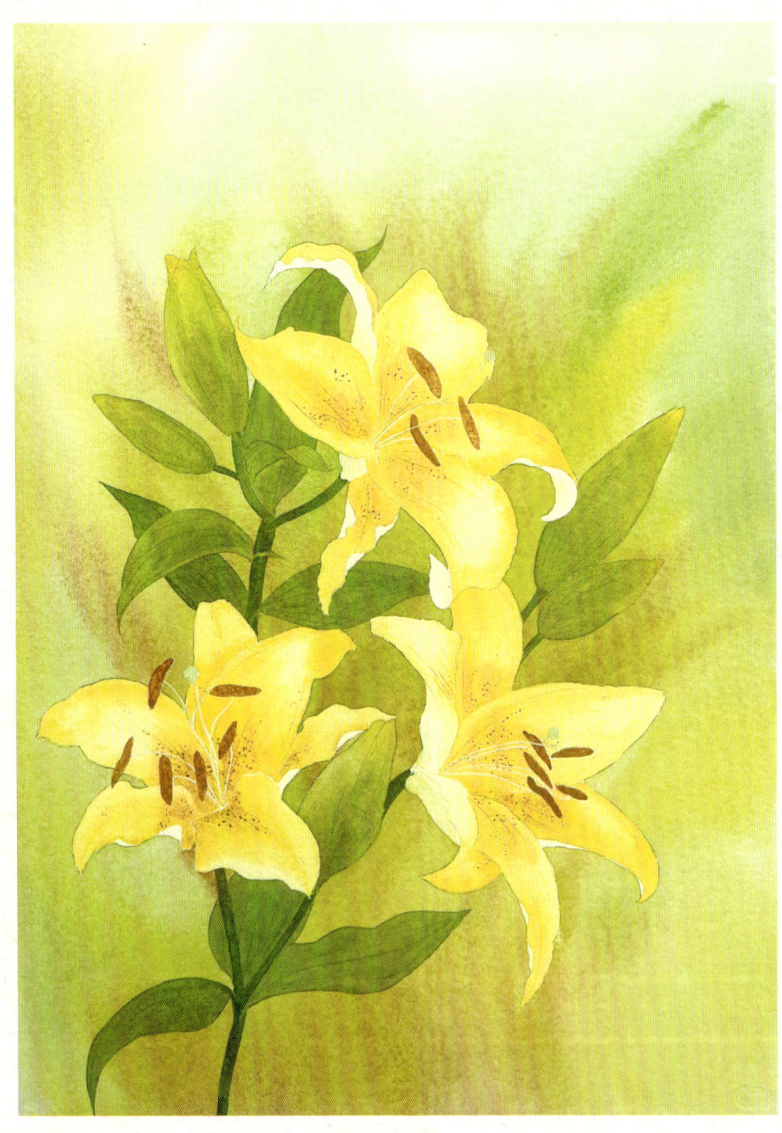

COLOURS NEEDED

Transparent Yellow	Sap Green	Burnt Sienna	Olive Green	White gouache

 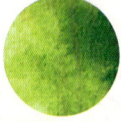 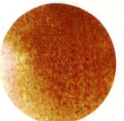 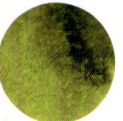

With their prevalence in florist's bouquets and flower arrangements, it's easy to overlook the wonderful variety of lilies that can be gathered from across the world. They arrive in a beautiful array of colours, from starry whites to rich pinks, fiery oranges and sunshine yellows.

The composition

Lilies are a surprisingly versatile subject when it comes to composing floral paintings. As well as being tall and statuesque enough to stand alone, lilies work well as companion plants for mixed bunches and bouquets.

In this painting only a handful of paints are required to emphasize the warmth and beauty of the lily flowers themselves. The simple, soft-focus background has been painted using just three colours, using clean, rhythmic brushstrokes that echo the natural curves of the leaves and unopened buds.

Setting up

Begin by transferring the outline from the template onto hot-pressed watercolour paper, using the method described on page 21. Mask out the lily flowers and buds using masking fluid and the old, small pointed brush (see page 13). Once the mask has set, tape your pencil outline onto a board and lay it flat, ready to begin.

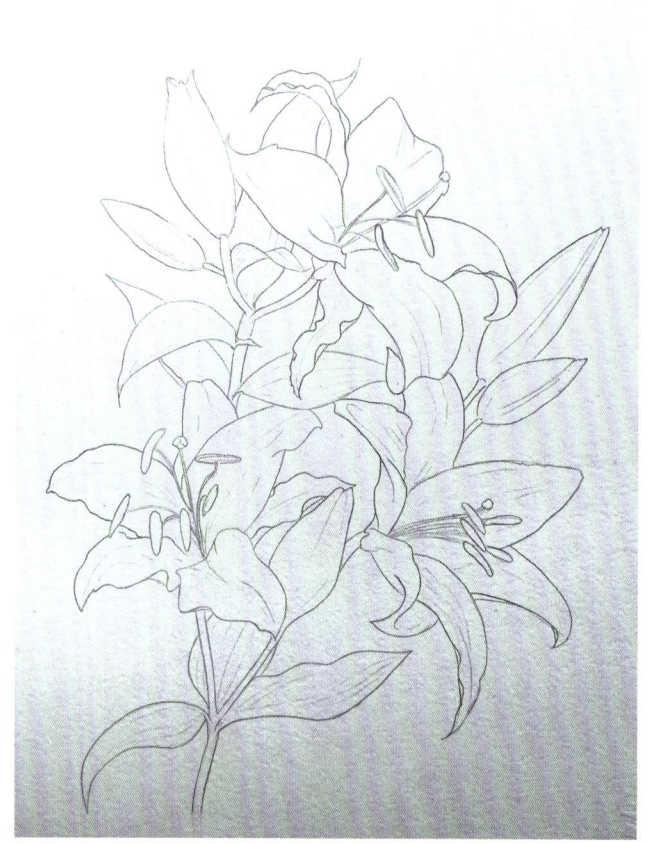

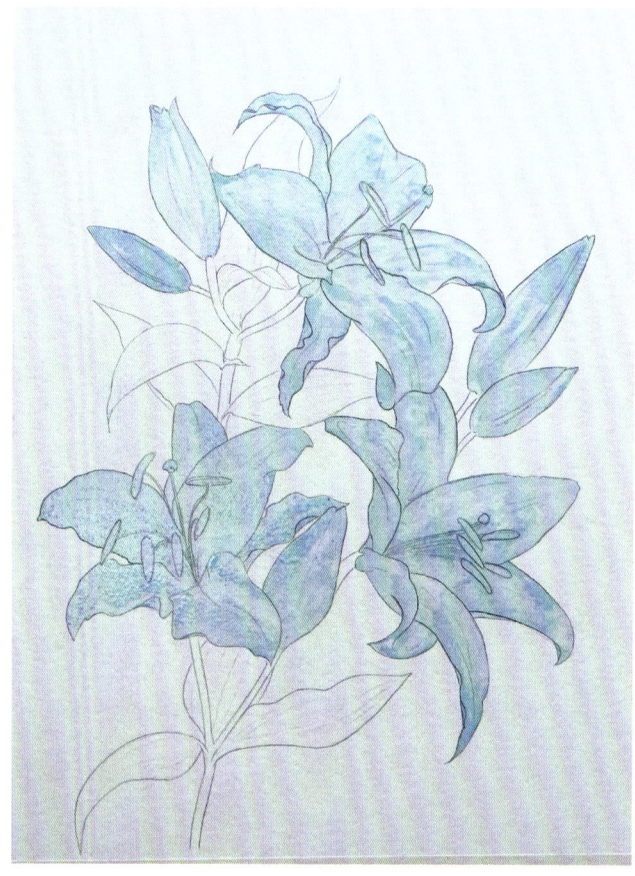

YOU WILL NEED

- *140lb (300gsm) hot-pressed watercolour paper*
- *Sketchbook or sketching paper and tracing paper*
- *Masking fluid and old, pointed small paintbrush*
- *Adhesive eraser*
- *HB pencil and eraser*
- *Painting board and decorator's masking tape*
- *Sponge and absorbent kitchen paper*
- *Palette with several mixing wells*
- *Size 20 mop brush*
- *½in (1.25cm) oval wash brush*
- *Size 3 round brush*
- *Size 0 round detail brush*
- *Size 2 synthetic quill brush*
- *Small sword liner brush*

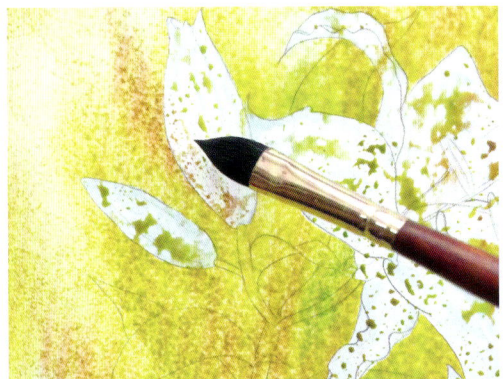

The oval wash brush is perfect for tasks such as this. Use the flat side of the brush to paint the soft-focus leaves, lifting it up as you reach the end of the brushstroke, so that the pointed tip creates a naturally tapered, flowing shape.

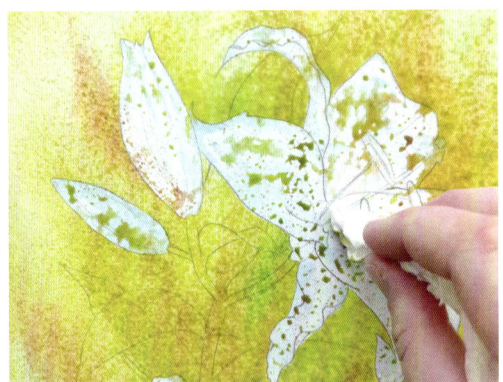

Use a small piece of kitchen paper to gently lift wet paint away from areas of masking fluid to help achieve a cleaner removal at a later stage.

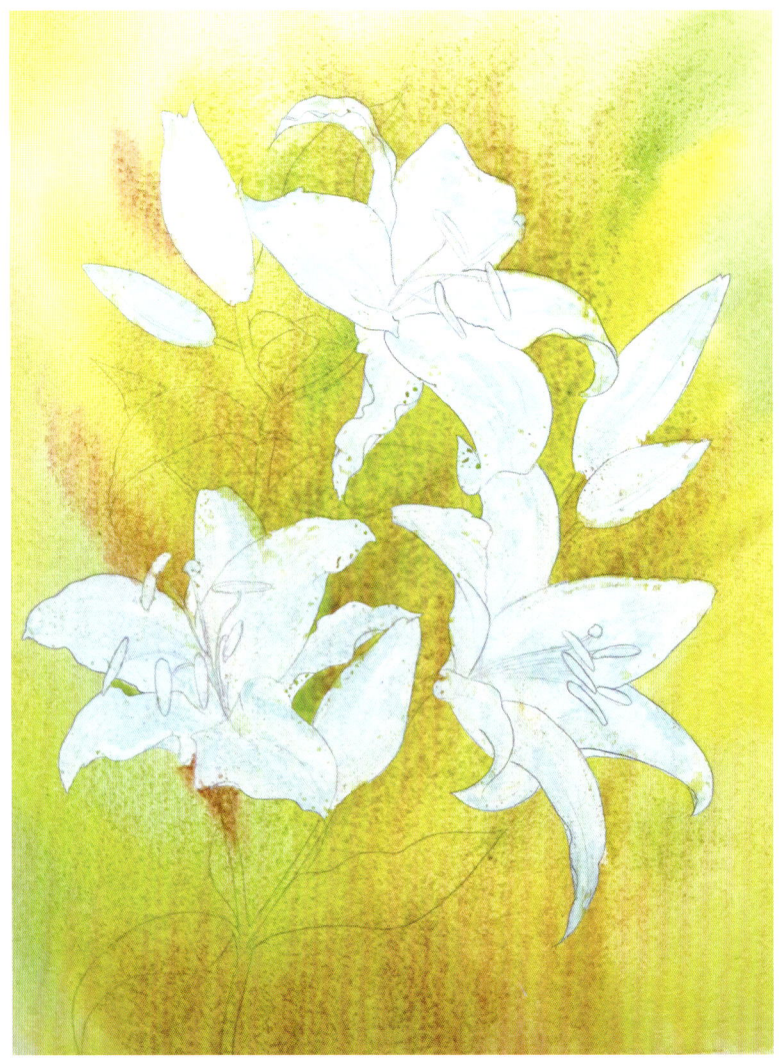

STAGE 1

Mix up three large wells of mid-value colour: Transparent Yellow, Sap Green and Burnt Sienna. Wet the watercolour paper all over, then use the size 20 mop brush to paint a soft-focus background, following the technique outlined on page 23.

Once the surface of the paper has been covered with colour, use the oval wash brush to dip back into the paints and add flowing, leaf-like shapes into the wet wash, mimicking the long, elegant shapes of the lily leaves and buds. Leave to dry.

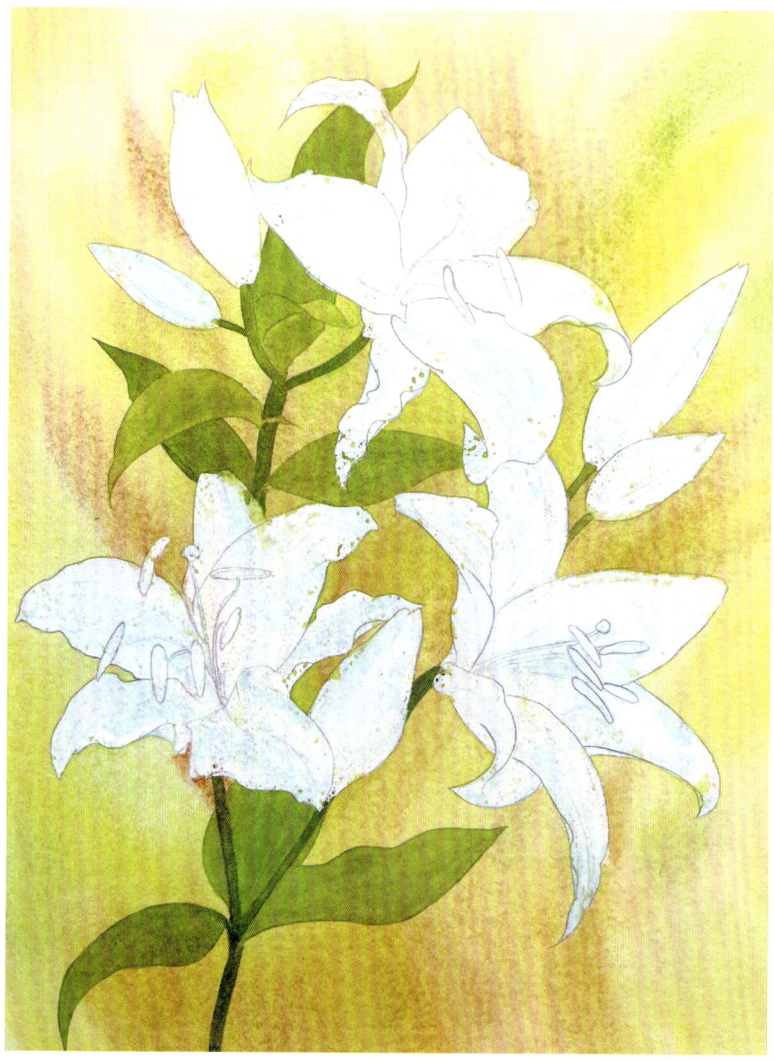

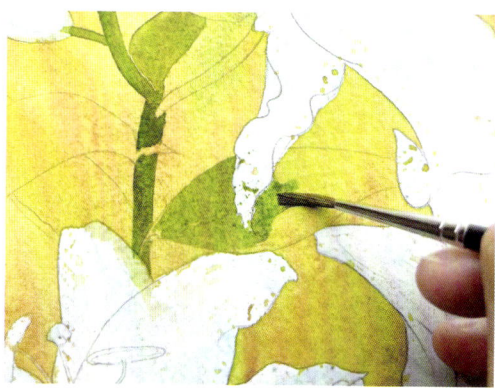

Painting in the leaves before removing the masking fluid from the flowers will make it easier to keep your painting neat.

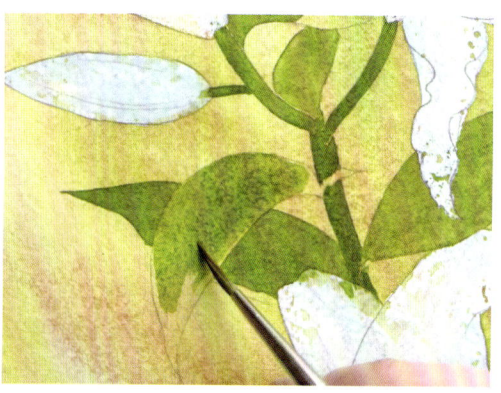

STAGE 2

Use the size 3 round brush to add colour to the leaves with some more Sap Green, using the size 0 detail brush if necessary to paint into the smaller, fiddly areas.

Use mid- and dark-value paint to vary the tone and to differentiate between areas where the leaves and stems overlap.

Use soft brushstrokes and paint lightly over the colour already present on the paper to avoid lifting or disturbing the dry pigment. This will also help avoid creating unwanted streaks.

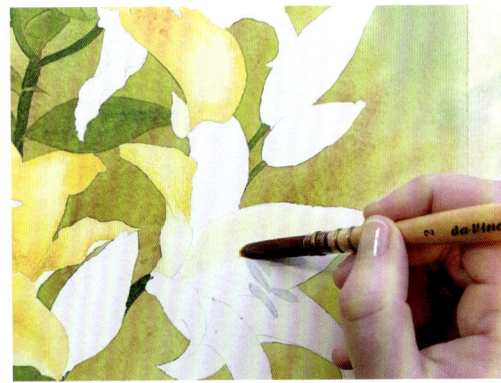

When painting the petals, concentrate paler colour on areas that curve outwards, and use the darker value paint in the areas that curl inwards.

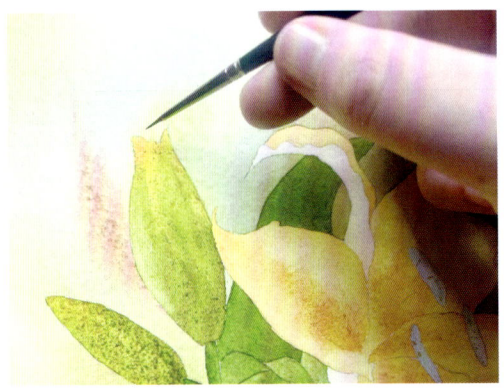

Dropping a little Transparent Yellow into the tips of the larger buds will help indicate that they're almost ready to open, revealing the sunny colour inside.

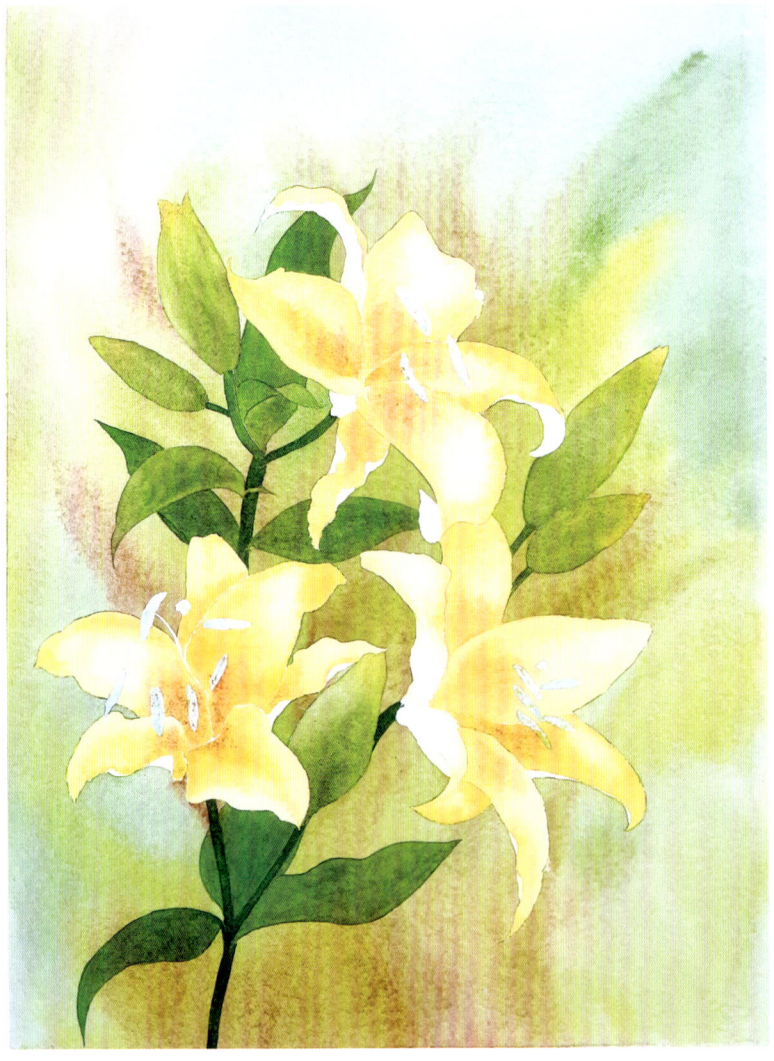

STAGE 3

Once the paint is fully dry, remove the masking fluid using the adhesive eraser, then re-mask the central anthers.

Mix two wells of Transparent Yellow, one dark and one mid-value, and mix one of mid-value Burnt Sienna. Use these mixes to add colour to the lily petals with the size 2 quill brush. Use the variegated wash technique on page 22 to achieve different tones of yellow in the petals.

Drop a little Burnt Sienna into the wet paint using the detail brush, close to the lower part of the petal, to create a hint of rust-coloured blush.

Once dry, use the same technique to paint the buds using Olive Green and more Transparent Yellow.

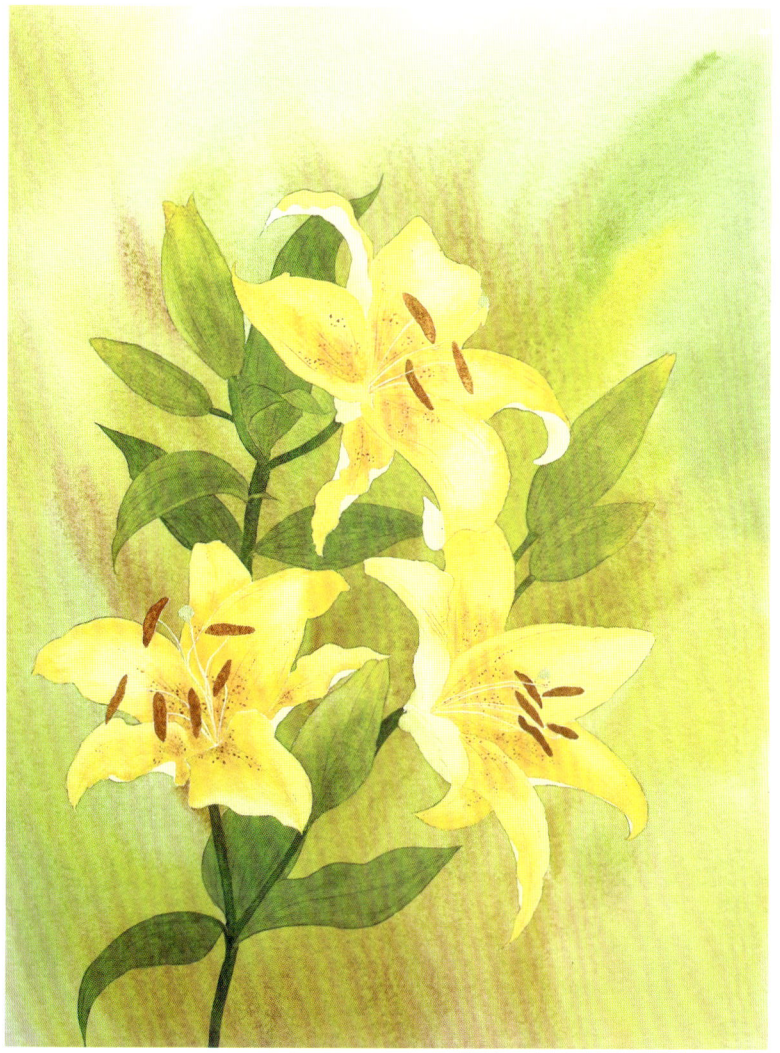

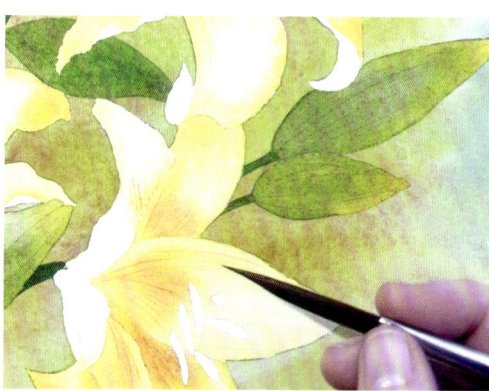

The long, springy bristles of a liner brush are designed to hold plenty of paint and water, in order to paint smooth unbroken lines. Hold the brush lightly against the paper so that only the pointed tip rests against the surface, and draw it upwards in one smooth, confident motion.

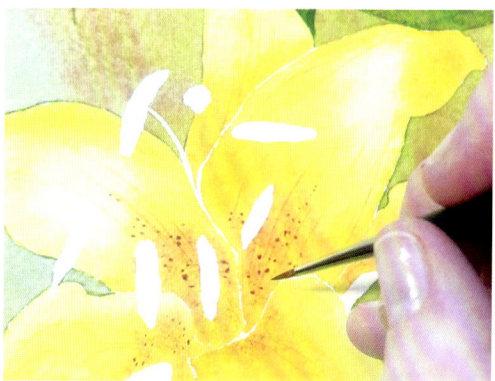

STAGE 4

Allow to fully dry, then remove the masking fluid from the anthers and add the final details. Use the point of the sword liner to add thin veins to the leaves, petals and buds, using mid-value Sap Green and Transparent Yellow, as well as a little Burnt Sienna for the petals.

Once dry, use the detail brush to scatter Burnt Sienna freckles across the petals, as well as to add colour to the anthers.

Tint a little white gouache with Sap Green, and use this to paint the thin connecting filaments and central stigma.

When adding freckles using the detail brush, concentrate them around the base and lower third of each petal, making them sparser the closer you get to the tip.

Windswept Japanese Anemones

These statuesque plants add colour and drama to autumn borders, with their delicate pink cup-shaped blooms that open wider and become flatter as the season progresses. Despite their delicate, ethereal appearance, they are strong enough to withstand gales.

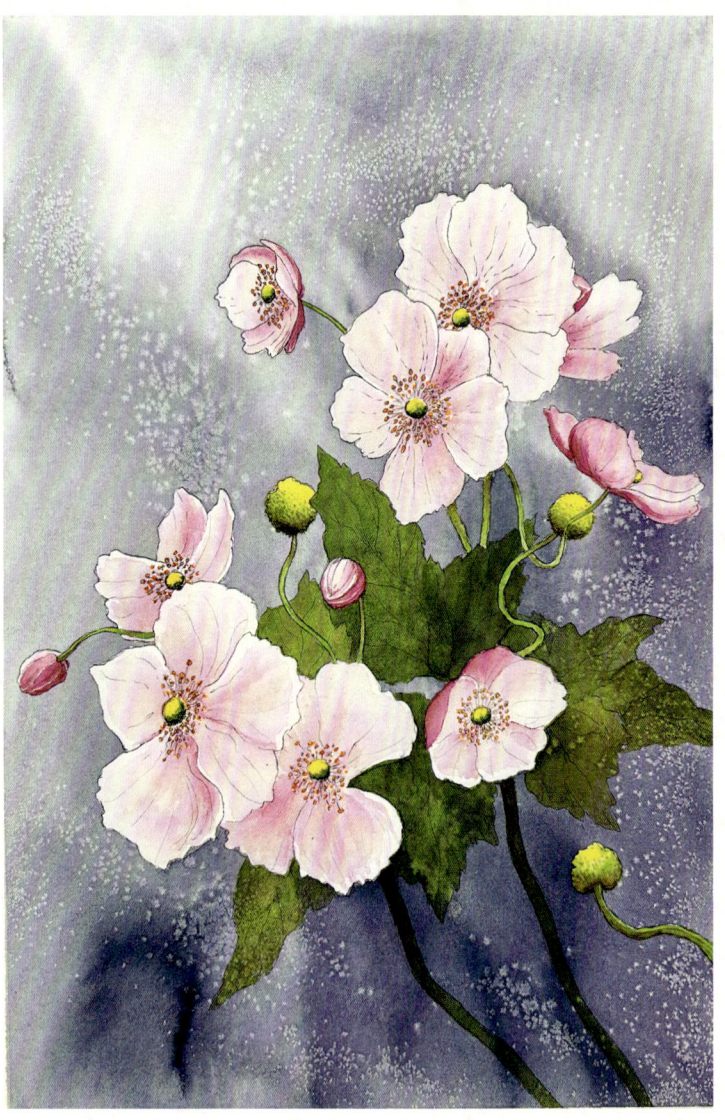

COLOURS NEEDED

Payne's Grey	Indigo	Dioxazine Purple	Transparent Yellow	Sap Green	Sepia	Quinacridone Magenta	Cadmium Orange Hue

 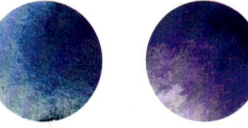   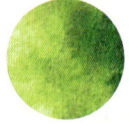 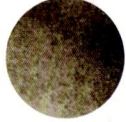 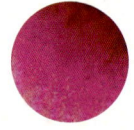 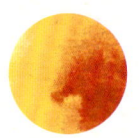

The inspiration for this painting came from a wet and windy autumn walk. During a break in the rain, I stopped to admire a cloud of gorgeous anemones swaying in the wind, their delicate pink petals and yellow seed heads making a stark contrast against the angry, violet-grey sky. I quickly took some photos just as it began to rain again, and began working on a couple of different versions of this painting as soon as I returned to my studio.

Setting up

Begin by transferring the outline from the template onto hot-pressed watercolour paper, using the method outlined on page 21. Go over the pencil outline with the 0.3mm waterproof fine-liner pen. Next, using a small old brush with a good point, mask out the flowers with masking fluid, using the method outlined on page 13. Tape the pencil outline onto your board and lay it flat, ready to begin.

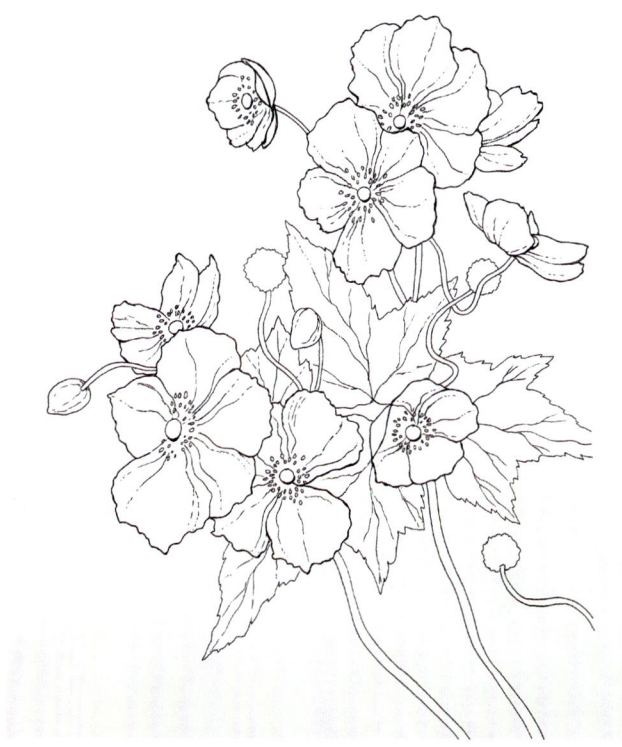

YOU WILL NEED

- *140lb (300gsm) hot-pressed watercolour paper*
- *Sketchbook or sketching paper*
- *Tracing paper*
- *HB pencil and eraser*
- *0.1mm and 0.3mm waterproof black fine-liner pens*
- *Painting board and decorator's masking tape*
- *Masking fluid and an old, small pointed brush*
- *Adhesive eraser*
- *Absorbent kitchen paper*
- *Palette with several mixing wells*
- *Water misting spray*
- *Fine table salt*
- *Clean dry brush (for removing salt)*
- *Size 20 mop brush*
- *Size 3 round brush*
- *Size 0 round detail brush*
- *Size 2 quill brush*
- *Oval wash brush*

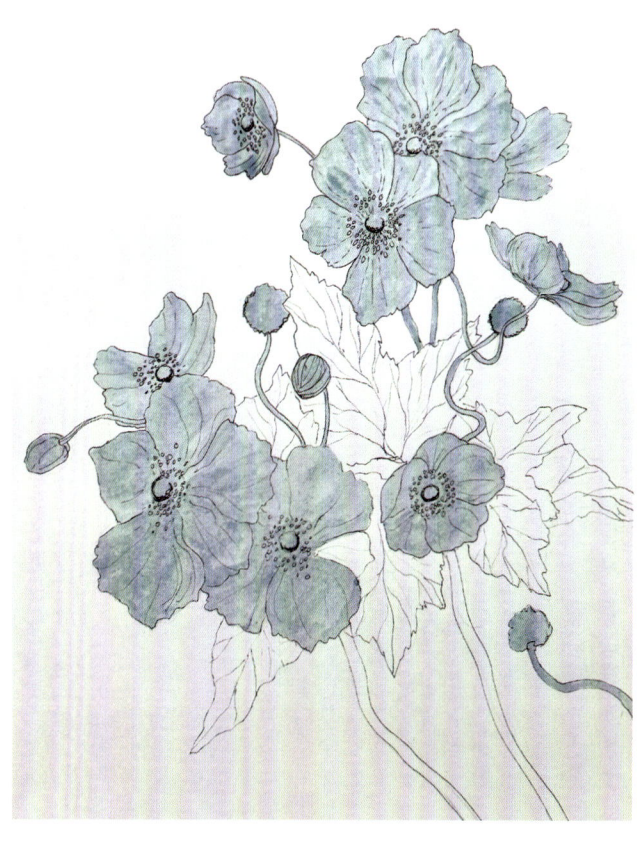

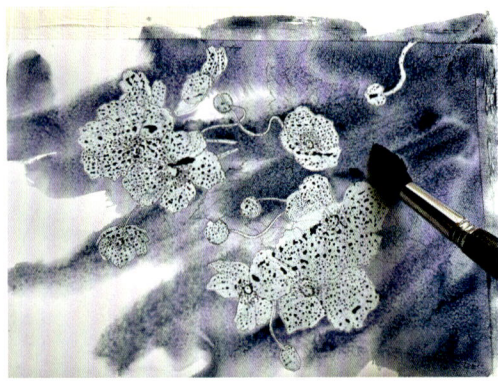

Tun the board sideways if you find it easier to make smooth, bold brushstrokes horizontally rather than vertically.

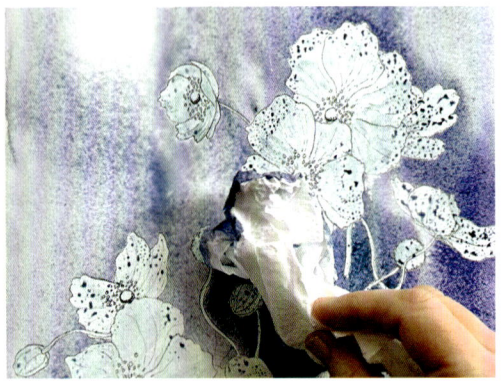

If you have excess water on your paper, dab lightly with clean kitchen paper. Use a delicate touch, otherwise it will lift colour as well!

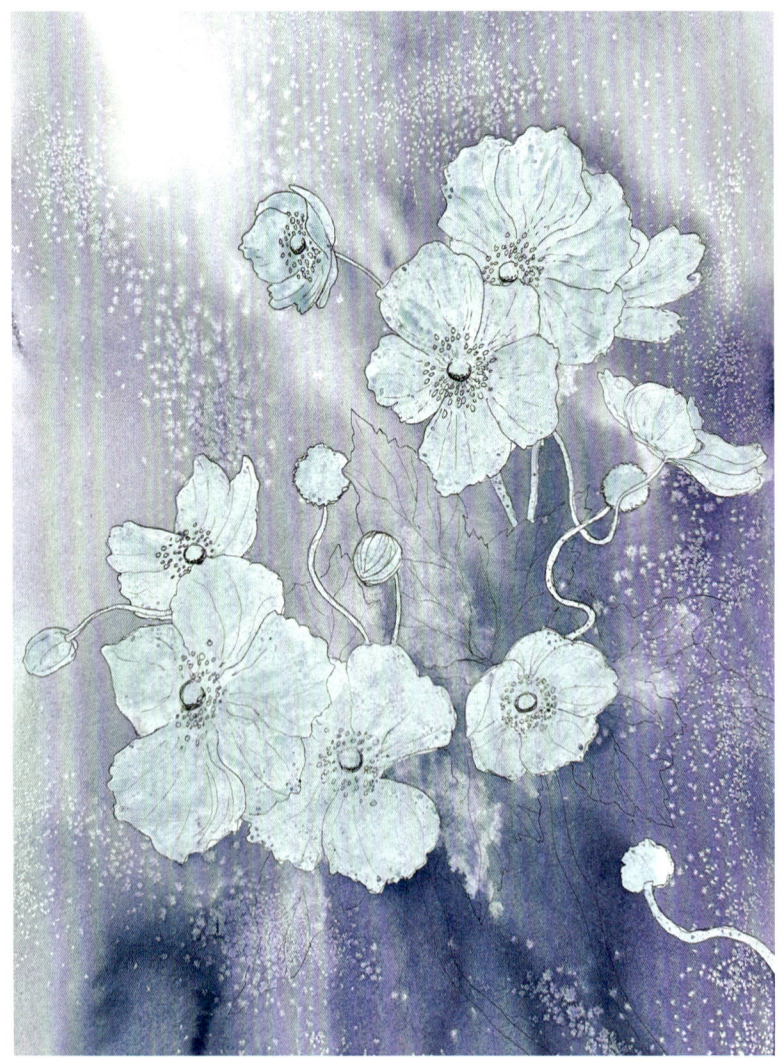

STAGE 1

Mix two large wells of mid- to dark-value colour: one of Payne's Grey and one of Indigo and Dioxazine Purple. Using the size 20 mop brush, wet the background with clean water and leave to soak for about 30 seconds.

Load the brush with the grey and starting at the bottom, sweep your brushstrokes up and over the masked flowers from bottom right to top left, to suggest a dramatic stormy sky.

Without rinsing the brush, dip it into the purple and continue with bold brushstrokes, allowing the grey and purple to blend together on the paper. Allow the paint to run out on the brush as you paint to create a graduated wash with a sky lighter at the top.

Leave briefly until the shine begins to go from the paper, then sprinkle a little salt into the damp wash (see page 23). Leave to dry completely.

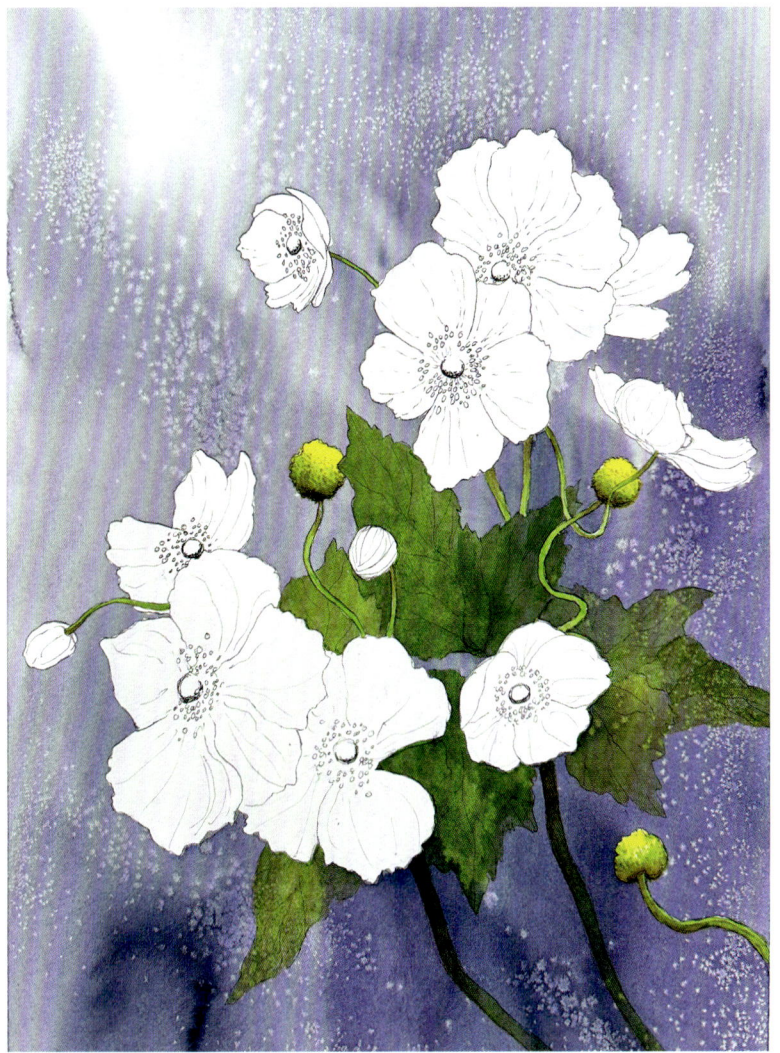

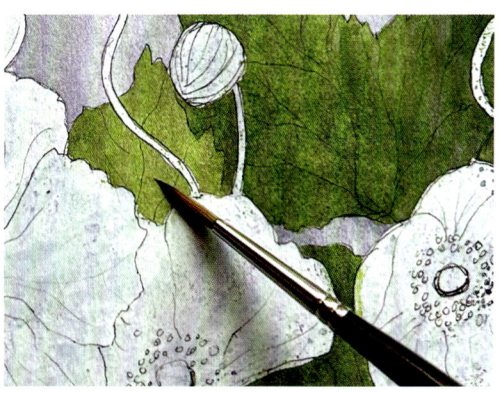

Where two leaves meet, brighten one by adding a touch of Transparent Yellow into the mix.

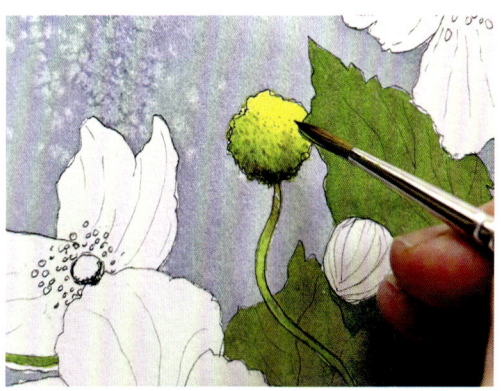

Dot in a little texture across the seed head using the tip of the brush.

STAGE 2

Brush off any salt that hasn't dissolved using a clean dry brush.
Mix two wells of mid-value paint: Sap Green and Transparent Yellow.
Paint the leaves one by one with the green using the size 3 round brush.
The underlying colour of the background wash will show through
and add variation to the leaves. Paint the two main flower stems.
Leave to dry completely.

Remove the masking fluid with the adhesive eraser. Mix more Sap Green
if you need it, and two small wells each of mid-value Lemon Yellow and
Sepia. Paint the stems with green using the size 0 detail brush.

Using the size 3 round brush, paint the seed heads with Lemon Yellow,
and drop in a little Sap Green along the bottom edge, allowing it to
diffuse into the yellow. Add a tiny touch of Sepia as a shadow at the base.
Leave to dry completely.

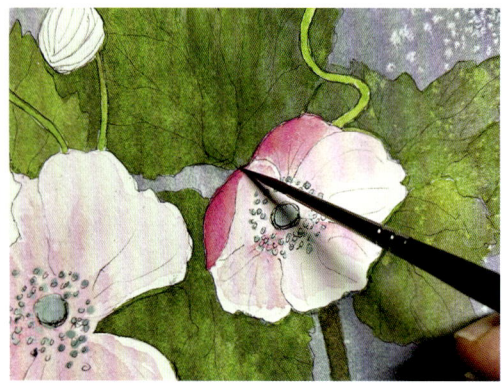

Use the mid-value mix of the magenta to paint the darker outer petals, graduating the colour from dark to light where necessary.

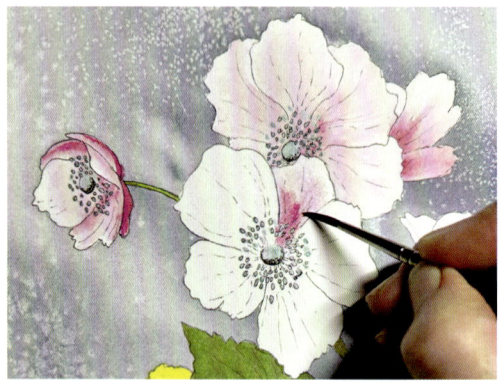

When deepening the pink around the flower centre, you can use a clean, damp brush to lift away excess colour, if it accidentally goes in too strong.

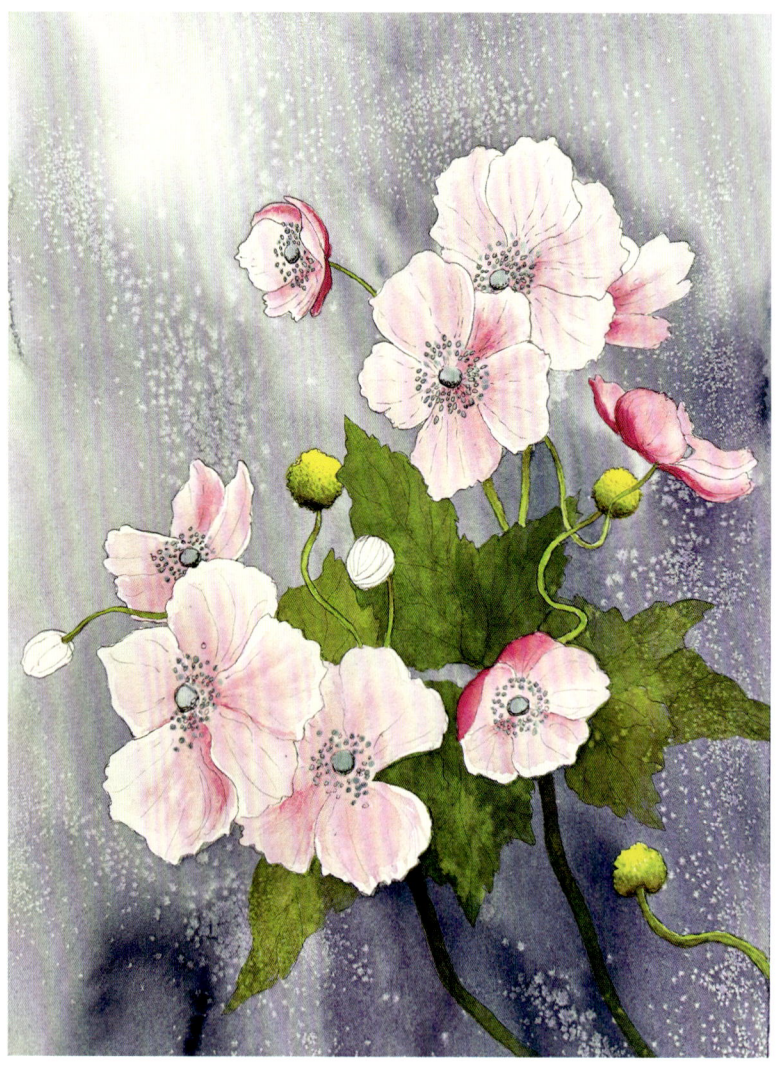

STAGE 3

Re-mask the flower centres and anthers. Mix three wells of Quinacridone Magenta: one a very watery light value with just a hint of colour, one a light value and one a mid-value. Paint the flowers one by one: dampen each petal with a little clean water, then add the paler mix, working from the flower centre towards the petal tip, graduating the colour and leaving a narrow margin of unpainted white paper at the edge. Add a little more of the deeper colour into the damp wash where the pink is slightly stronger. Leave to dry.

Once dry, remove the masking fluid with the adhesive eraser.

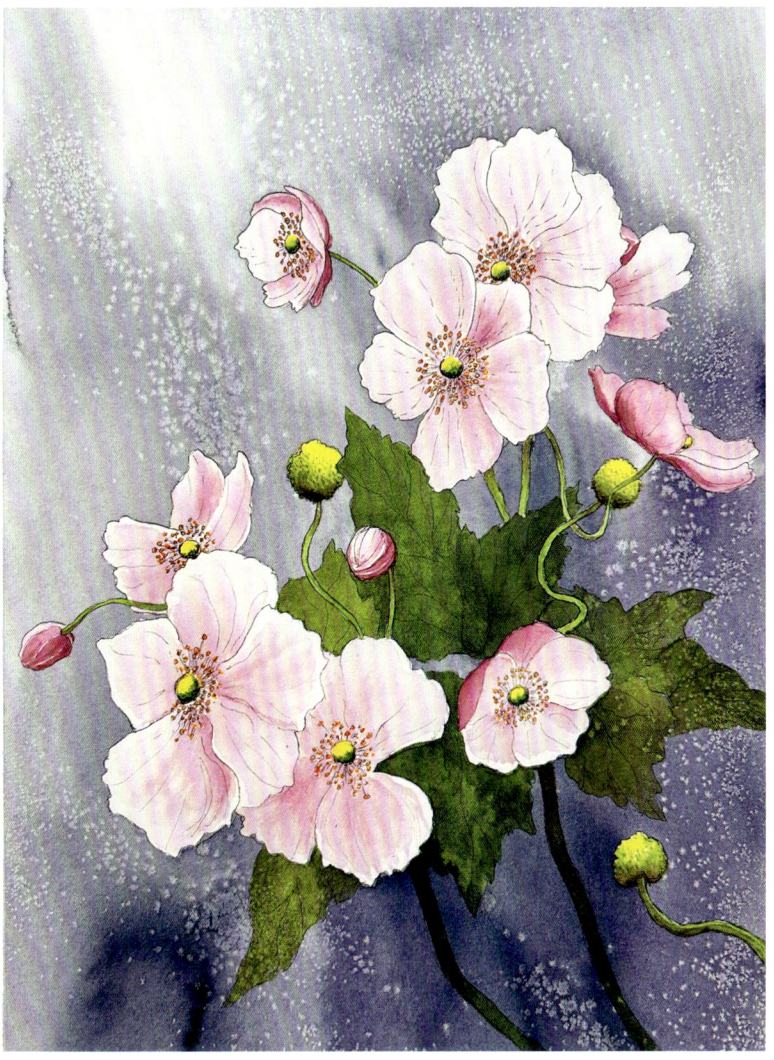

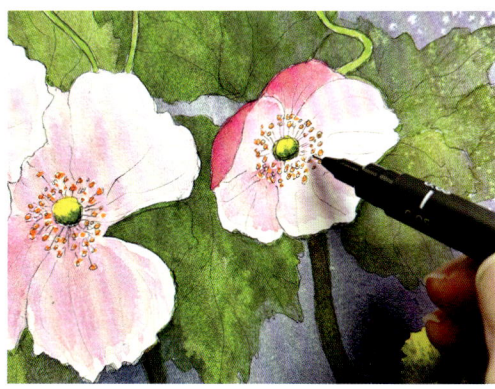

If your washes have obscured the line work, you can carefully go over it again at the end to bring more clarity if needed.

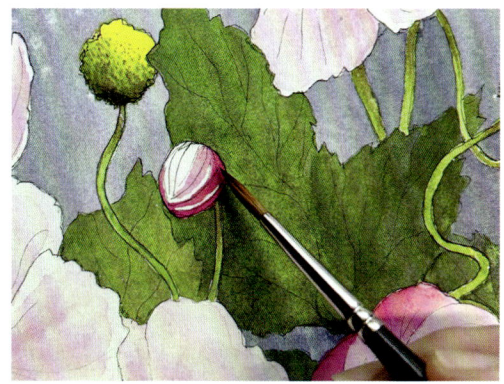

Leaving some white, unpainted highlights on the buds helps to give them shape and form.

STAGE 4

Mix two small wells of mid-value paint: Lemon Yellow and Sap Green. Paint the flower centres with Lemon Yellow, with a little Sap Green added to the base while damp. Mix a small well of Transparent Yellow and Cadmium Orange Hue. Use the tip of the size 0 detail brush to paint the tiny anthers surrounding the centres. Leave to dry.

To paint the buds, mix two small wells of Quinacridone Magenta, one light value and one mid-value. Using the size 3 round brush, paint the buds with the light-value mix leaving some fine unpainted highlights. Drop in a little of the mid-value magenta while still damp to deepen the colour on the shadow side. If the two main flower stems are looking a little light, mix a small well of Sap Green darkened with a little Sepia and paint them using the size 3 round brush. Leave to dry.

Join the anthers to the flower centres using a 0.1mm fine-liner pen.

Tip

Hold the detail brush at a 90-degree angle to the paper to get really small dots of colour for the anthers.

FOCUS ON
Floral Arrangements

Setting up and painting your own still life flower arrangements can be a lot of fun. It's a great way to create expressive paintings with your own personal stamp, as you can choose flowers from your garden or local florist, and use unique vases and props from your home.

Creating the scene

You can find or set up an area for arranging your still life quite easily, basically anywhere with enough room for a vase of flowers and a few props. Maybe pin up a fabric backdrop that spreads across a table: you can use a tablecloth or striped tea towel to add pattern and interest, or use plain backgrounds – the possibilities are endless!

I love to use vintage vases and props for my floral arrangements. I find them cheaply in charity shops and thrift stores, and the addition of bright citrus fruit, berries or leaves can complement the arrangements beautifully.

Lighting

You can use natural light from a window, or light your subject with artificial light from a lamp. The light source is often best placed top left or right, which will provide a strong light on one side and shadow on the other side. In other words, you will have enough contrast and tonal value variation to give shape and form to the painting.

Take photos from different angles to find a composition that pleases you, and try out different composition ideas in your sketchbook, cropping in or zooming out. Most importantly, use your creative licence and have fun!

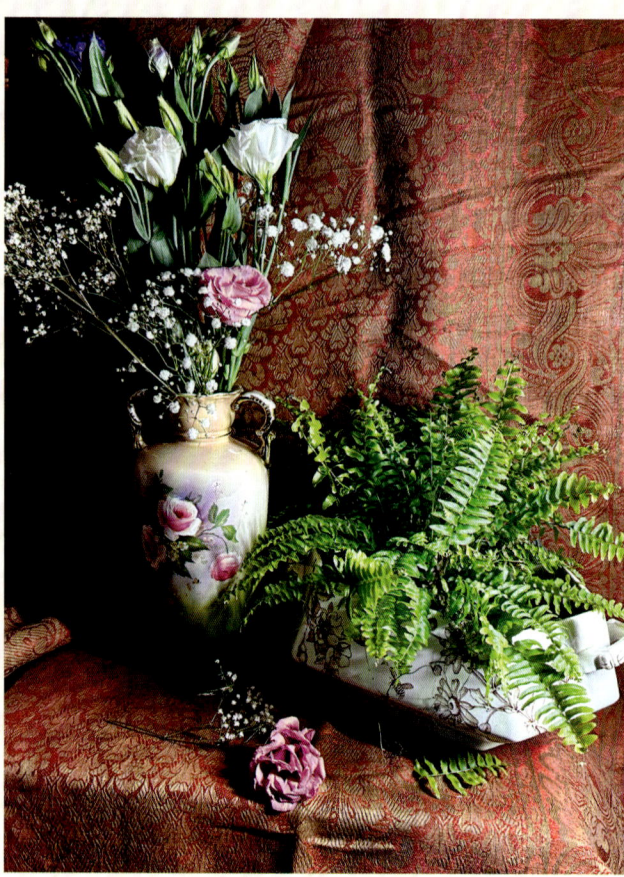

An old vintage curtain acts as an effective backdrop for the rose-like lisianthus blooms and ferns.

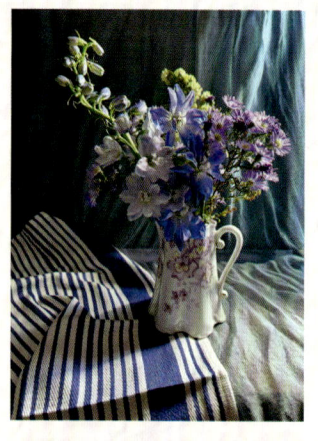
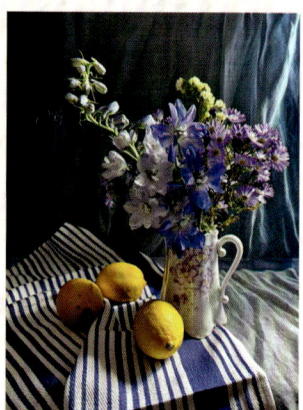
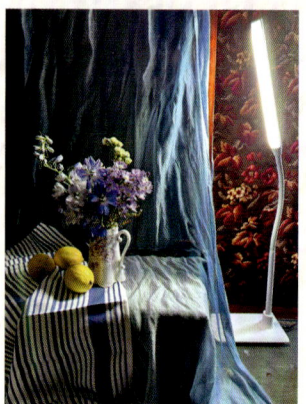
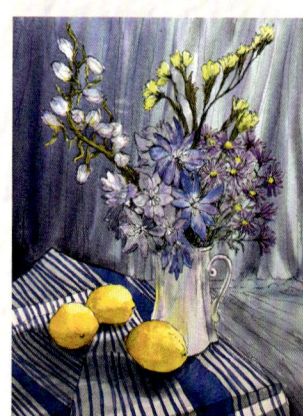

Try out different ideas and take photos from different angles, including or excluding some elements to see what works.

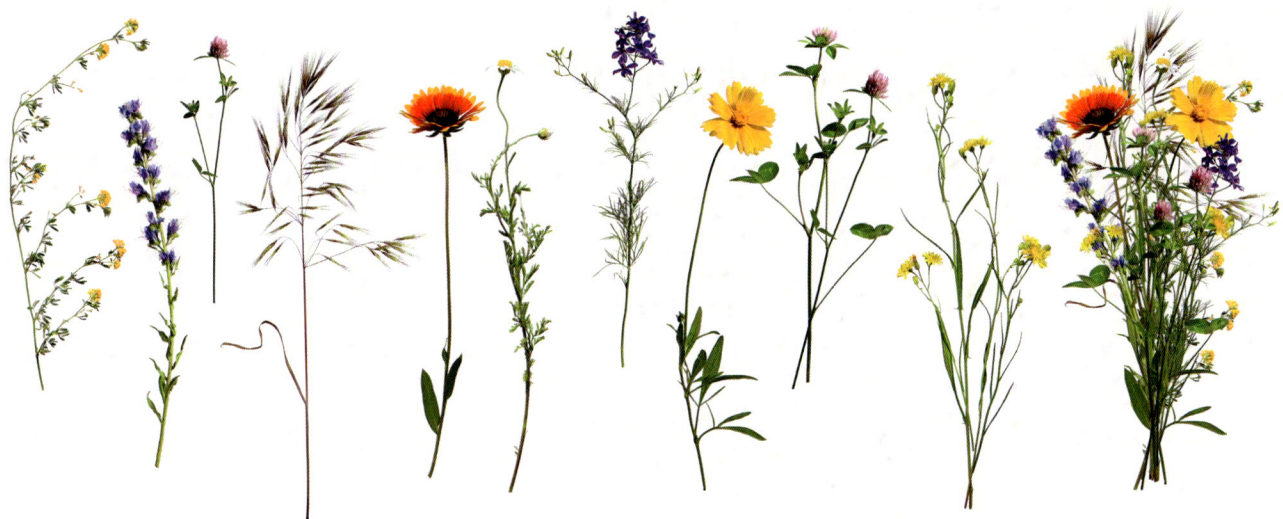

Simplifying floral arrangements

It's possible to use layered images to simplify complex flower arrangements. To create mixed flower compositions using this idea, sketch several different plant stems in your sketchbook, then transfer them individually to tracing paper.

Play around with layering these individual components in different configurations until you find a composition that you like. Secure the result with a little decorator's masking tape, then trace them to create a template. The finished layered design can now be transferred onto watercolour paper using the technique on page 21.

Winter Hellebores with Ferns and Ivy (see pages 46–51) uses this technique to combine three separate elements into a pleasing floral arrangement. The sketching of the complex stems and leaves becomes simpler and less confusing when each element is considered and sketched separately. This makes it much easier to create a pleasing arrangement, which can then be traced and transferred to watercolour paper.

A selection of single flower stems can be seen individually and then all layered together to create a pleasing arrangement.

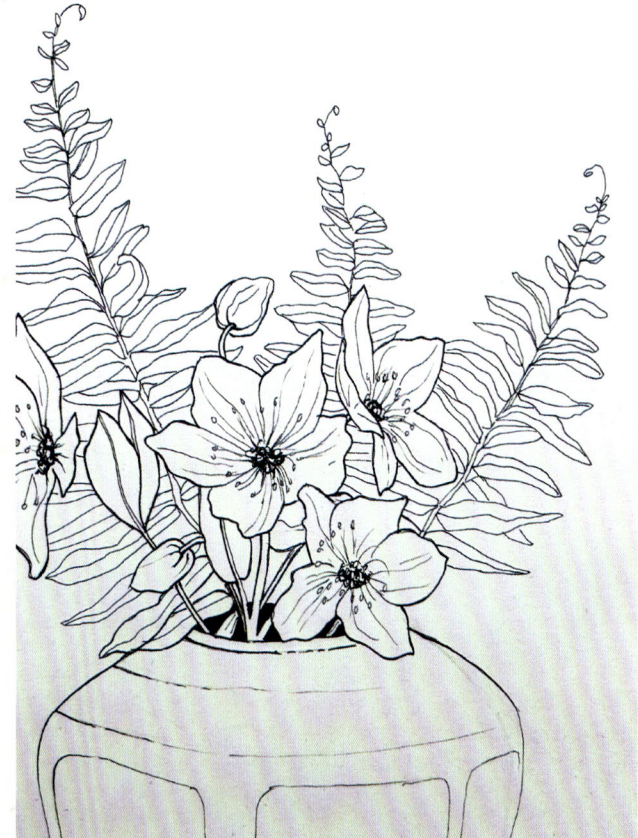

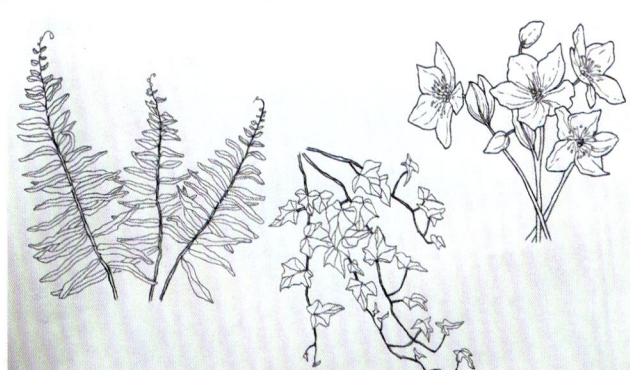

Experiment with the positions of the individual groups of flowers and leaves before positioning them in your vase or other prop, ready for tracing.

Winter Hellebores with Ferns and Ivy

Winter hellebores, also known as Christmas roses, come in many different colours;
I love those with cool green petals, veined and limned with pinkish red. The fern
fronds and ivy complement them perfectly.

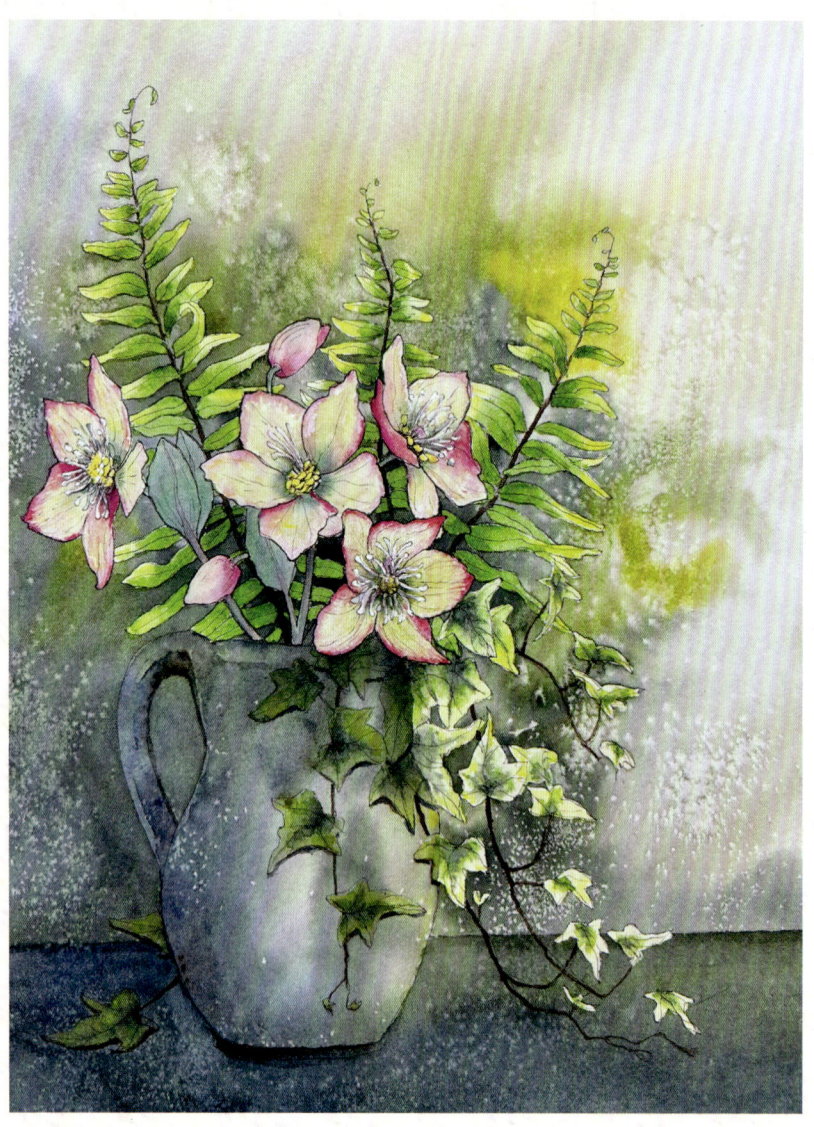

COLOURS NEEDED

Indigo	Perylene Green	Olive Green	Lemon Yellow	Sepia	Quinacridone Magenta	Hooker's Green

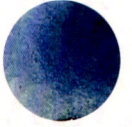 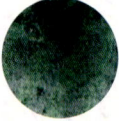 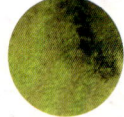  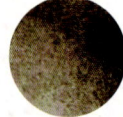 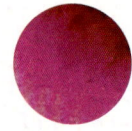 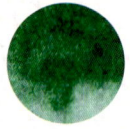

This project uses the layered approach described in 'Focus On: Floral Arrangements' (see page 45) to create the outline of the sketch. Templates for the ivy, the ferns and the hellebores are provided there as separate elements, so you can combine them more easily into the line work for the painting.

Setting up

Once you are happy with the arrangement from the three templates, draw the vase and transfer the outline onto hot-pressed watercolour paper, using the method outlined on page 21. Go over the pencil outline with the 0.1mm and 0.3mm waterproof fine-liner pens. Use the 0.1mm fine liner for the ferns, ivy and vase, and use a slightly bolder line with the 0.3mm fine liner to outline the hellebores so that they stand out a little more against the foliage.

Mask out the flowers and ferns with masking fluid and an old, small pointed brush, using the method outlined on page 13. Tape the outline onto your board and lay it flat, ready to begin.

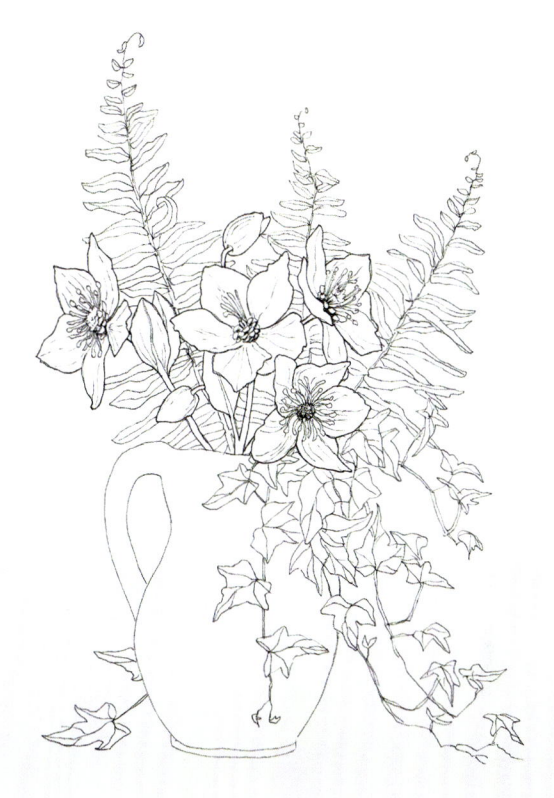

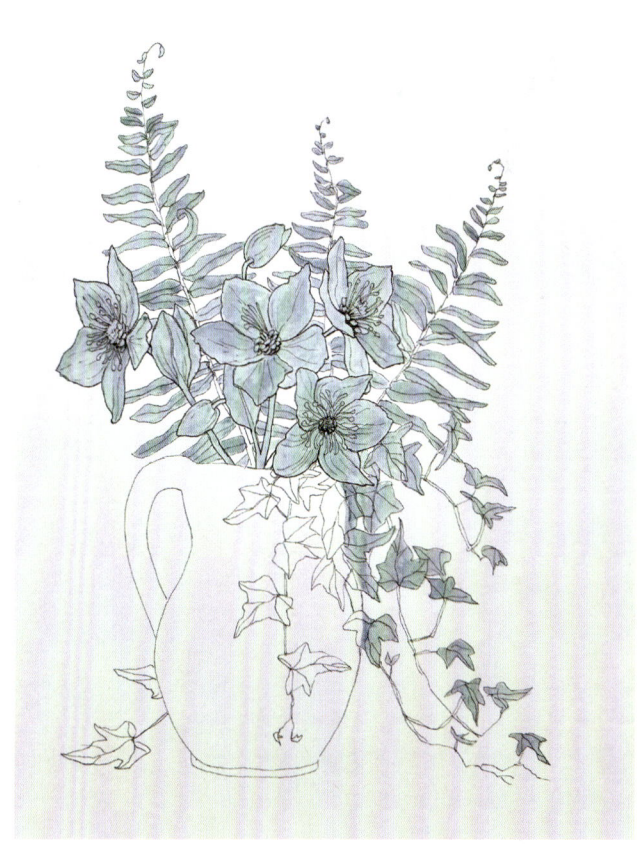

YOU WILL NEED

- *140lb (300gsm) hot-pressed watercolour paper*
- *Sketchbook or sketching paper*
- *Tracing paper*
- *HB pencil and eraser*
- *0.1mm and 0.3mm waterproof black fine-liner pens*
- *Painting board and decorator's masking tape*
- *Masking fluid and an old, small pointed brush*
- *Adhesive eraser*
- *Absorbent kitchen paper*
- *Palette with several mixing wells*
- *Water misting spray*
- *Fine table salt*
- *Size 20 mop brush*
- *Size 2 quill brush*
- *Oval wash brush*
- *Size 3 round brush*
- *Size 0 round detail brush*

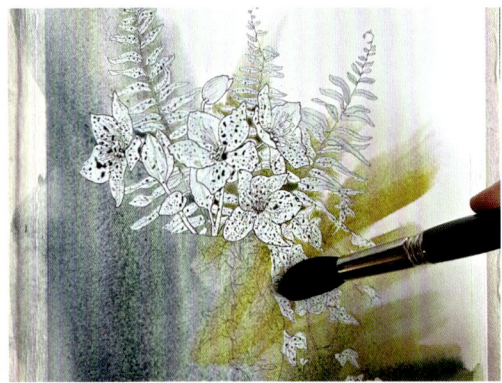

Use sweeping brushstrokes to complement the upward sweep of the ferns.

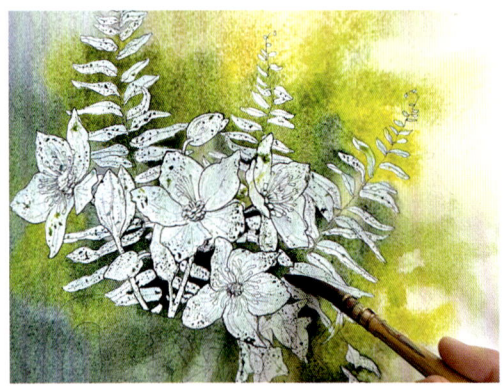

Using the smaller quill brush allows for greater control when deepening the colour around the vase.

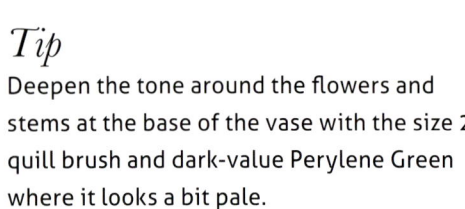

Tip

Deepen the tone around the flowers and stems at the base of the vase with the size 2 quill brush and dark-value Perylene Green where it looks a bit pale.

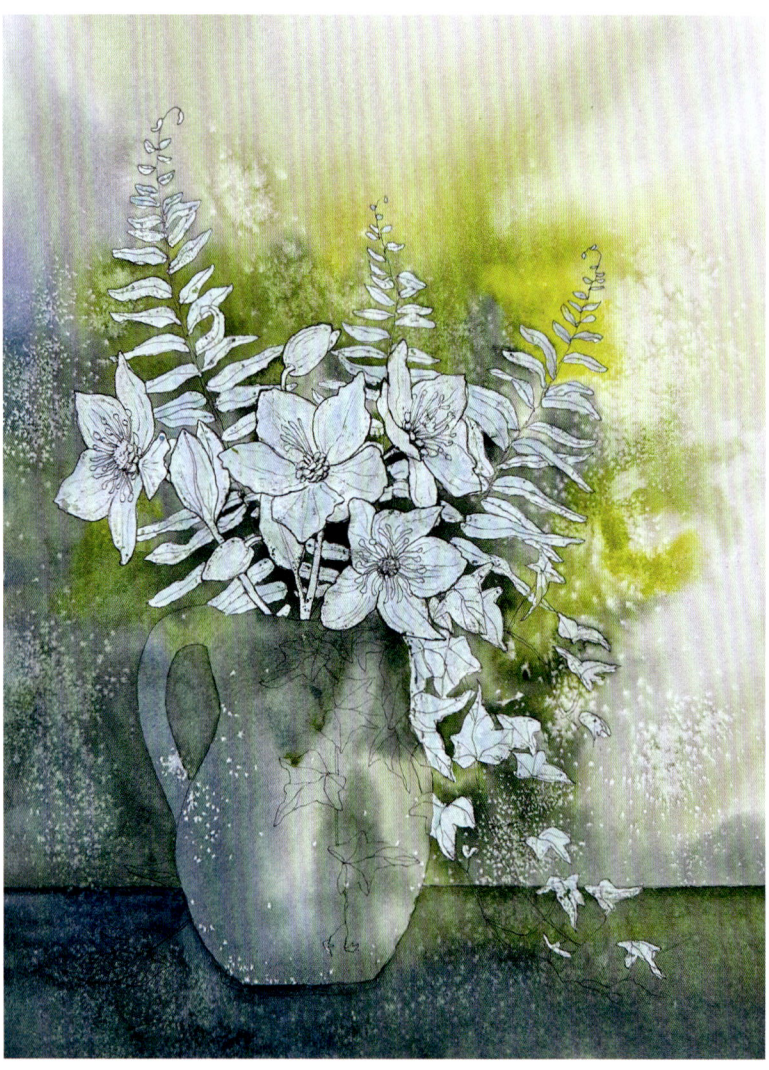

STAGE 1

Mix four large wells of mid-value Indigo, Perylene Green, Olive Green and Lemon Yellow, and a small well of dark-value Perylene Green. Wet the page with clean water with the size 20 mop brush. Leave to soak for 30 seconds.

Start with sweeping brushstrokes of Indigo across the bottom and left edge. Without rinsing the brush, dip it into the Perylene Green and add around the vase area, allowing the colours to blend on the paper. Rinse the brush and complete the wash with Olive Green and Lemon Yellow, keeping it brighter and yellower top right to indicate the source of light.

Once the shine starts to go from the wash, sprinkle with a little fine table salt (see page 23) and leave to dry. Once dry, paint a band of Indigo behind the vase. Allow to dry, then lighten the Indigo mix with a little water and negatively paint around the left of the vase, softening it into the rest of the wash with a clean damp oval wash brush. Leave to dry.

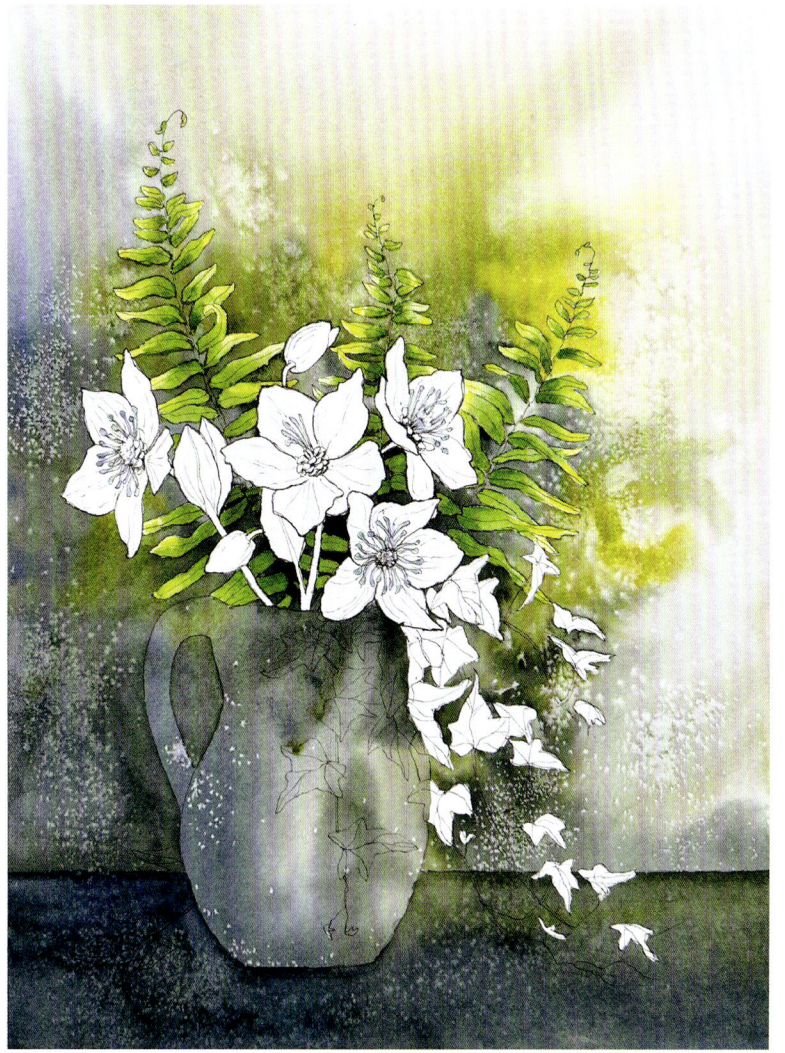

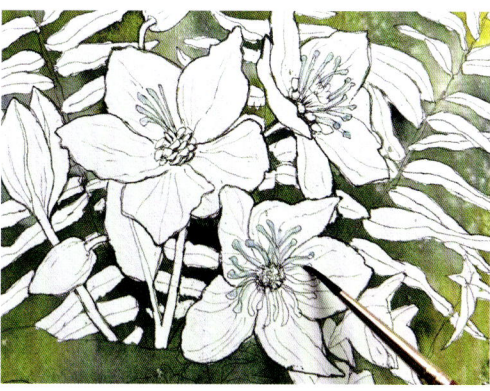

If you make a mistake applying the masking fluid, or splash some onto the paper, avoid wiping it off while still wet – this can leave traces and spoil subsequent washes. Allow to fully dry before removing it with the adhesive eraser; re-apply the correct mask if needed.

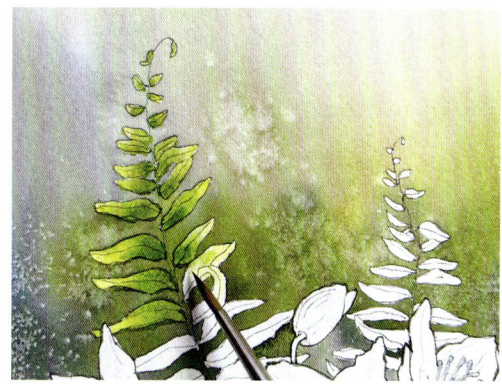

STAGE 2

Brush away any salt that hasn't dissolved from the painting using a clean dry brush, then remove the masking fluid with the adhesive eraser. Re-mask the fine stamens and stigmas in the middle of each flower.

Mix two light-value wells of paint for the ferns: one of Lemon Yellow and one of Sap Green. Using the size 3 round brush, dampen a few fern fronds at a time with clean water, then drop the yellow into the top and the green into the base of each frond, allowing the paint to softly diffuse and mix. Continue in the same way until all the ferns fronds are painted. Leave to dry.

Take care not to add too much green into the yellow; the colours should meet and blend, not overtake or overwhelm one another.

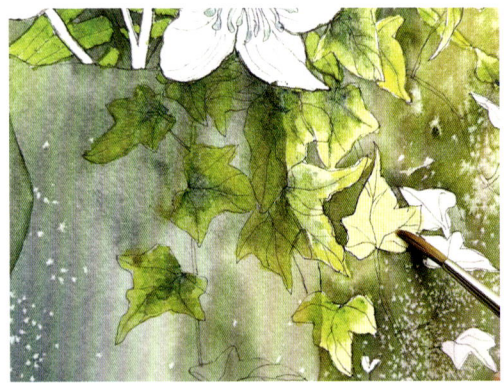

The Lemon Yellow provides a base that will allow the other colours in the variegated ivy to glow.

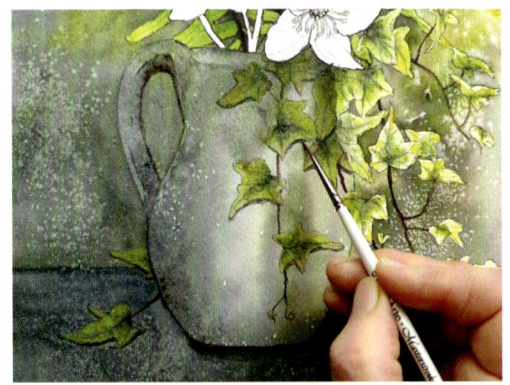

Adding touches of Perylene Green around the underside of the shaded ivy leaves will help them to lift away from the vase.

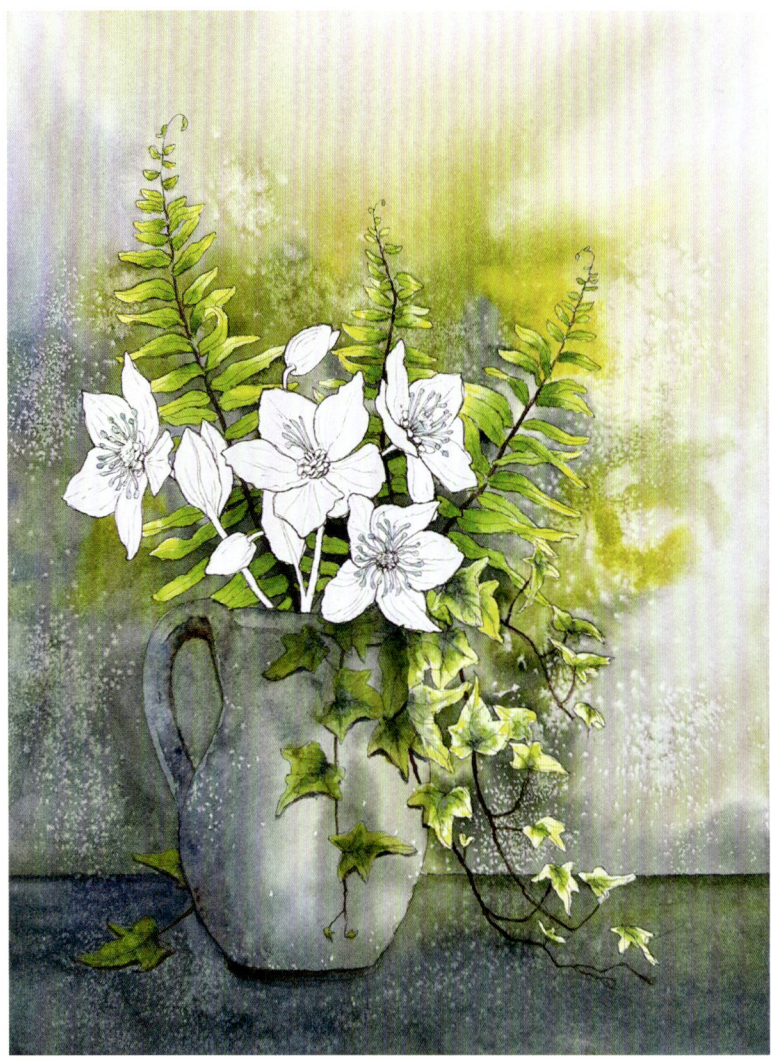

STAGE 3

Mix three small light-value wells of Lemon Yellow, Sap Green and Sap Green darkened with a little Indigo. To paint the variegated ivy leaves on the right side of the vase, paint a whole leaf with the yellow using the size 3 round brush, then add a touch of the light-value green at the base of the leaf while still wet. After waiting a few seconds, touch in a small dab of the darker green mix at the base. Repeat for the rest of the leaves in this area.

For the ivy leaves in shadow on the vase and left, add a dab more Lemon Yellow to the mix to brighten it, and use this to paint the leaves. Touch a little of the dark green into the centres. Leave to dry.

Mix two wells of mid-value colour: Sepia and Indigo. Paint the fern and ivy stems with Sepia using the size 0 detail brush. Brush a little clean water across the base, handle, rim, and left edge of the vase with the oval wash brush. Dab Sepia and Indigo into these areas while damp to add shadows. Leave to dry.

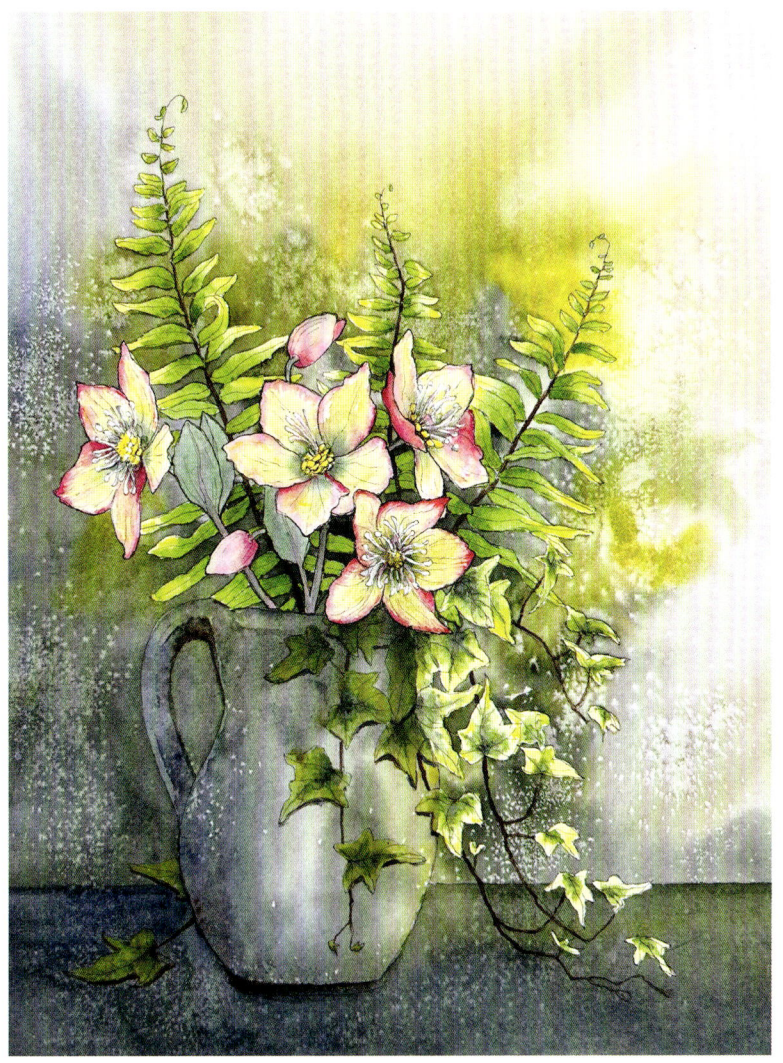

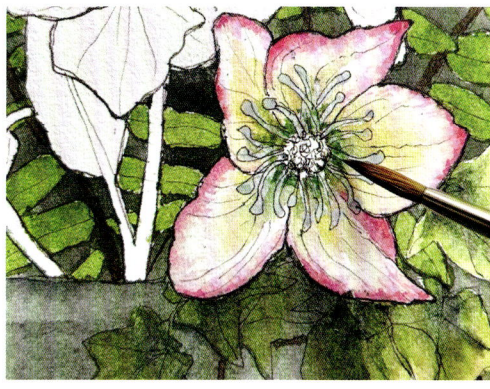

Using bluer-toned Hooker's Green to colour the hellebores will help differentiate the delicate blooms from the more yellow-toned greenery in the rest of the painting.

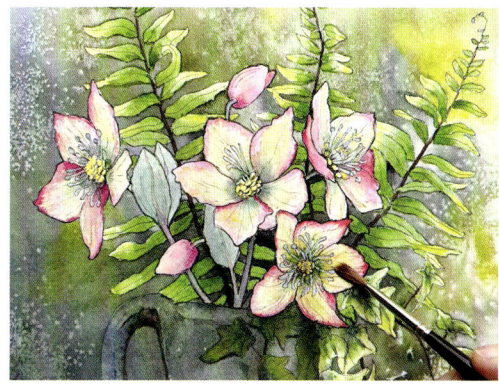

When glazing over the flowers, make sure that they are bone dry and use a very light touch to avoid lifting any paint.

STAGE 4

Mix three wells of mid-value Olive Green with a touch of Lemon Yellow, Quinacridone Magenta and Hooker's Green. To paint a flower, dampen each petal with clean water using the size 3 round brush, and paint the middle part of the petal with the Olive Green/Lemon Yellow mix. Add delicate edges to each petal with the magenta. While still wet, add a dab of Hooker's Green around the masked-out stamens. Repeat for all flowers. When completely dry, glaze over the whole flower with watery, light-value lemon yellow to add an ethereal glow.

Paint the hellebore leaves and stems with Hooker's Green, adding a little magenta in the leaf vein and stems to redden them. Paint the buds with magenta, graduating the tone from light to dark to suggest their shape and form. Once dry, glaze the buds with the watery Lemon Yellow. Remove the masking fluid from the stamens with the adhesive eraser, and add a little light-value Indigo to them here and there to indicate subtle shadows.

Peonies in a Glass Jar

Peonies have a timeless elegance, making them beloved by artists and gardeners alike. Here, this rosy-hued bouquet is painted in a simple glass jar, where the delicate curves of the flower shapes are complemented by the curved edges of the vessel.

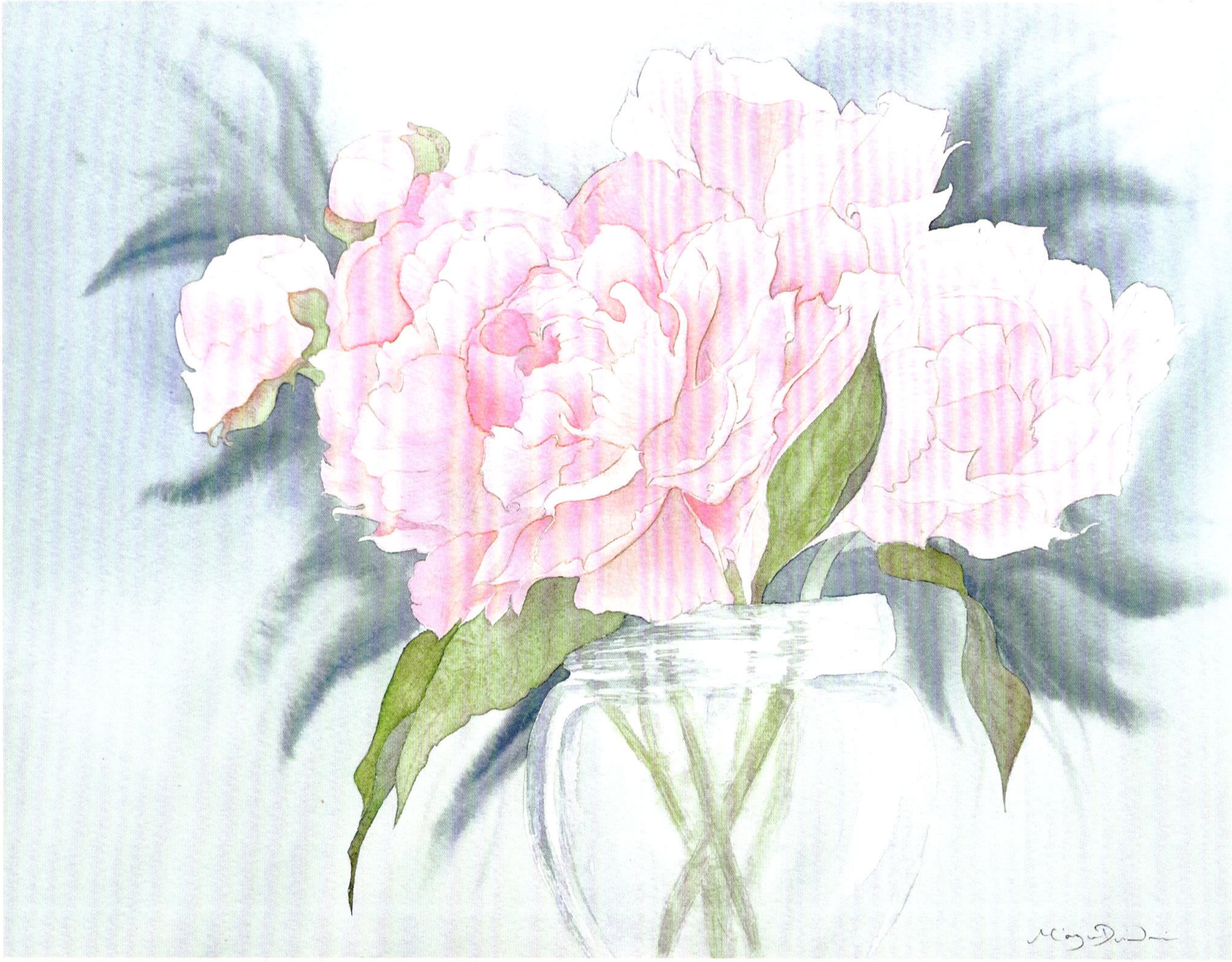

COLOURS NEEDED

Indigo	Perylene Green	Sap Green	Quinacridone Magenta	Rose Dore	French Ultramarine
	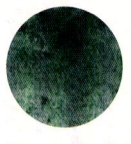	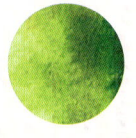		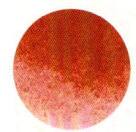	

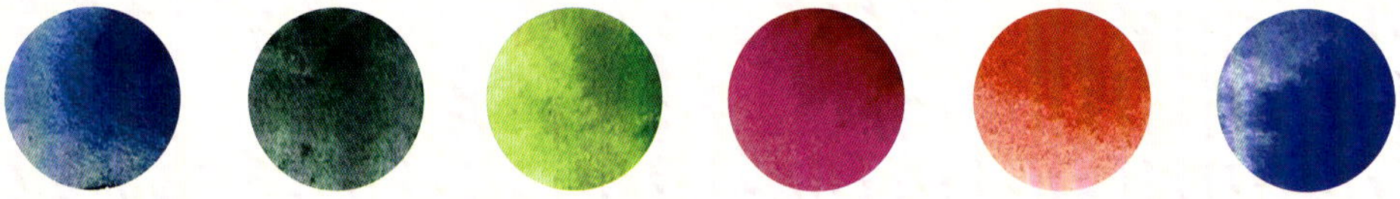

Peonies are one of summer's perpetual delights, with their bright, blowsy flowerheads that come in an array of delicate whites, palest pinks and rich crimsons. I have a personal fondness for the pink variety, which always remind me of ballerinas, with their frothy abundance of layered petals.

This layering of petals can sometimes give painters pause when it comes to capturing the beauty of flowers such as these, as it can be a tricky process to get right. It requires focus and concentration, but when broken down into stages, it becomes a relatively simple process. The key is to make sure you don't lose track of which way the petals are curving, as this dictates the shape of the overall bloom. This is a handy thing to remember when tackling other flowers that have their petals layered in a similar fashion, such as roses, dahlias and chrysanthemums.

Setting up

Begin by transferring the outline from the template onto hot-pressed watercolour paper, using the method described on page 21. There is no need to mask out the entire flower shape here: a simple outline of masking fluid will suffice, in order to protect the pale glass jar and outer peony petals from the background wash. Tape your pencil outline onto your board and lay it flat, ready to begin.

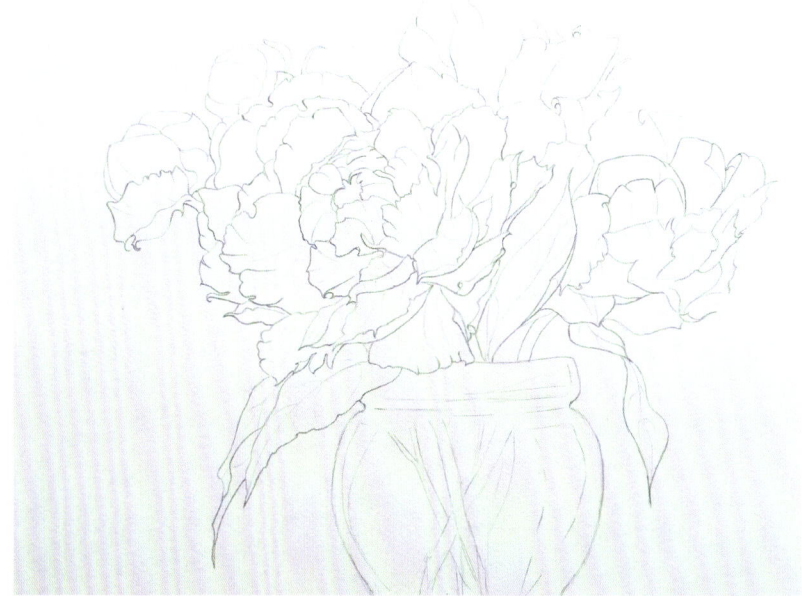

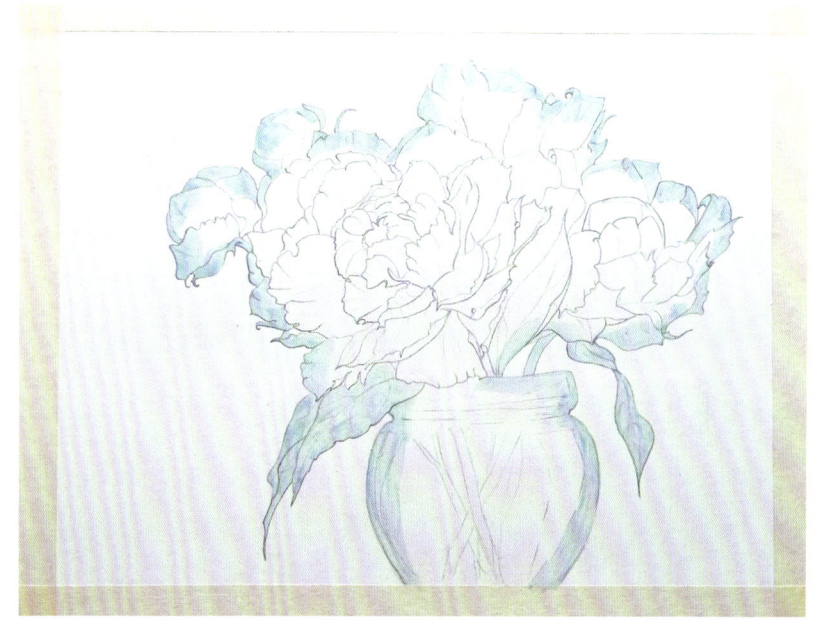

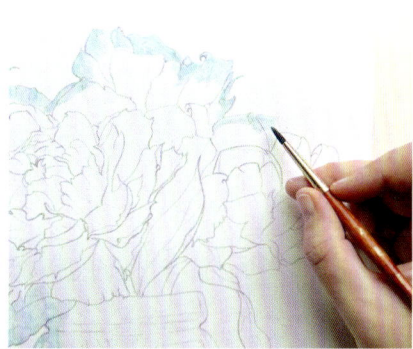

YOU WILL NEED

- *140lb (300gsm) hot-pressed watercolour paper*
- *Sketchbook or sketching paper and tracing paper*
- *Painting board and decorator's masking tape*
- *Sponge and absorbent kitchen paper*
- *HB pencil and eraser*
- *Palette with several mixing wells*
- *Size 20 mop brush*
- *Size 2 quill brush*
- *Size 3 round brush*
- *Size 0 round detail brush*

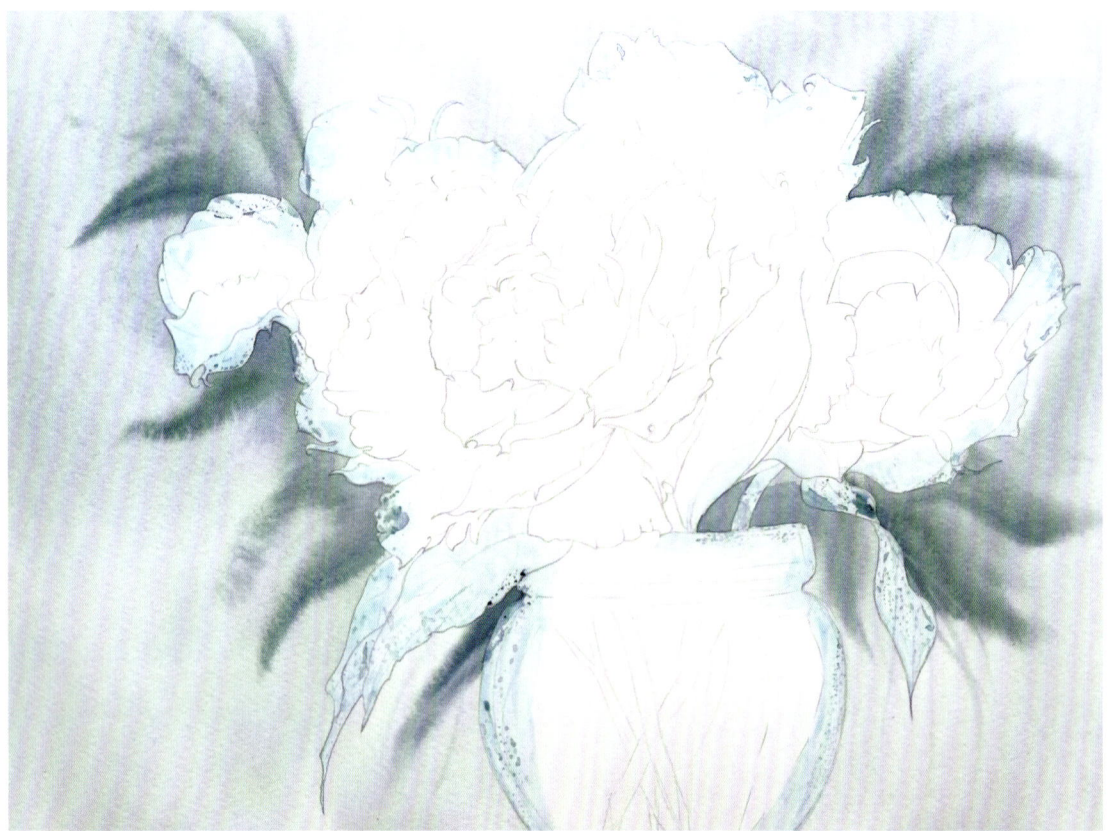

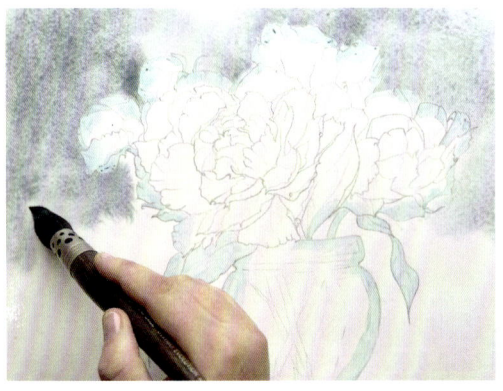

Painting from the top downwards and allowing the colour to run out on the brush as you paint is a simple method for achieving a dark-to-pale graduated wash.

Tip

Paint the leaves by starting at the masked area, then flicking your brush outwards in a shallow curve; this will minimize the chance of accidentally painting over the masking fluid and into the petal area.

STAGE 1

Paint a soft-focus backdrop using the technique outlined on page 23. Wet the background area all over with clean water using a size 20 mop brush and allow 30 seconds for the water to sink in.

Mix four wells of colour: one light and mid-value each of Indigo and Perylene Green. Use the two light-value mixes to paint a softly mottled graduated wash, still using the size 20 mop, concentrating more colour at the top edge of the page and fading it down towards the lower edge of the paper.

While the wash is still wet, take a little of the mid-value green and use the quill brush to paint loose leaf shapes around the masked-out peony blooms. Next, use some mid-value Indigo to paint a few shadows along the lower edge of the leaf shapes. The richer paint should sit nicely in the wet wash, blurring at the edges but not fully diffusing out. Allow to dry completely.

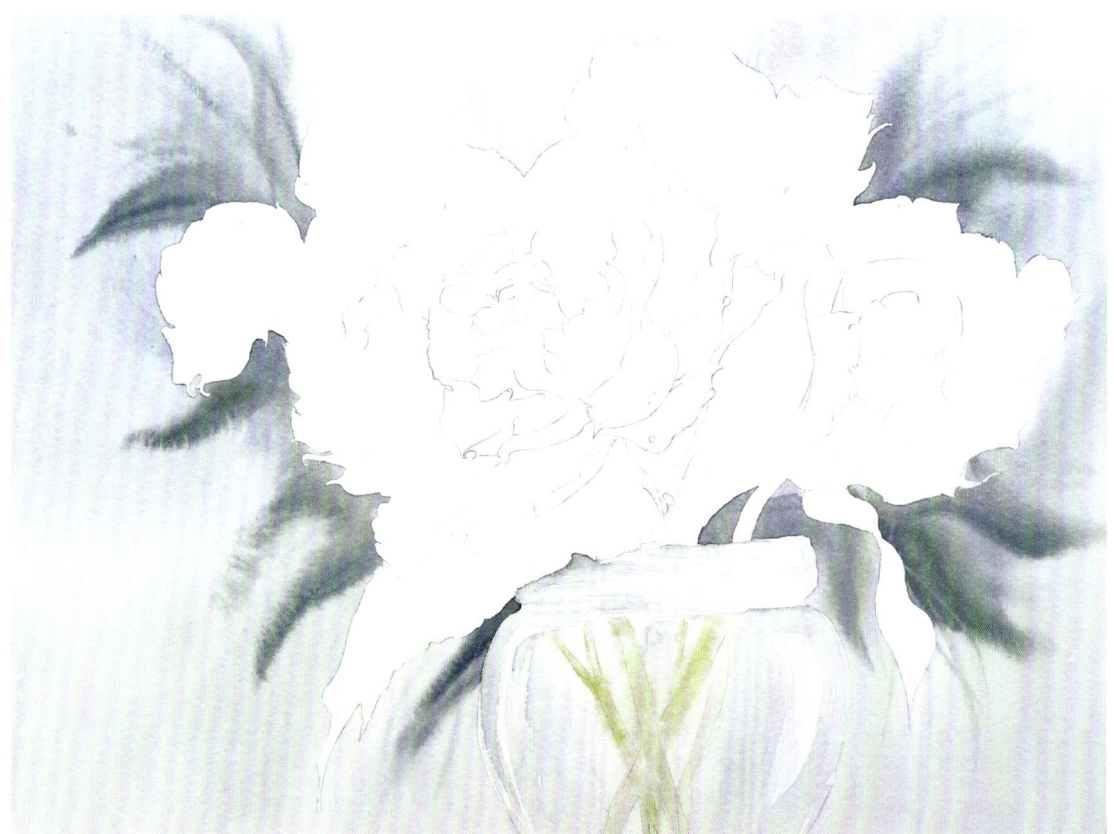

STAGE 2

Remove the masking fluid with an adhesive eraser. Using very pale Indigo and your quill brush, wash some colour loosely over the glass jar, but leave some areas of the paper unpainted around the curved edges to create patterns of reflected light.

Use the size 3 round brush and a touch of Perylene Green to add some areas of deeper colour wet-in-wet, including some shadows around the top edge of the jar, where the blooms overhang.

While the paint is still damp, use a little light value Sap Green and the size 3 round brush to add colour to the peony stems inside the jar. Do this loosely, as the idea is for the stems to appear blurred and indistinct, as if viewing them through both water and curved glass.

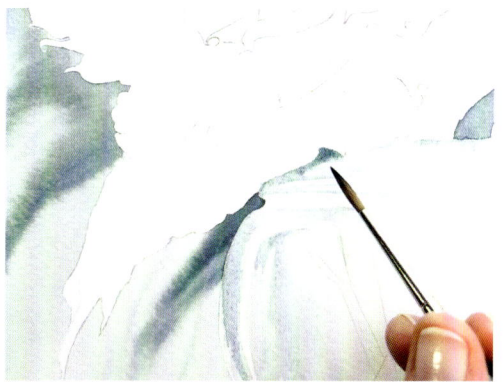

Use your size 3 round brush to paint a series of thin horizontal lines to create the loose impression of a threaded rim on the glass jar.

Tip
Use light pencil strokes to re-draw any pencil marks you still need that may have been lifted away when the mask was removed.

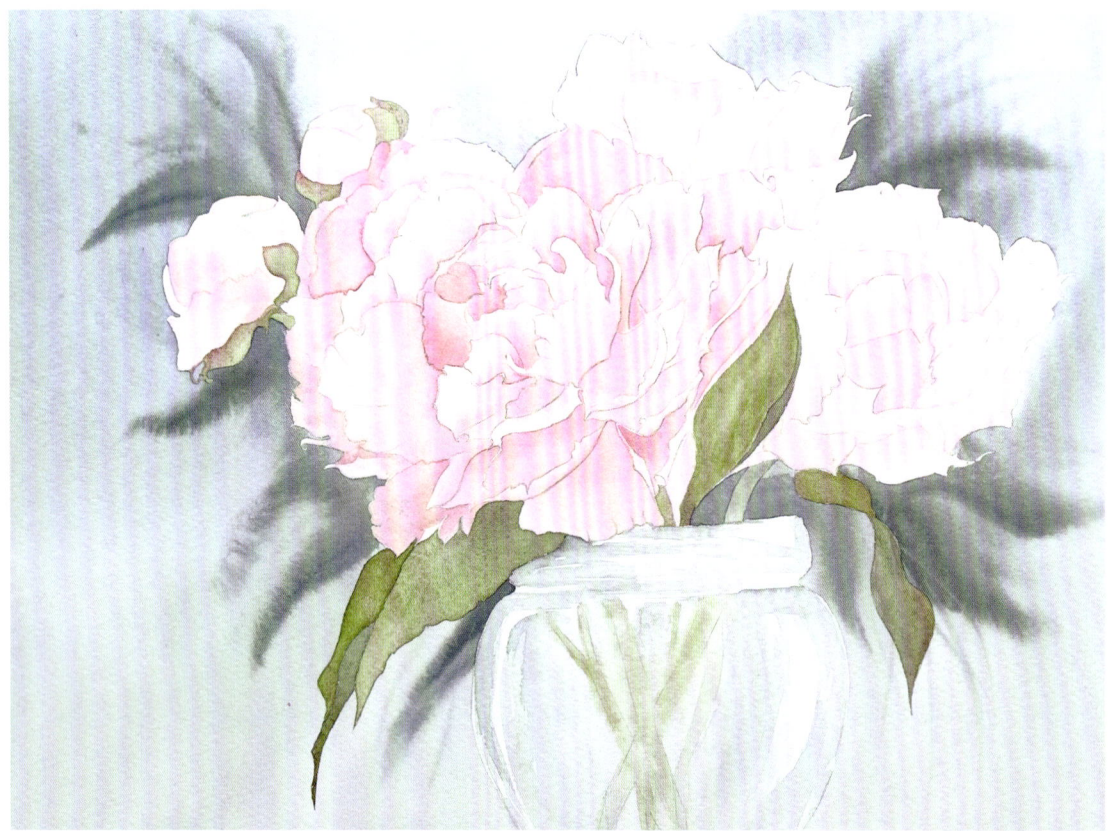

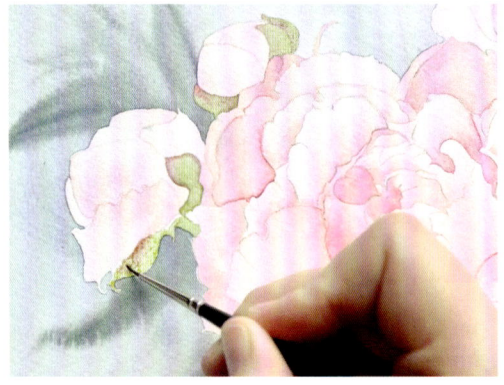

For the smaller buds, use the size 0 detail brush to dab Rose Dore into the leaf edges to achieve the characteristic peony bud blush.

STAGE 3

Add the first layer of colour to the flowers and leaves. Paint the petals using a combination of Quinacridone Magenta and Rose Dore; these are both potent colours, so mix light-value wells of each paint to achieve a delicate, rosy hue. Paint each petal one at a time, using the size 3 round brush to fill colour and the size 0 detail brush to tidy the edges.

Graduate the colour as you go, adding deeper colour to the part of the petal that is closest to the flower centre, allowing the colour to run out on the brush so that the edges of the petal appear paler. Doing this consistently will help achieve a sense of directionality among the layers of petals, which can otherwise become confusing.

Use mid-value Sap Green, Perylene Green and a touch of Rose Dore to add colour to the leaves, again using the size 3 brush to fill and the size 0 detail brush for clean neat edges.

Tip
Paint alternating petals, so you don't have to wait for one petal to dry before beginning another. This is the slow part of the painting, so take your time and enjoy the process!

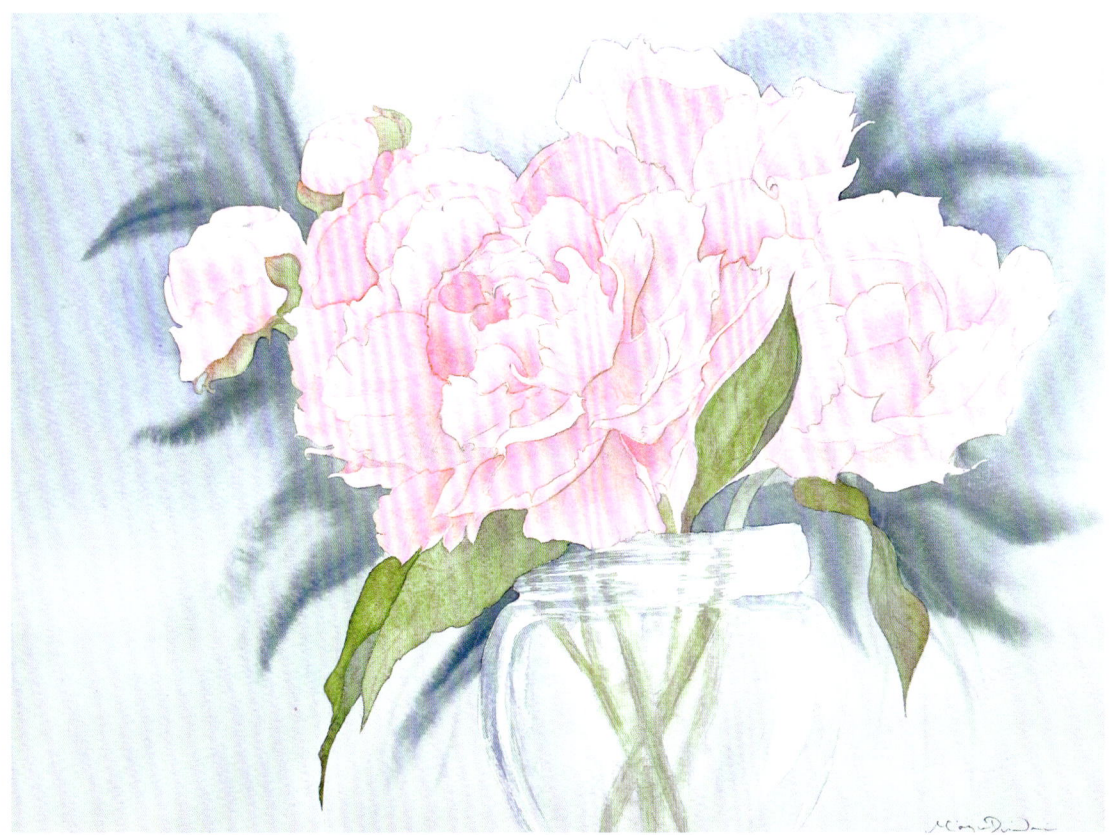

STAGE 4

Add the finishing darks and details to the painting, using the size 0 detail brush. Mix up a little light-value French Ultramarine, and use it to paint subtle shadows in the recesses of the petals where necessary. Once dry, use some mid-value Rose Dore to add fine directional lines to the petals and some delicate vein detail into the leaves.

Finish the glass jar by mixing up some mid-value Indigo and using it to add darker values around the edges of the jar where necessary. Use a combination of the two greens to strengthen the colour of the stems, and add a series of loose, lightly connected lines showing the stems through the jar's threaded rim.

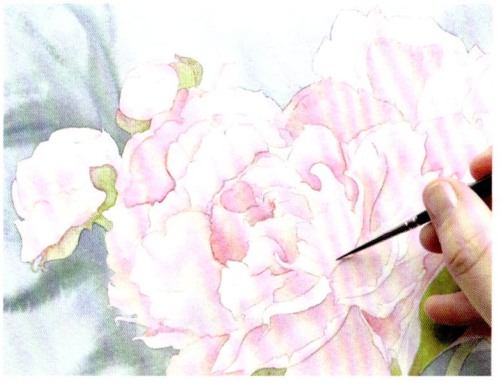

Pay attention to the direction in which each peony petal is unfurling, and use the fine finishing lines to convey this. A few simple brush marks at the edge or centre of each petal are usually sufficient for this.

Tip

When painting loose lines, try holding your brush further away from the ferrule, towards the middle of the handle. This can help give more spontaneity to your brush marks.

FOCUS ON
Wild Flowers

Painting wild flowers can be a challenging process, but it can also be all the more rewarding for this very reason. Their humble beauty can often be overlooked in favour of the larger, showier garden variety of blooms; but considering their delicacy, colour and astonishing variety, wild flowers are compelling compositional subjects.

Seasonality

One of the many challenges faced in painting wild flowers is their seasonality. Some of these flowers, such as English bluebells, flower for only a few weeks during spring, and are nowhere to be found at any other time of year. Considering their very nature of being wild, these are blooms that will be difficult (or impossible) to source from your local florist. However, luckily, it is possible to buy wild flower seeds and sow them in your own garden, providing an easily accessible painter's paradise of your very own. Alternatively, a well-lit and sunny window-box can be put to similar use, for those without access to a garden or outdoor space.

Wild flowers in situ

It is important to note that in some areas, picking wild flowers is illegal – so ensure you check your local laws before gathering any specimens. In any event, as wild flowers are often fragile creatures, they are usually best painted en plein air, i.e. in their outdoor setting. More often than not, you'll find that even when gathering them with the greatest of care, they will begin to wilt even before you get them to the studio. The best answer to these challenges is to paint wild flowers in situ or take their photograph, wherever you find them. In this manner, you can build up your own library of beautiful, everlasting reference blooms.

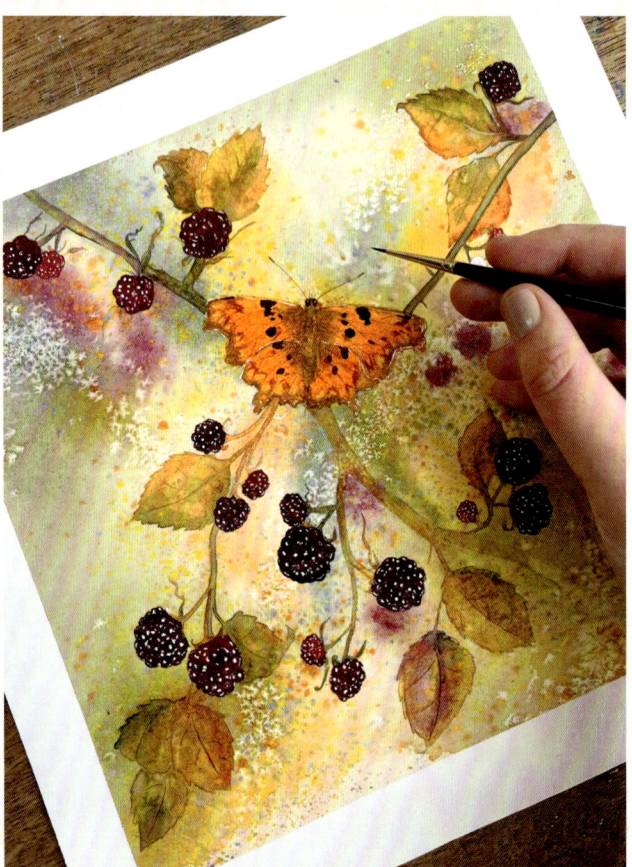

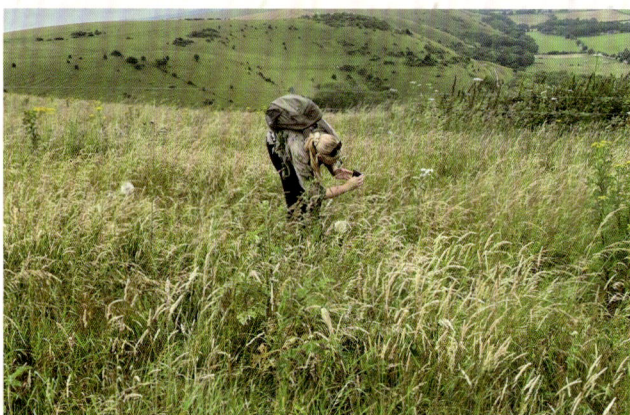

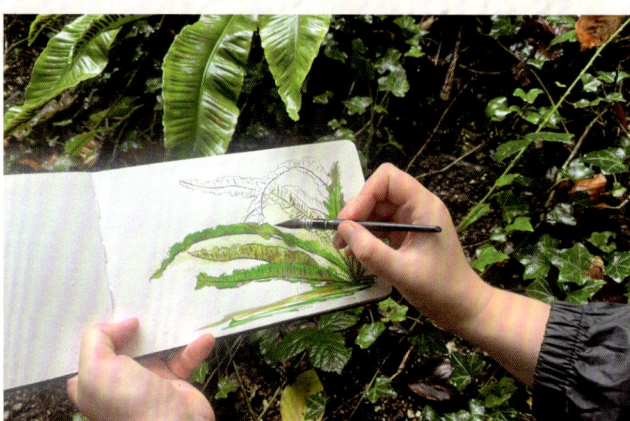

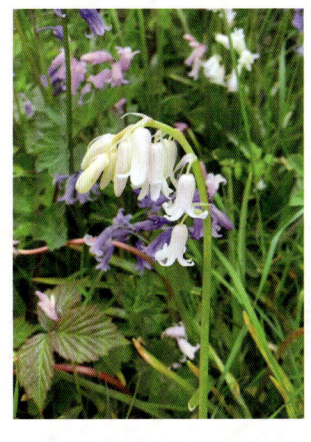
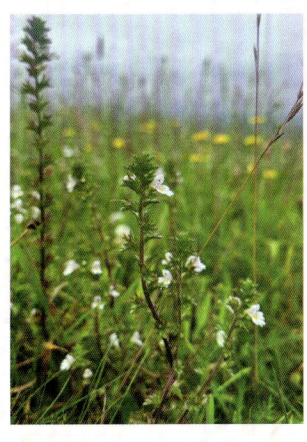
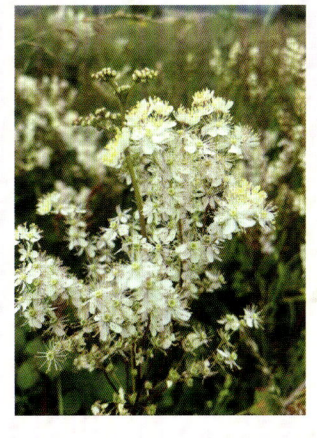
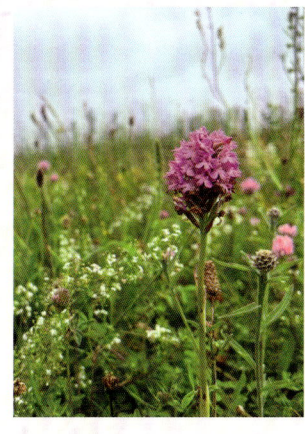

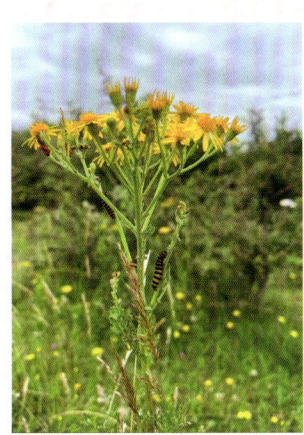
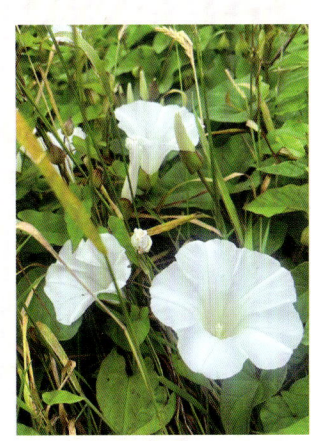
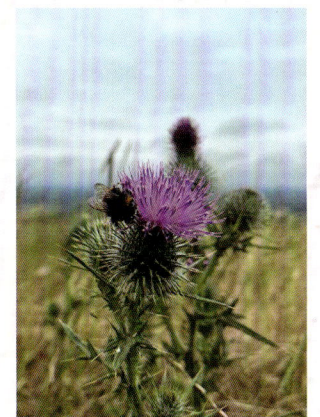
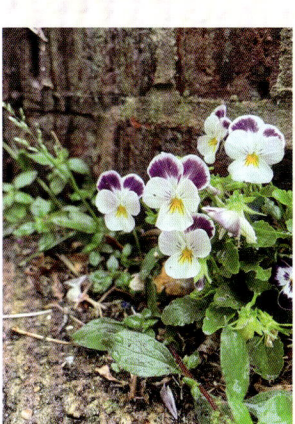

Vagabonds

Another consideration is that what constitutes a wild flower often overlaps with the gardener's enemy: weeds. A perfect example lies with the hedge bindweed featured in the Bramble Ramble project on pages 86–91. As a hardy, strangling climber, it is seldom welcome in any manicured garden setting, as its voracious growing tendencies are deadly to other plants; however, there is no denying that its pale, heart-shaped leaves and luminous white blooms are of staggering beauty. Similarly, yellow ragwort offers a bright, vivacious splash of summer colour; yet its toxicity to livestock makes it an unwelcome presence in most pastures.

There are also the roguish, incidental wild flowers to consider such as the dandelion at home in a flower bed, ivy that trails its green fingers up the sides of abandoned buildings, or even a garden flower that has readily self-seeded elsewhere such as pansies growing in a crack in the pavement. Ivy in particular is a remarkable plant, as its late autumn flowers provide vital nectar for all manner of insects, and it makes an excellent compositional addition to virtually any flower painting. These often-overlooked green elements that sit quietly beside the brighter blooms, that give body and life to a painting, allow the flowers themselves to shine.

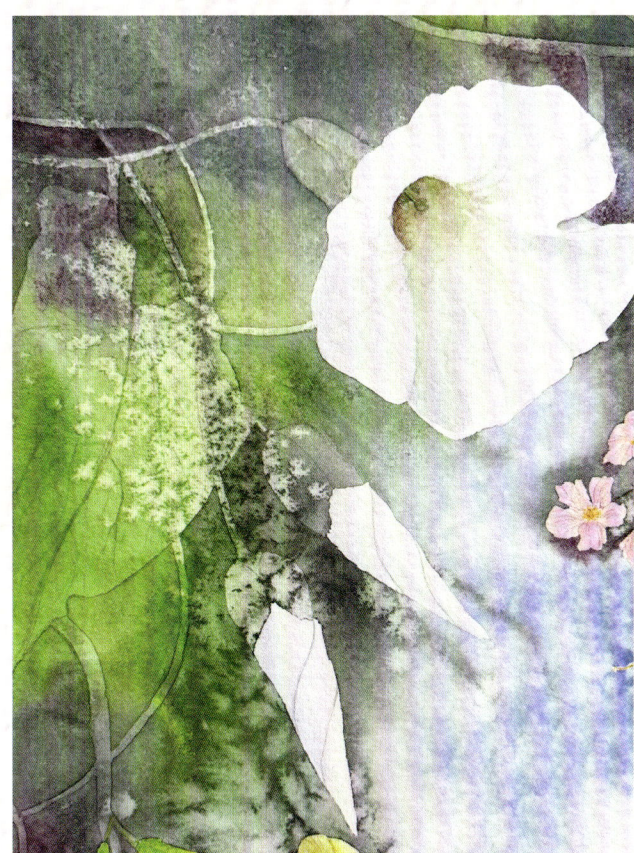

Wistful Wild Flowers

Bluebells are a firm favourite among wild flowers – there is something so enchanting about their delicacy, their astonishing colour, and the way they can transform entire swathes of woodland into a sea of luminous blue. When placed alongside other spring blooms, they provide height and eye-catching colour as part of a composition.

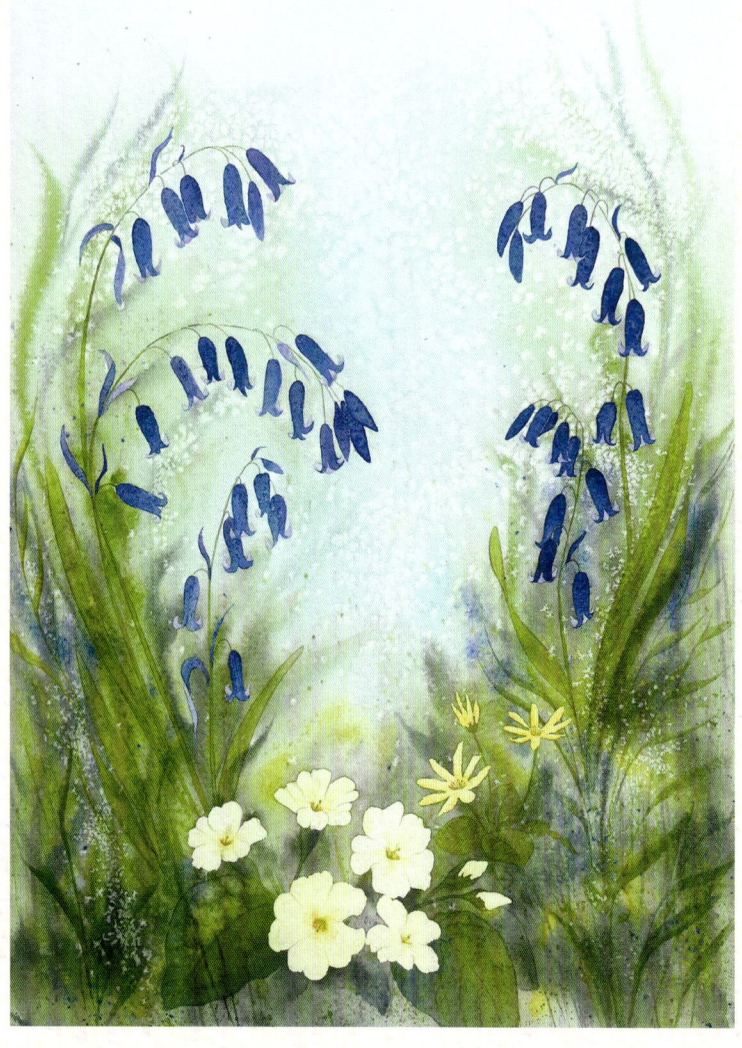

COLOURS NEEDED

Perylene Green	Sap Green	Winsor Blue	Transparent Yellow	French Ultramarine	Lemon Yellow	Dioxazine Purple

 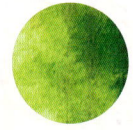   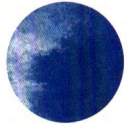 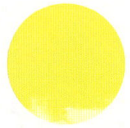 

The intense colour and the charming daintiness of each slender bell make bluebells an ideal subject for a watercolour painting; however, trying to capture the essence of an entire bluebell wood is a formidable task, so it is perhaps a simpler matter to paint a handful of individual stems. Consider complementing the bluebells with a handful of wild primroses – their sweet, flattened faces that provide much-needed contrast – along with lesser celandine flowers to provide delicate pops of intense yellow colour, which also contrasts nicely with the deep blue hues.

When painting the background, don't be afraid to go a little bit wild! As long as the deeper greens are concentrated around the lower third of the paper (in the areas where the flowers would naturally grow), there is room for some freedom of expression when using the sword liner brush. Try experimenting with the sword liner in your sketchbook, practising long, flowing lines that change width without breaking, using the 'belly' of the brush.

Setting up

Begin by transferring the outline from the template onto hot-pressed watercolour paper, using the method described on page 21. Mask out the individual bell shapes on each bluebell stem, as well as the primrose and lesser celandine flowers, using masking fluid and the old, small pointed brush (see page 13). Once the mask has set, tape your pencil outline onto a board and lay it flat, ready to begin.

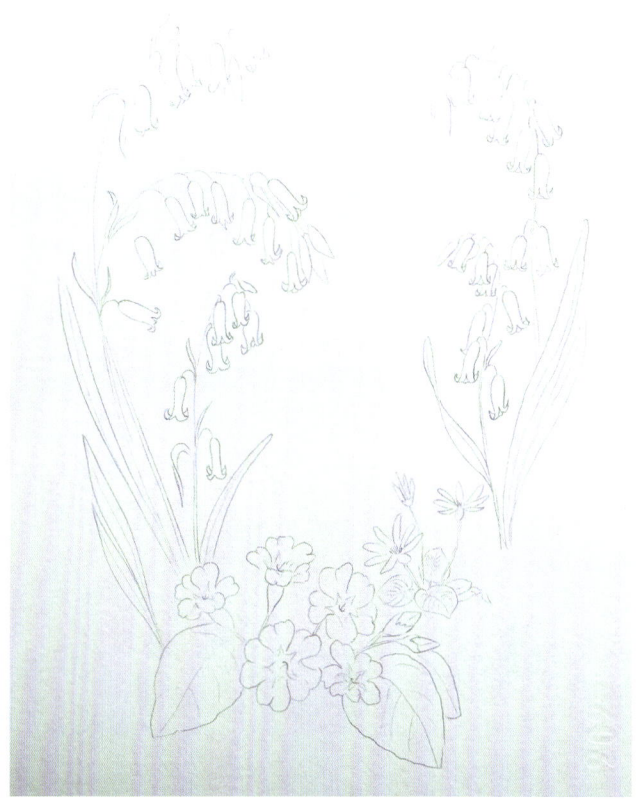

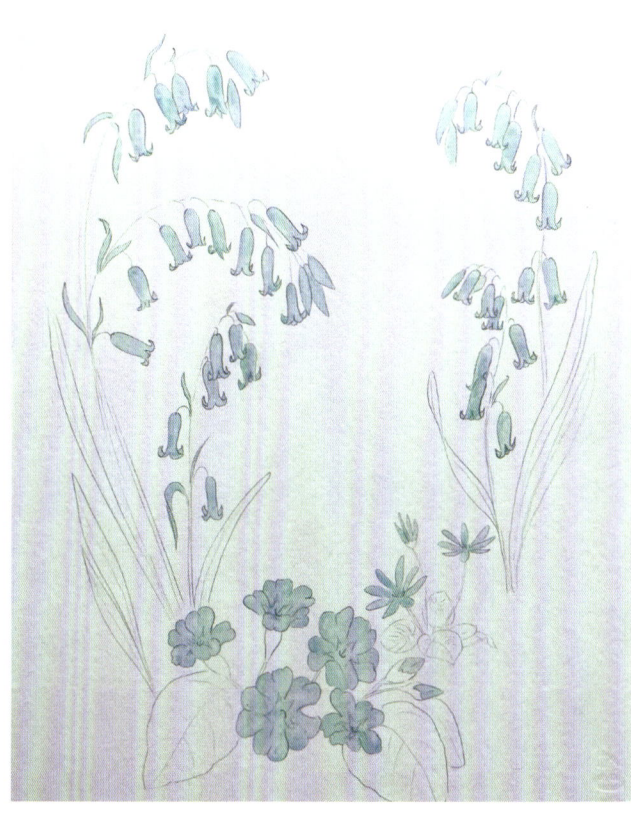

YOU WILL NEED

- *140lb (300gsm) hot-pressed watercolour paper*
- *Sketchbook or sketching paper and tracing paper*
- *Masking fluid and old, small pointed brush*
- *Adhesive eraser*
- *HB pencil and eraser*
- *Painting board and decorator's masking tape*
- *Sponge and absorbent kitchen paper*
- *Palette with several mixing wells*
- *Fine table salt*
- *Size 20 mop brush*
- *Size 2 synthetic quill brush*
- *Small size fan brush*
- *Small size sword liner brush*
- *Size 3 round brush*
- *Size 0 round detail brush*

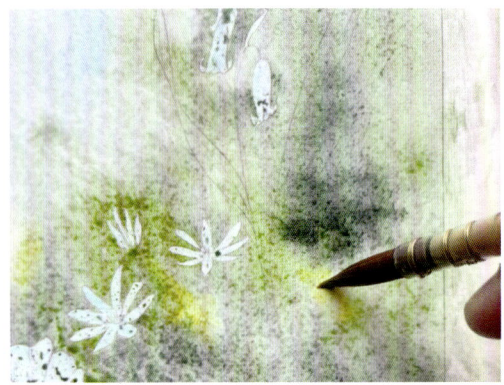

Using a separate brush to add light colours into the wash will help to keep them looking clean and bright against the darker greens.

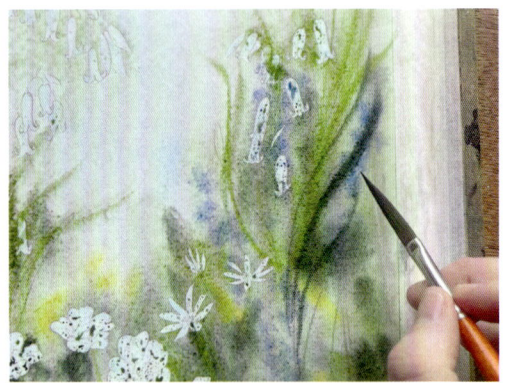

Use the belly of the sword liner brush to broaden your lines, pressing it against the paper to create different thicknesses within the same stroke.

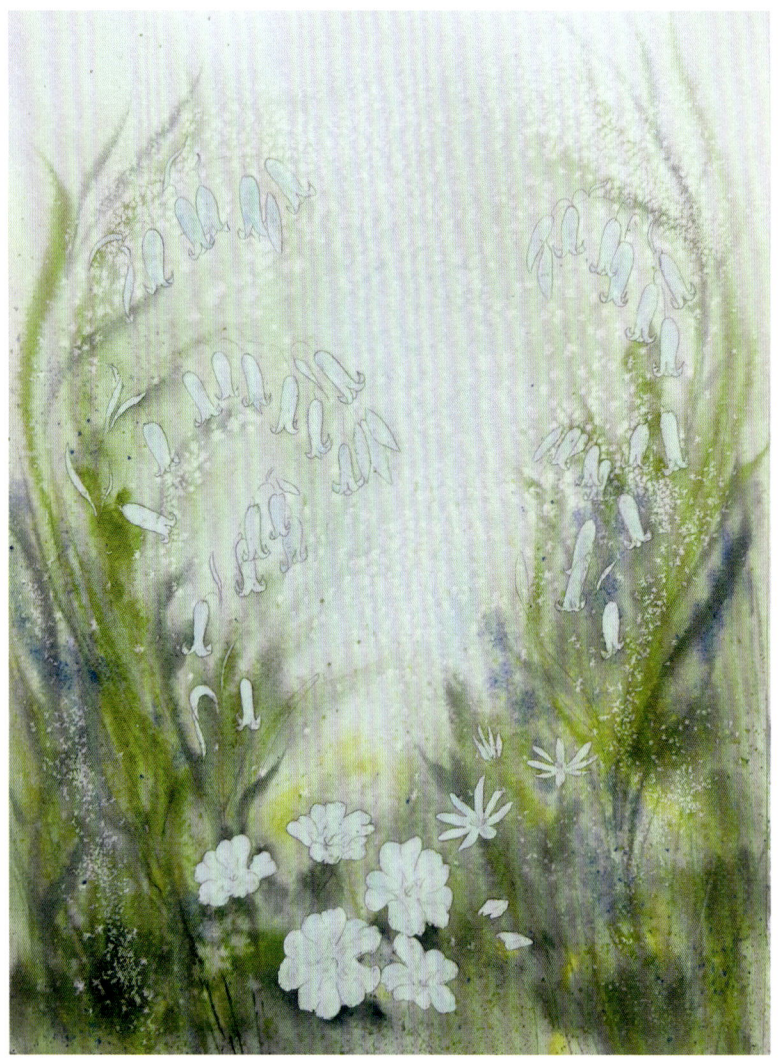

STAGE 1

Prepare three wells of light-value Perylene Green, Sap Green and Winsor Blue. Wet the paper all over and allow it to sink in for 30 seconds. Using the size 20 mop brush, begin by adding patches of the two greens to the lower third of the paper. Layer the colours to create interesting wet-in-wet blends, building the greens up the sides of the paper. Thoroughly rinse your brush, dip it into the blue and use this to create a soft, pale sky.

Switch to the size 2 quill brush to pick up a little rich-value Transparent Yellow, and add some bright dabs of colour into the paint while it is still wet; do the same with some mid-value French Ultramarine. Use the fan brush to spatter a little Transparent Yellow to lighten any areas that are too dark. Finally, dip back into your green paints with the sword liner brush, and draw sweeping, elegant marks into the wet wash, bringing the colour up the sides of the paper in a way that mimics the curve of the bluebell stems, almost 'framing' the composition. Add a sprinkle of fine salt and leave to dry.

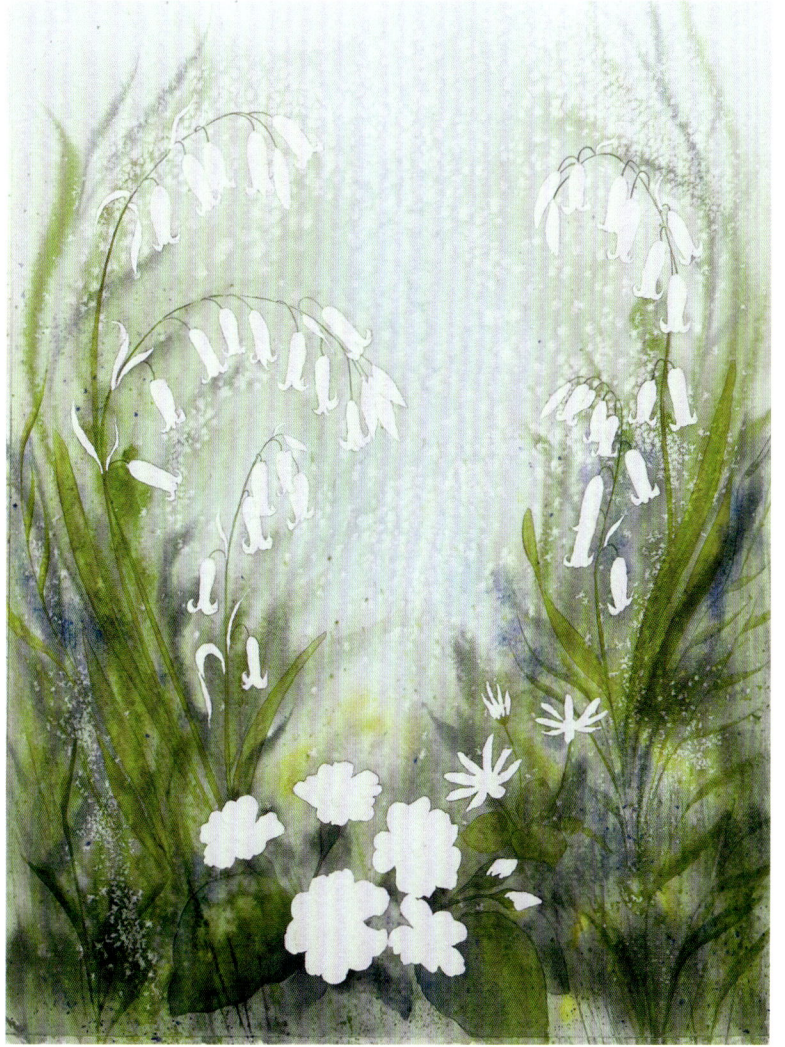

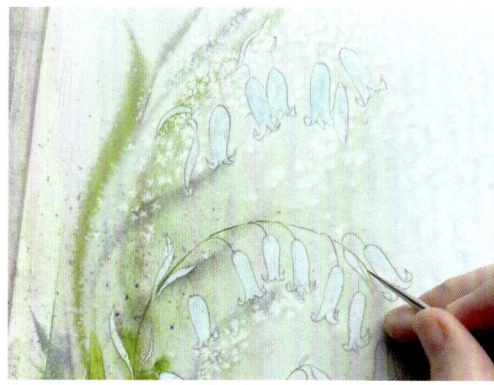

The size 0 detail brush is ideal for handling delicate areas such as the thin stems around the bluebell flowers.

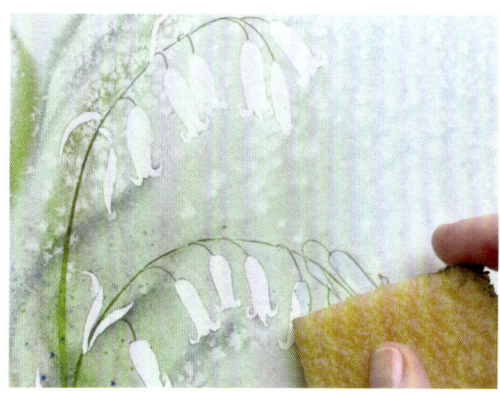

Use the corner of the adhesive eraser to carefully remove the mask from the blooms one at a time.

STAGE 2

Once dry, brush away any salt that hasn't dissolved from the painting using a clean dry brush, then mix up two wells of light-value Sap Green. Tint one with Transparent Yellow, and the other with a dab of French Ultramarine, and use these and the size 3 round brush and size 0 detail brush to paint the foliage. Use the pencil marks as a guide for the first few leaves and stems. Leave to dry completely.

Now take the sword liner brush and add another layer of sweeping, elegant shapes across the foliage, creating a pleasing contrast of soft and hard edges. Leave to dry fully, then remove the masking fluid from the blooms using the adhesive eraser.

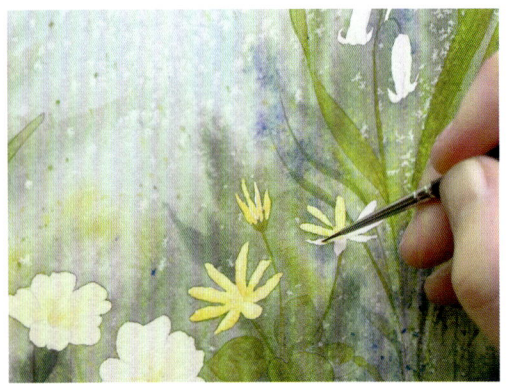

The size 0 detail brush is perfect for getting into the fiddly details in the delicate lesser celandine petals.

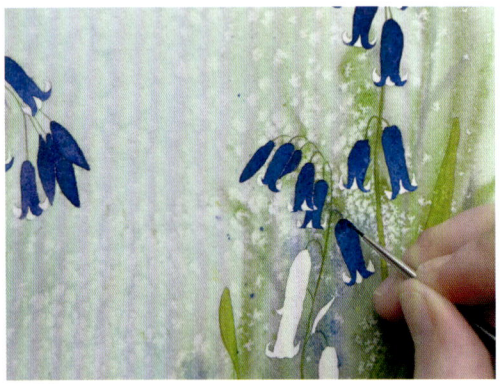

Place the deeper blue-violet colour at the base of the bell, closer to the stem.

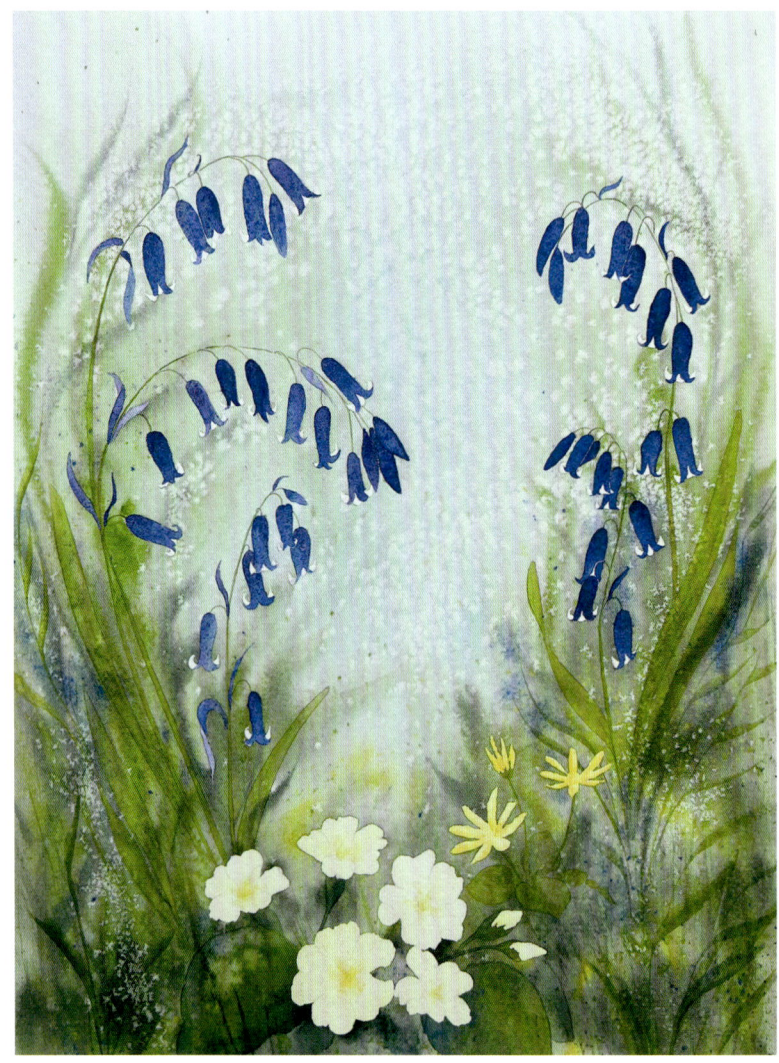

STAGE 3

Paint the flower petals using soft washes of colour and a combination of the size 3 and 0 round brushes. For the primroses, tint the petals lightly with light-value Lemon Yellow, before touching a little rich Transparent Yellow to their centres. Use this Transparent Yellow to add a pop of colour to the lesser celandine petals.

For the bluebells, mix up two wells of mid-value French Ultramarine, and tint one with a little Dioxazine Purple to create a blue-violet hue. Use these to paint the individual bell flowers.

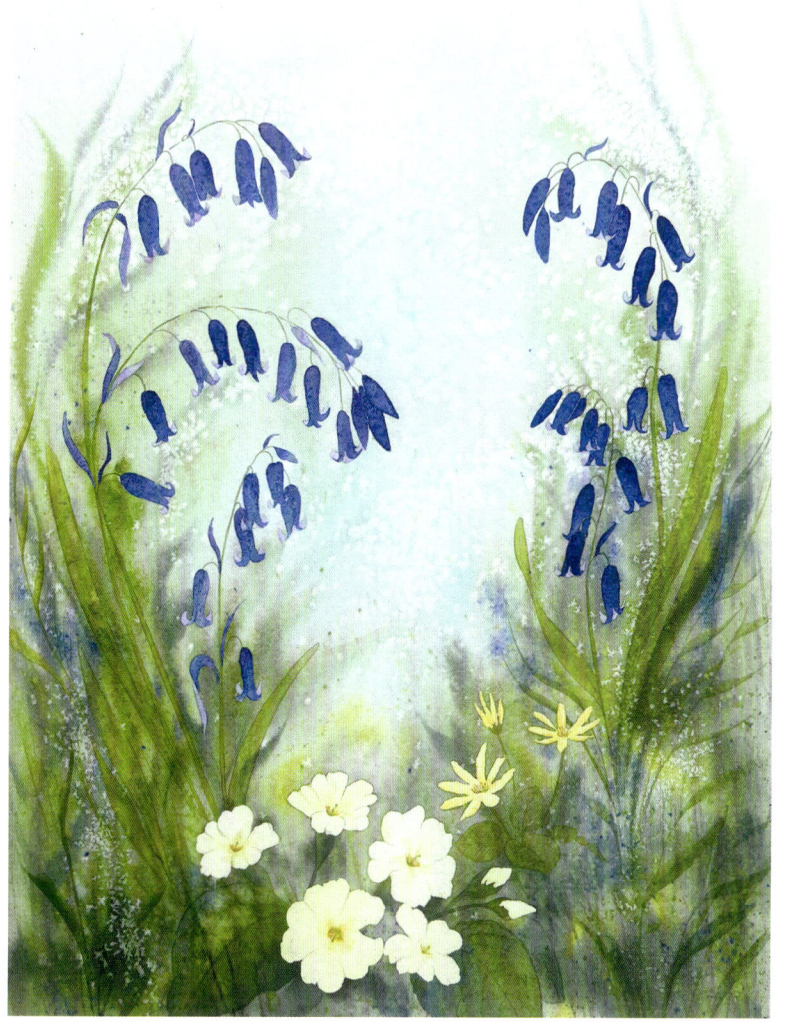

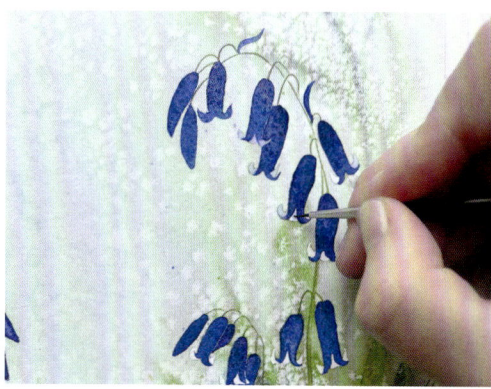

Patience and a steady hand will be needed for this stage; taking your time will pay dividends.

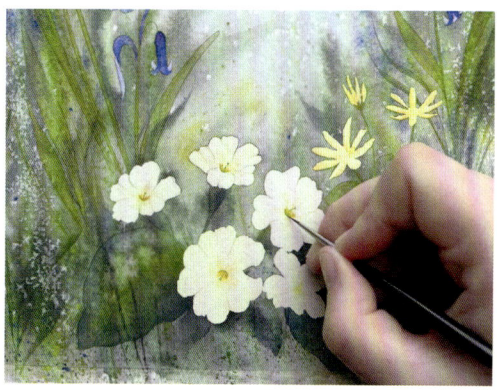

Adding a little green into the yellow flower centres will help to make them pop.

STAGE 4

Once dry, use the size 0 detail brush to add dark-value details to the centres of the primroses and lesser celandine using Transparent Yellow and Sap Green.

Using some light-value French Ultramarine, tint the curled-back parts of the bluebell petals.

Finally, add some texture and veining to the primrose leaves using a mid-value mixture of Sap Green and Lemon Yellow.

Sunset Poppies

The rich burnt orange and violet background in this painting evokes the heat of a sultry summer evening, and perfectly complements the fiery sunset warmth of giant oriental poppies.

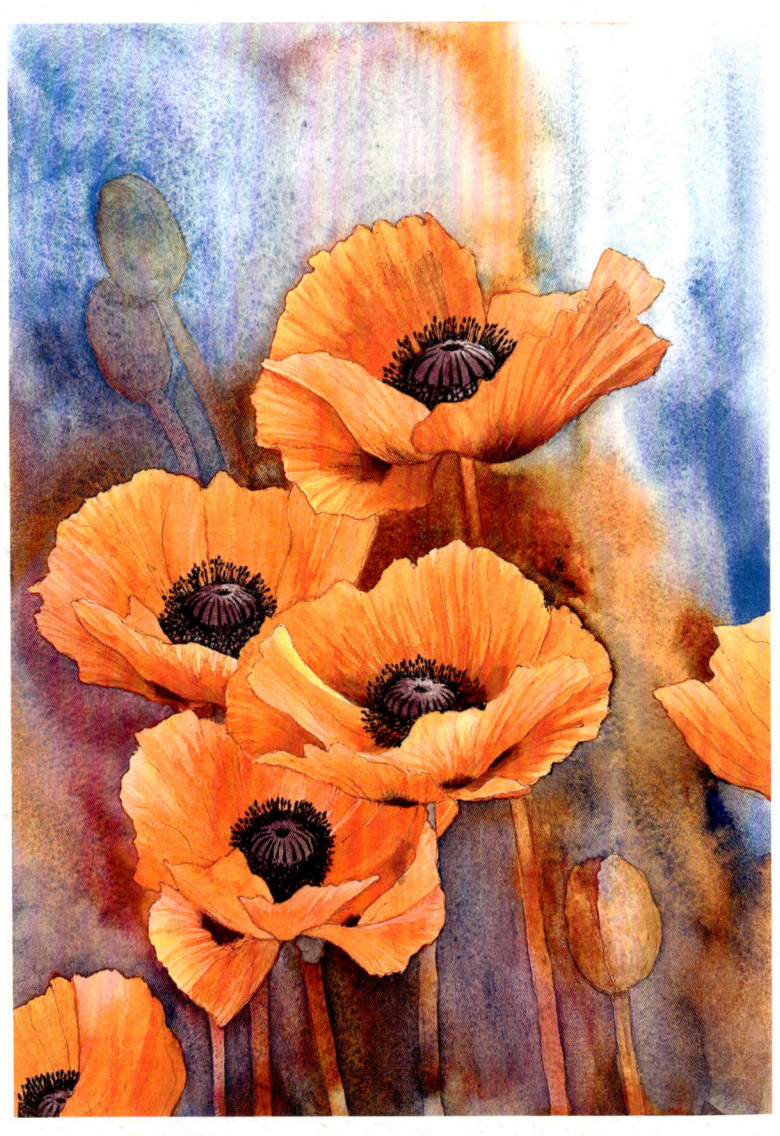

COLOURS NEEDED

French Ultramarine   Transparent Orange   Pyrrole Red   Transparent Yellow

 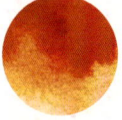 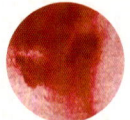 

In this dramatic line and wash painting, the complex shapes that form the oriental poppy centres are simplified and blocked in at the line work stage, creating a strong contrast. This adds shape and form to these spectacular blooms, so that you can focus on painting the play of colour across the silken petals.

Setting up

Begin by sketching the outline from the template in pencil and transferring it onto hot-pressed watercolour paper, using the method described on page 21. Using the 0.1mm waterproof black fine-liner pen, go over the outline to create the line work, using the following steps to simplify and shade the poppy centres:

1 Sketch the position of the central stigma and stamens roughly in pencil.

2 Refine the shapes of the stigma and stamens using the 0.1mm fine-liner pen.

3 Use the 0.3mm fine-liner pen to shade the grooves on the stigma and the deep shadows surrounding it, pulling out a few dark stamens and anthers behind it. Shade around the dotted stamens in front of the stigma leaving the white paper showing through.

When you've finished, mask out the poppy flowers around their edges with masking fluid and a small old brush, using the approach outlined on page 13. Tape your paper to the painting board and lay flat, ready to begin.

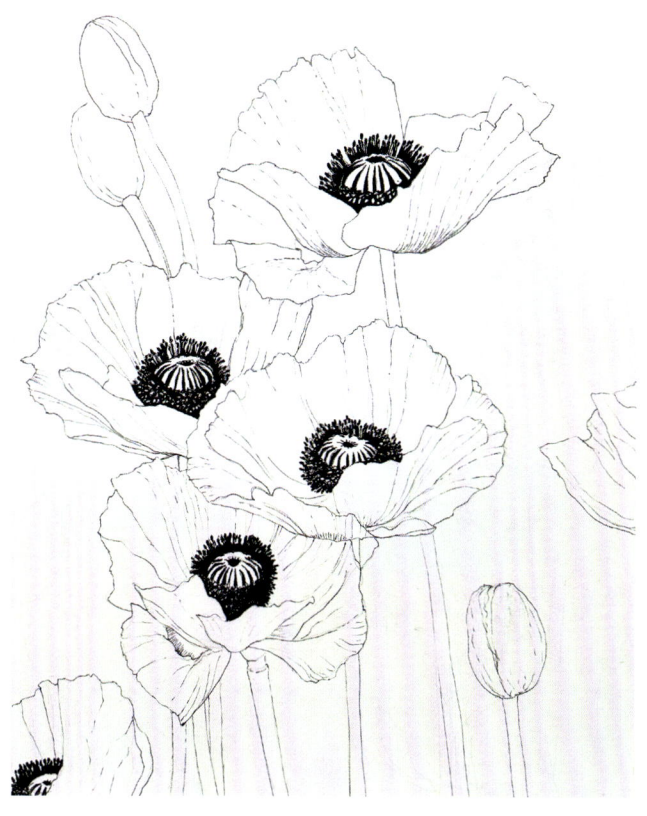

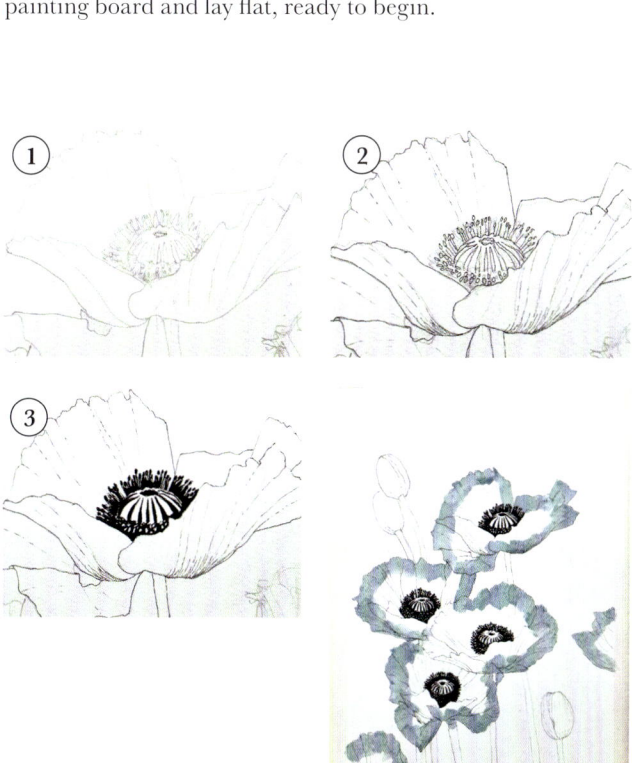

YOU WILL NEED

- *140lb (300gsm) hot-pressed watercolour paper*
- *Sketchbook or sketching paper*
- *Tracing paper*
- *HB pencil and eraser*
- *0.1mm and 0.3mm waterproof black fine-liner pens*
- *Painting board and decorator's masking tape*
- *Masking fluid and an old, small pointed brush*
- *Adhesive eraser*
- *Absorbent kitchen paper*
- *Palette with several mixing wells*
- *Size 20 mop brush*
- *Size 2 quill brush*
- *Oval wash brush*
- *Size 3 round brush*
- *Size 0 round detail brush*

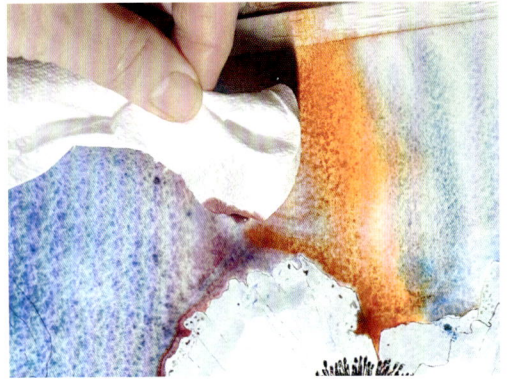

When painting around the poppy shapes, use the kitchen paper to quickly dab off any colour that strays into the petals.

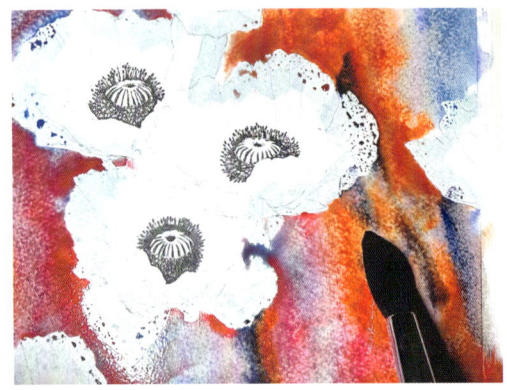

French Ultramarine is a granulating colour, so the pigment particles will settle as the washes dry and create beautiful effects, even when mixed with other colours.

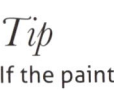

Tip
If the paint isn't flowing, spray a few small bursts with the misting spray, then tip and tilt the board gently to get the washes to flow.

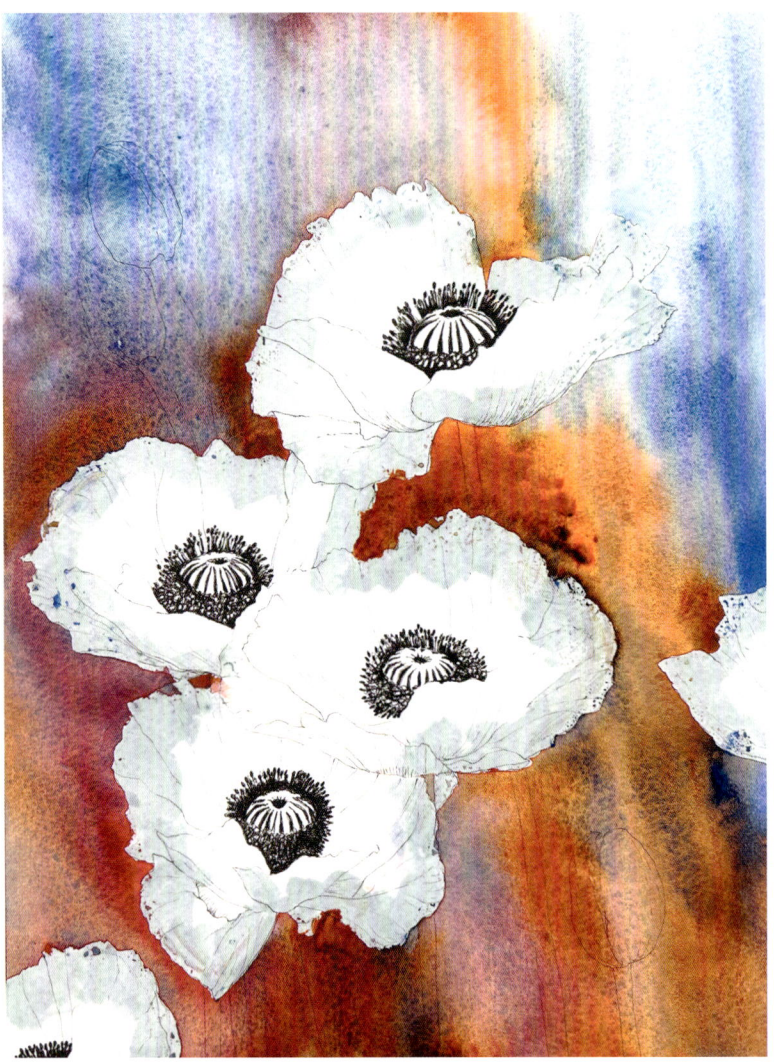

STAGE 1

Mix three large wells of mid to dark-value French Ultramarine, Transparent Orange and Pyrrole Red. Ensure you have plenty of rich creamy paint for this strongly coloured background wash. Thoroughly wet the background with clean water and the size 20 mop brush, working around the unmasked poppy middles, leaving them dry. Leave to soak for about 30 seconds.

Load the brush with ultramarine, and starting at the top, paint around the poppies to suggest sky, bringing a few brushstrokes further down. Rinse the brush and paint around the lower half of the poppies with the orange, allowing it to blend with the blue in places. Without rinsing the brush, dip it into the red and work this into the wash in the same way until the background is done. Try to keep it bluer at the top and darker behind the flowers where the colours mix and blend to create burnt orange and deep violet hues. Allow to dry completely.

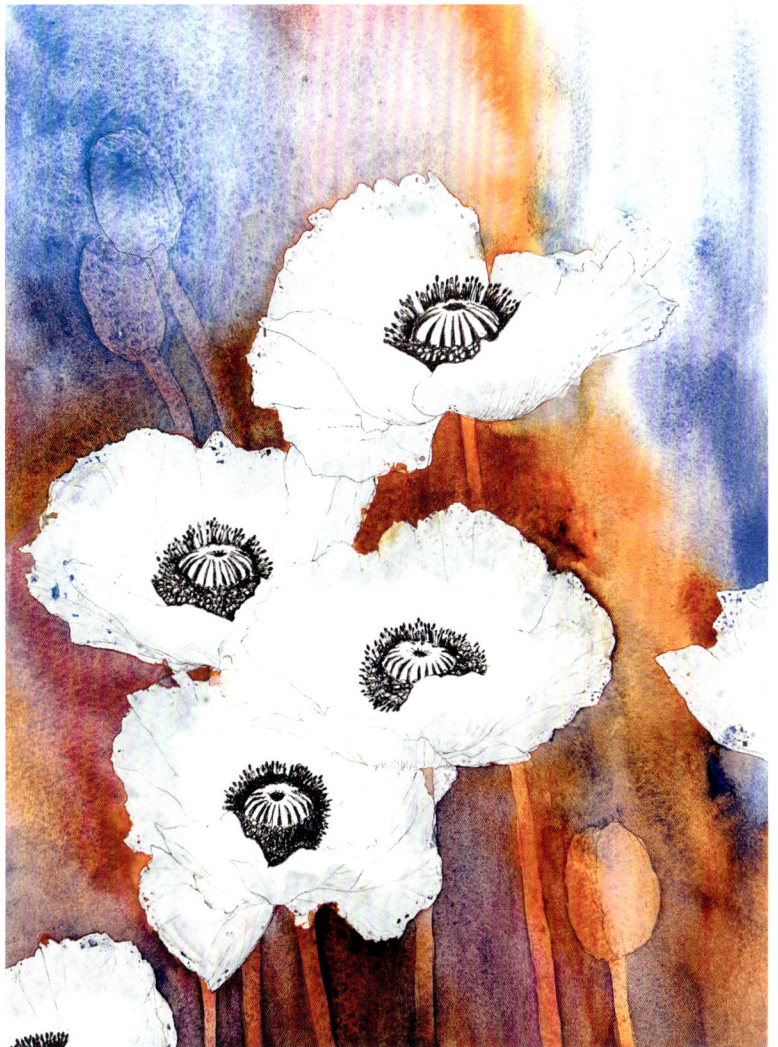

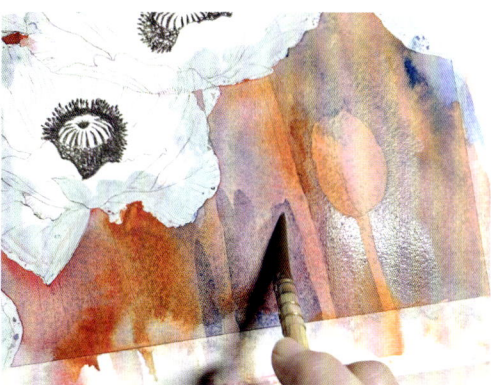

Layering the ultramarine over the rich red tones around the base of the painting will introduce a variety of lovely violet shadow hues.

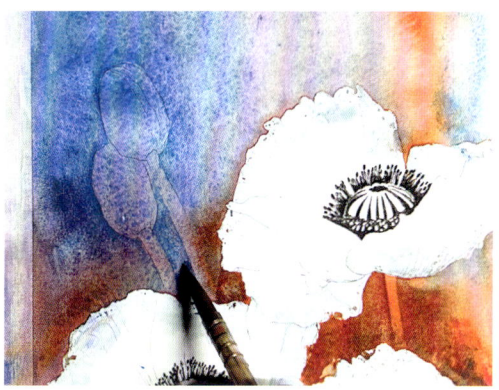

Keep the glazes very pale when using the negative painting technique.

STAGE 2

This stage involves painting around the poppy buds and stems using the negative painting technique (see page 25). This technique is wonderful for creating loose, atmospheric suggestions of detail.

Mix two light-value watery wells of paint to use as glazes (see page 24): one of French Ultramarine and one of Transparent Orange. Paint around the stems and buds with ultramarine, using the size 2 quill brush so that the background wash negatively reveals the stems and buds. Soften the edges into the background wash with the clean, damp oval wash brush if needed.

Repeat with the orange and negatively paint around the buds at the top, again, carefully softening the edges into the background with the oval wash brush if needed. Leave to dry completely.

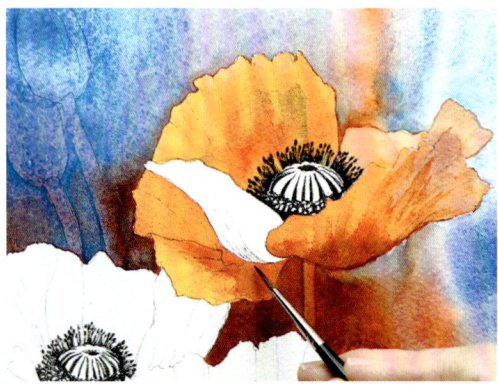

Your brushstrokes should follow the direction of the petal veins, dragging darker colour over them to start to suggest the pleated petals.

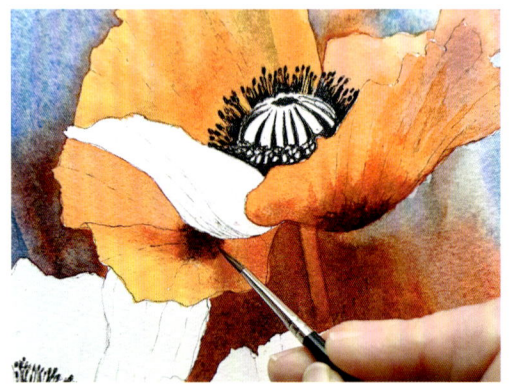

Adding the violet while the paint is still wet will help the colours to diffuse together, creating a soft blended edge.

Tip

The ink outline defines the shape of the petals and buds, while the veins help to define the form. Follow the direction of these veins as you paint to help achieve the appropriate gradations of colour and tone for each petal.

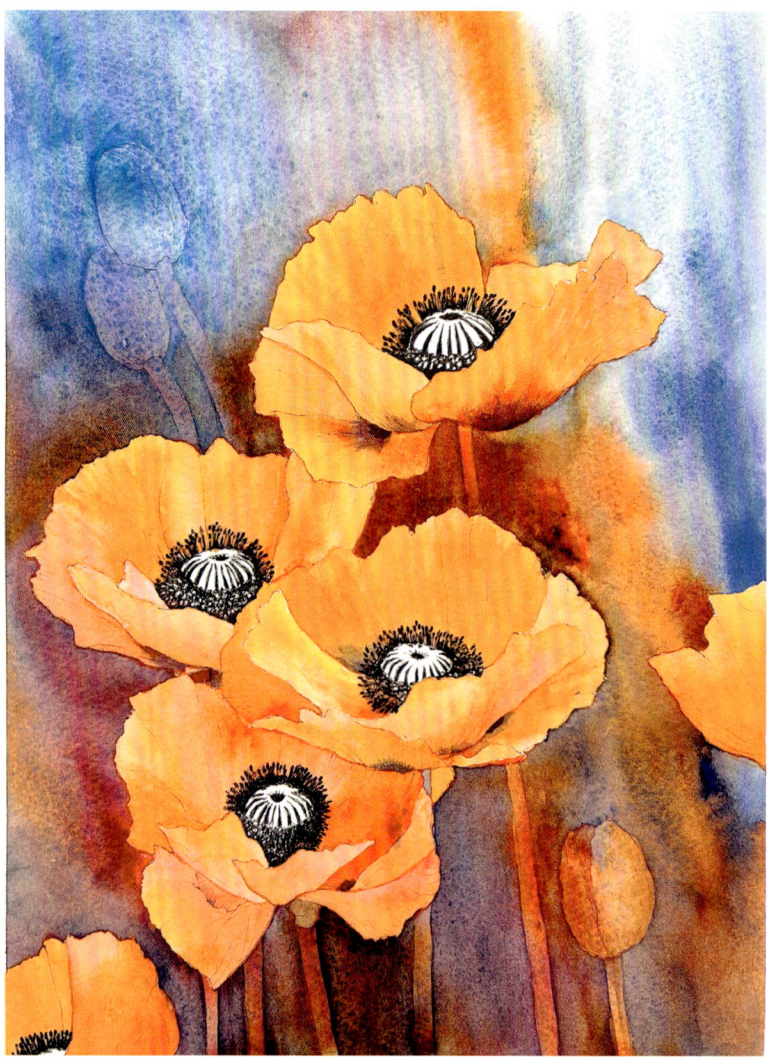

STAGE 3

Mix three different shades of light-value orange: Transparent Yellow with a touch of Transparent Orange, equal amounts of the two colours, and equal amounts of yellow, orange and Pyrrole Red. Mix a small well of mid-value violet from French Ultramarine and Pyrrole Red. Paint each petal separately: start by painting the petal with clean water to dampen it using the size 3 round brush. While still damp, alternate between the three mixes to create subtle gradations in each petal: the yellower mix where the light catches the petals near the edges, softly blending into the second mix to deepen the colour, and the redder mix around the base of the petals where they are in shadow. Soften any hard edges with a clean, damp oval wash brush.

Just before the paint dries, use the size 0 detail brush to add a little of the violet mix to suggest the distinctive dark spots at the base of the petals. Repeat this process until you have painted this first layer on all the flowers, then leave to dry.

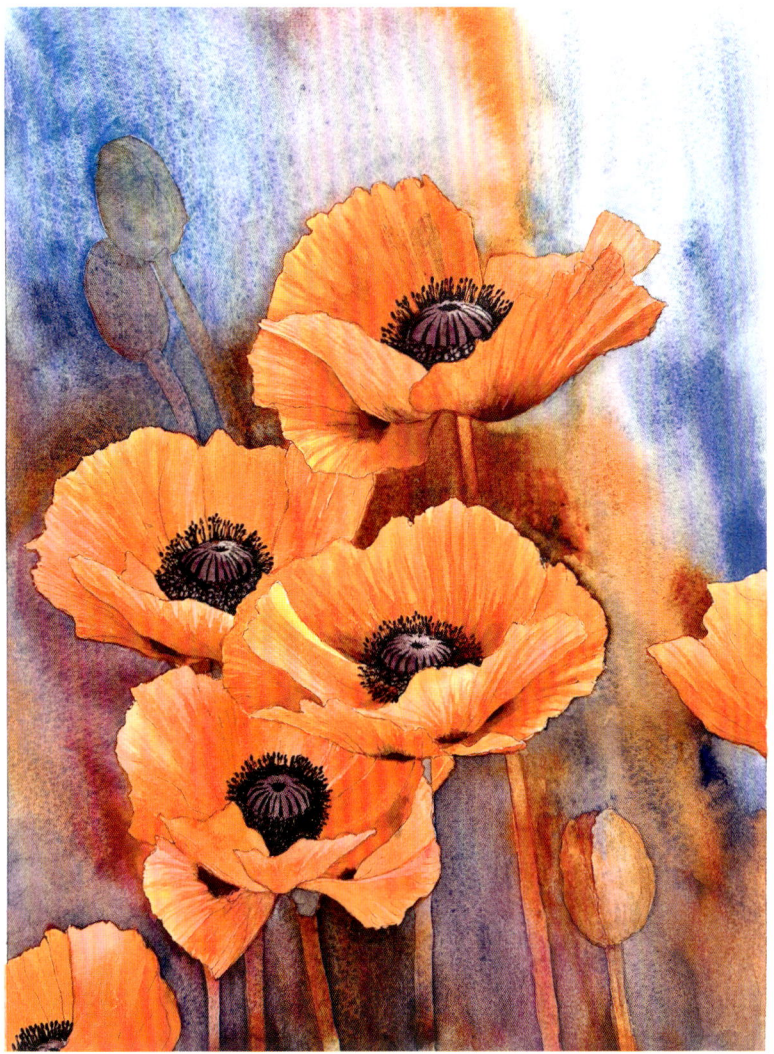

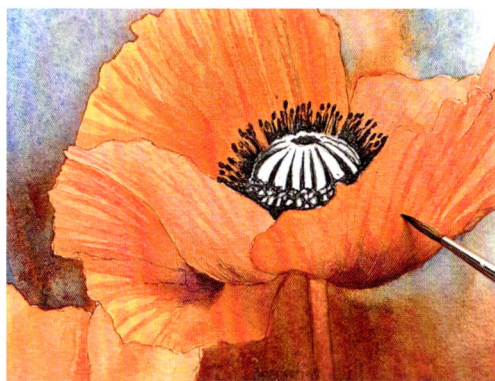

Allow the petal to almost dry before painting in the finest veins, always following the direction you indicated with the inked line work.

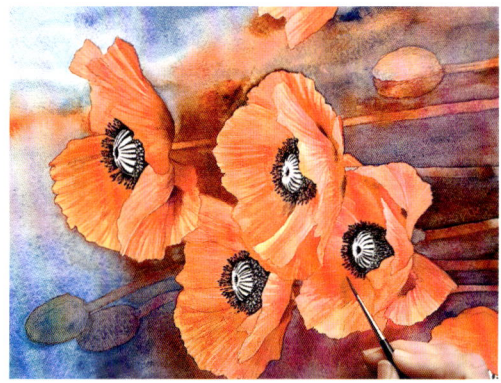

Feel free to turn the board around to find a more comfortable angle at which to paint the delicate, detailed veins.

STAGE 4

Mix more of the colours used in stage 3 if you need to, plus a well of light-value pure Pyrrole Red. Work on each petal separately in a similar way to Stage 3, but don't wet the petals first. Starting with the pure red, deepen the colour at the base with the size 3 round brush, pulling out finer lines to accentuate the veins with the fine tip of the brush. Alternate between the orange mixes to graduate the red into the paler areas, leaving some of the lighter parts of the underpainting showing and using the oval wash brush to soften edges as necessary. Repeat for all the poppy petals and leave to dry.

Mix a mid-value violet from French Ultramarine and Pyrrole Red, then paint the stigmas and stamens in the middle of each poppy. Lift out a highlight on each stigma with kitchen paper while still wet. If you need to adjust a colour, paint a light glaze of transparent colour over the area; here I used the orange over the buds in the top left, which were too blue. Leave to dry completely.

Hummingbird Fuchsias

Also known as Fuchsia magellanica, *hummingbird fuchsias have slender bell-shaped flowers that blossom profusely throughout the summer season, showing wild splashes of deepest red and purple against the dappled sunlight.*

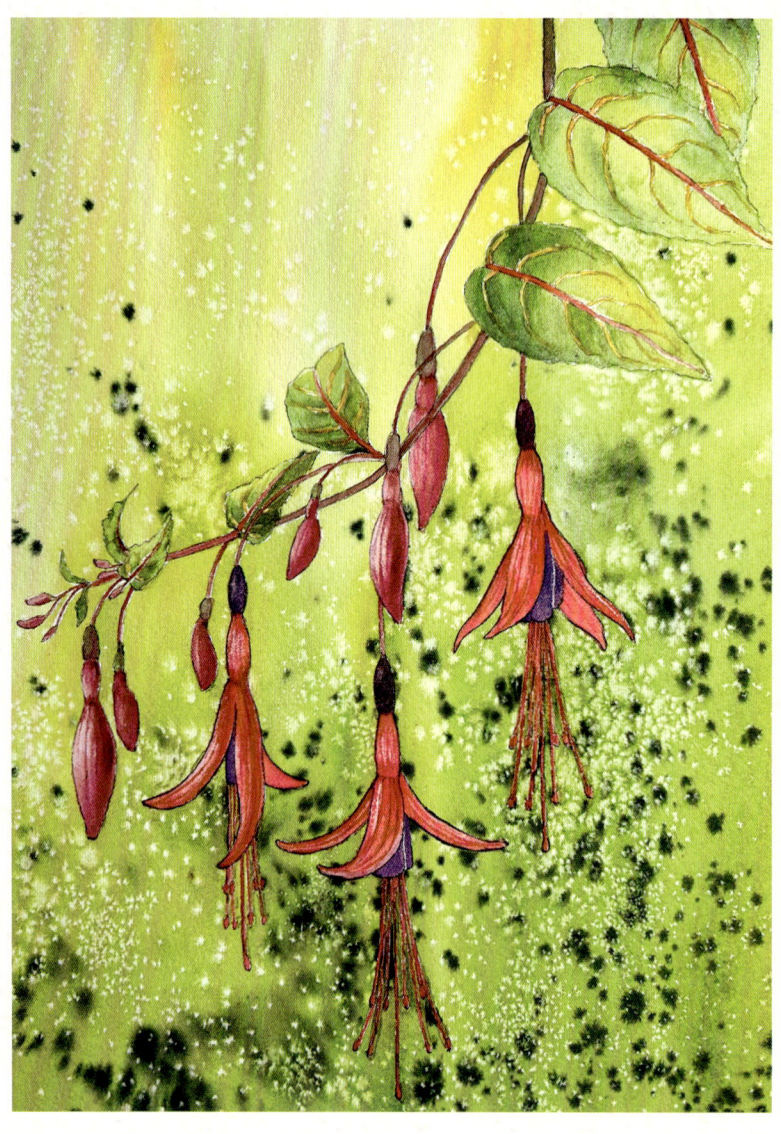

COLOURS NEEDED

Transparent Yellow	Sap Green	Perylene Green	French Ultramarine	Pyrrole Red	Permanent Alizarin Crimson	Quinacridone Magenta
	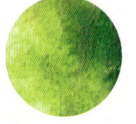	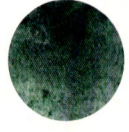		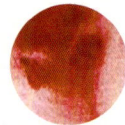	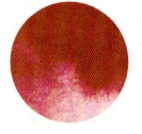	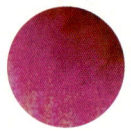

The curve of the reddish stems, and the multitude of pendant flowers and buds are characteristic of this species of fuchsia, a member of the evening primrose family. When sketching from life or a reference photo, try to simplify things wherever possible. A composition will often be greatly improved by focusing on a few buds, flowers and leaves in different stages of growth rather than trying to include everything you see.

Setting up

Begin by transferring the outline from the template onto hot-pressed watercolour paper, using the method outlined on page 21. Go over the pencil outline with the 0.1mm waterproof fine liner. You can change to a 0.3mm fine liner if you prefer the flowers to be slightly more defined than the rest of the plant. Next, using an old, small pointed brush, mask out the flowers with masking fluid, using the method outlined on page 13. Tape the outline onto your board and lay it flat, ready to begin.

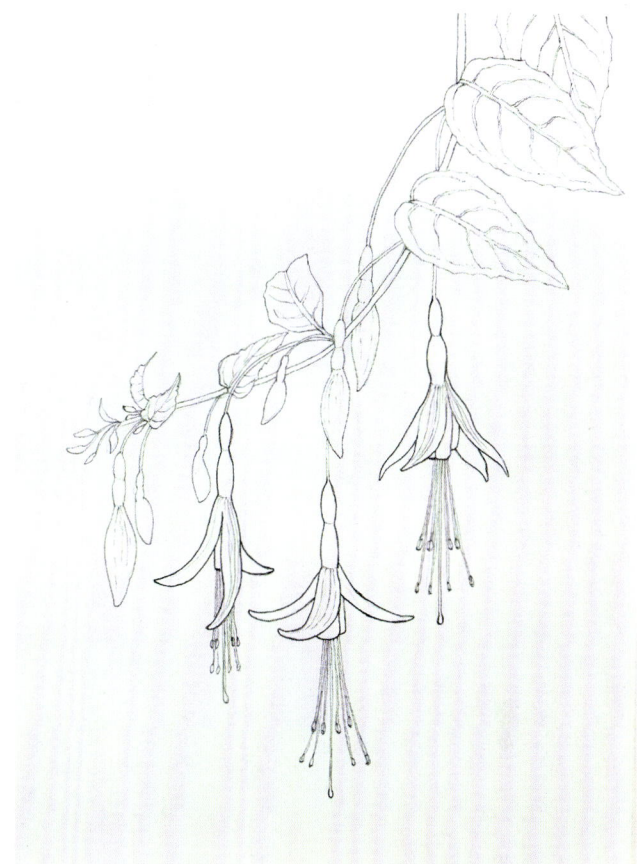

YOU WILL NEED

- *140lb (300gsm) hot-pressed watercolour paper*
- *Sketchbook or sketching paper*
- *Tracing paper*
- *HB pencil and eraser*
- *0.1mm and 0.3mm waterproof black fine-liner pens*
- *Painting board and decorator's masking tape*
- *Masking fluid and an old, small pointed brush*
- *Adhesive eraser*
- *Absorbent kitchen paper*
- *Palette with several mixing wells*
- *Water misting spray*
- *Fine table salt*
- *Cotton buds*
- *Size 20 mop brush*
- *Small fan brush*
- *Size 3 round brush*
- *Size 2 quill brush*
- *Oval wash brush*
- *Size 0 round detail brush*

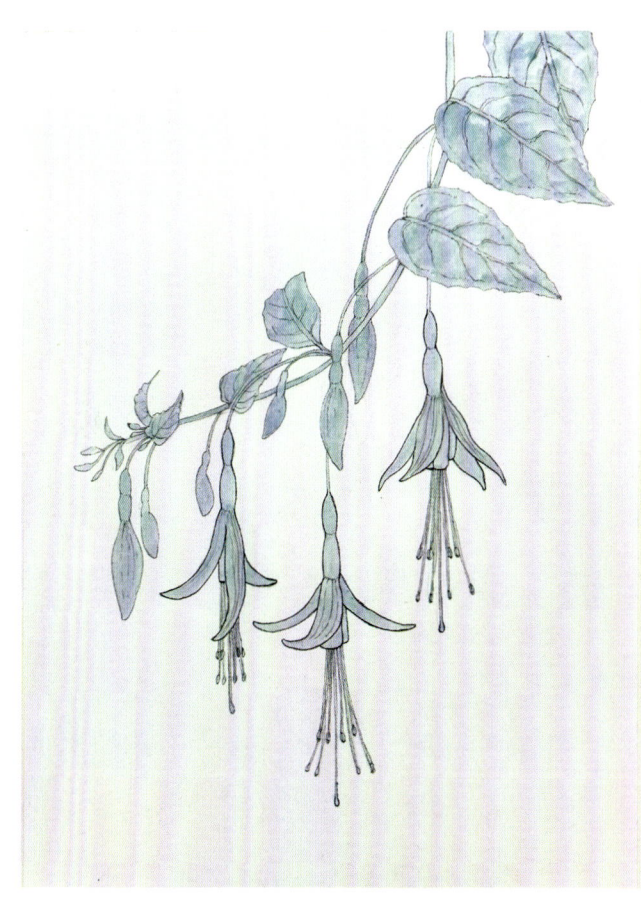

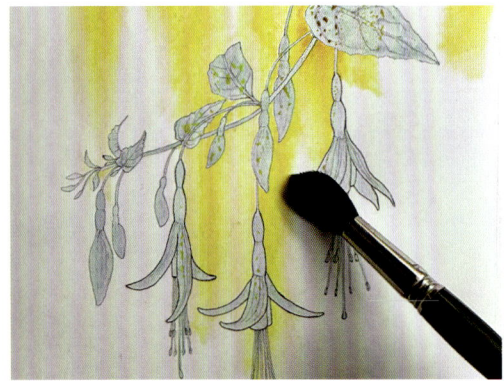

Beginning with a bold yellow in the wash will help to give a sunny luminosity to the green backdrop.

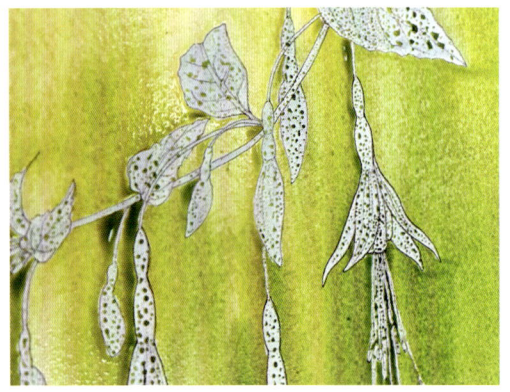

Spray lightly with the water mister, and tip the board from side to side to even out the wash if it looks patchy.

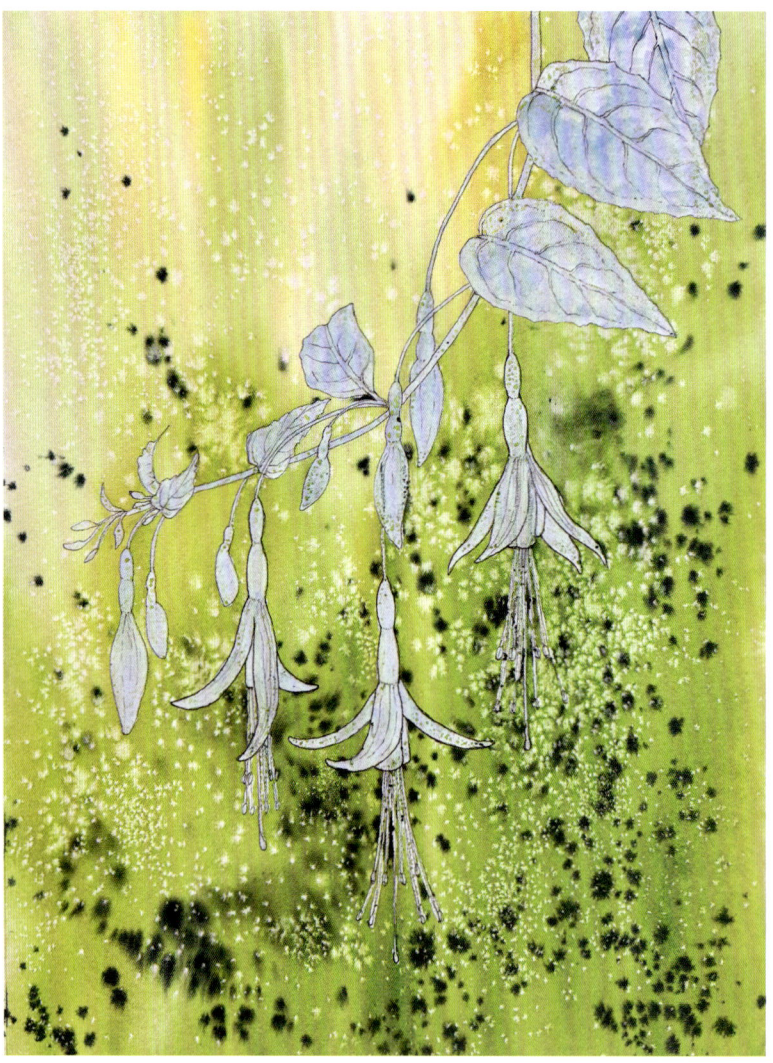

STAGE 1

For the background wash, mix two large wells of dark-value paint: Transparent Yellow and Sap Green, and a small well of mid-value Perylene Green. Wet the whole page with clean water using the size 20 mop brush and leave to soak for about 30 seconds.

Dip the brush into the yellow, and starting from the top, paint vertical brushstrokes towards the middle of the paper. Without rinsing the brush, dip it into Sap Green and sweep the brush from the bottom towards the middle, letting the colours blend and diffuse on the page where they meet. Try to keep it yellower at the top, and greener towards the bottom. Lay the board flat, and using the fan brush and Perylene Green, create spatter patterns across the lower half of the painting by tapping the brush to release the spatter droplets into the wet wash. Wait for the shine to begin to go from the paper and sprinkle a little salt into the background to suggest the effect of dappled light. Leave to dry.

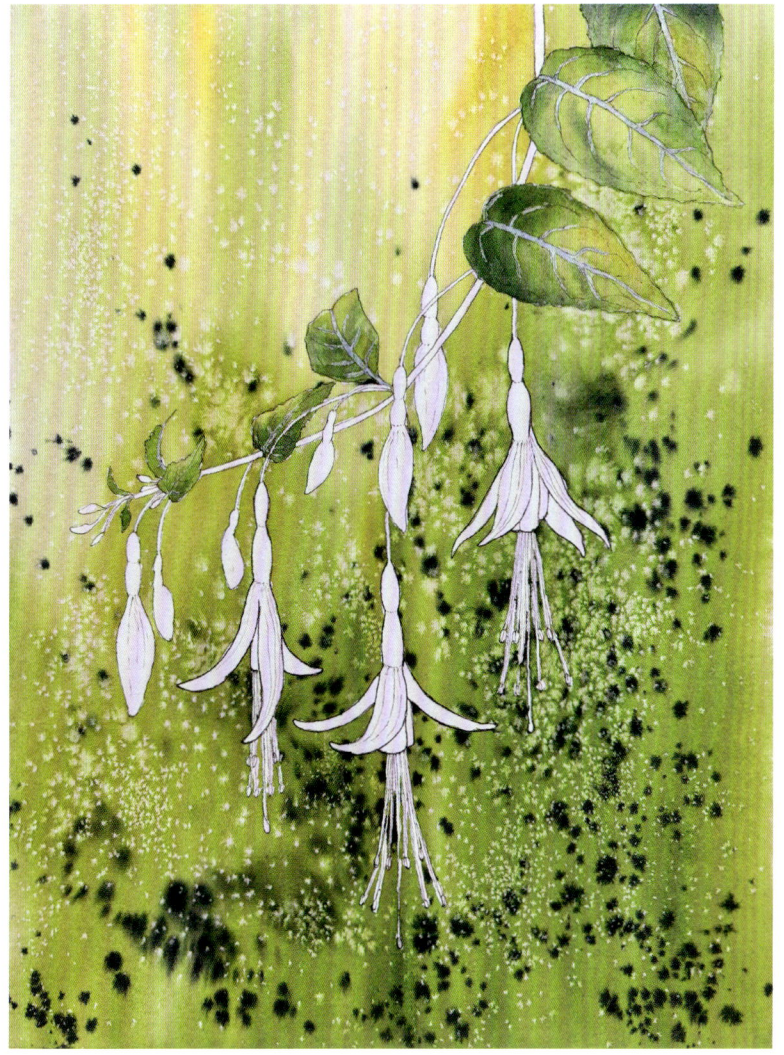

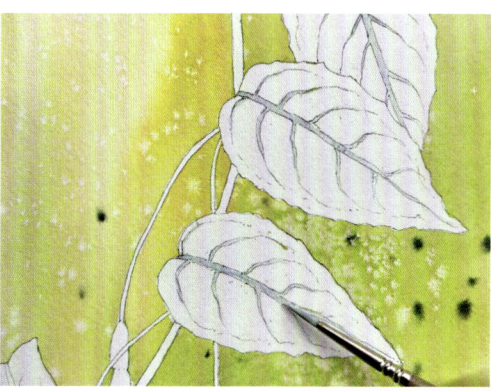

Re-masking the veins will help in adding clean, bright colour to them during the next stage.

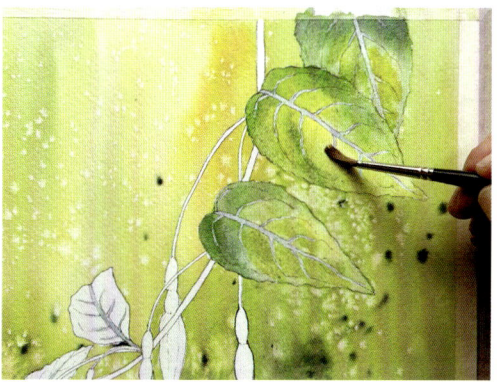

Keep the leaves yellower where the sun would naturally catch them.

STAGE 2

Brush away any remaining salt crystals with a clean dry brush. Re-mask the veins on the leaves with masking fluid and a small old brush.

Mix a well each of mid-value Transparent Yellow and Sap Green, and one of light-value Sap Green mixed with French Ultramarine.

Paint the leaves one by one with a variegated wash: dampen the whole leaf with clean water with the size 3 round brush. Dab yellow into the damp leaf, add the green and allow to blend. While still damp, touch in some of the darker green mix into the darker parts to deepen the tone. Repeat for all leaves and allow to dry.

Tip

Switch to the size 0 detail brush to tidy the edges as you paint, and keep a rolled-up piece of kitchen paper nearby to gently lift out any excess paint if it looks a bit too dark in places.

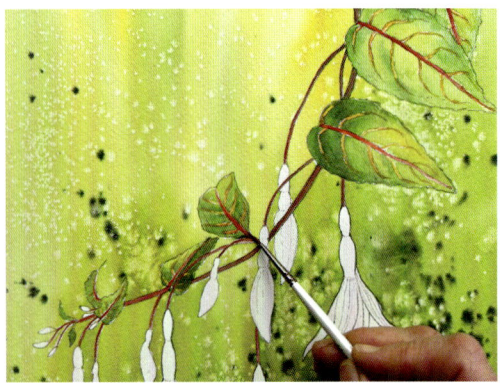

If the stems and veins are a little pale when fully dried, glaze over them with a light coat of the same colour.

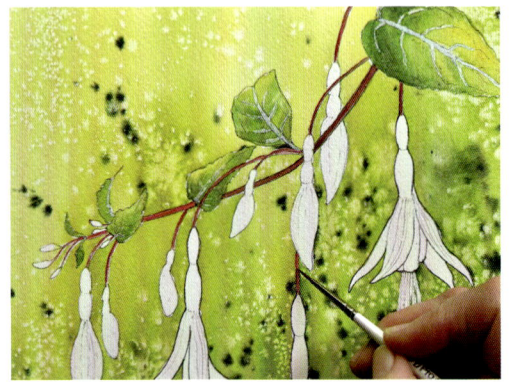

Use the size 0 detail brush to maintain nice fine stems.

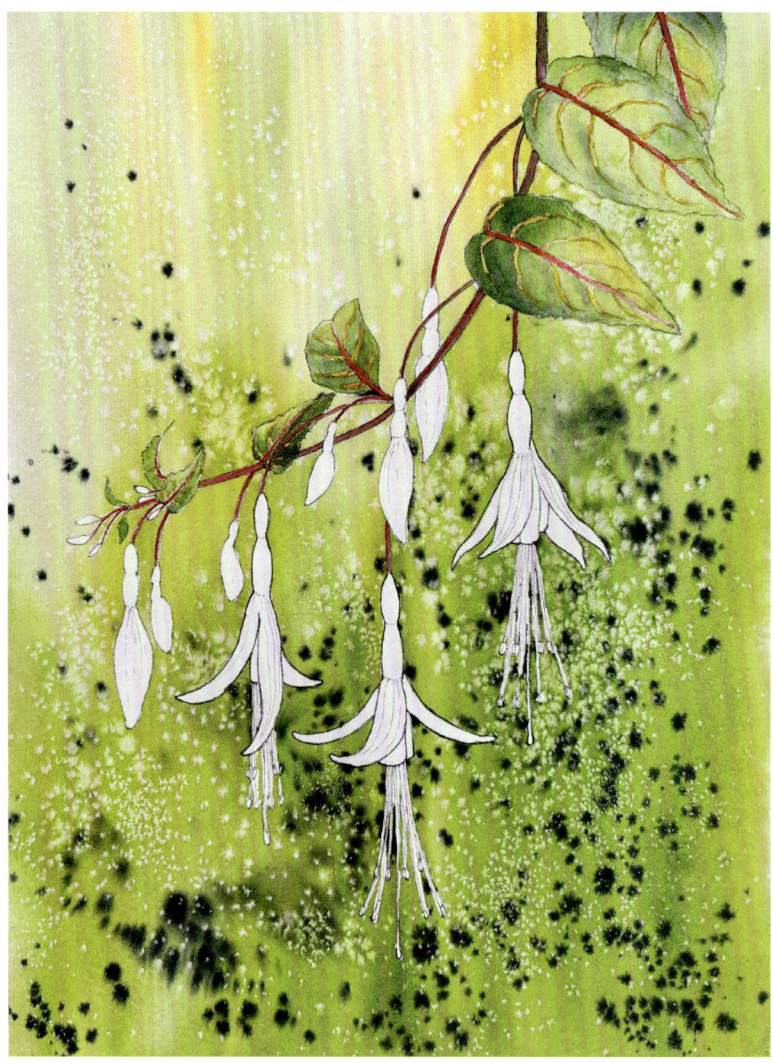

STAGE 3

Mix two wells of light-value paint: Sap Green and Pyrrole Red. Dampen the stems with the size 0 detail brush. Starting with the thicker, darker stems top right, add a light wash of the green, and drop in a little red while still wet to create a greenish red. Paint the rest of the stems, adding less green and more red to those in the sunlight, and to the younger stems on the left.

Remove the masking fluid from the leaf veins using the adhesive eraser. Mix two small wells of mid-value Pyrrole Red and Transparent Yellow, and paint the leaf midribs red. Allow these to dry, then paint the leaf veins with the yellow. Leave to dry.

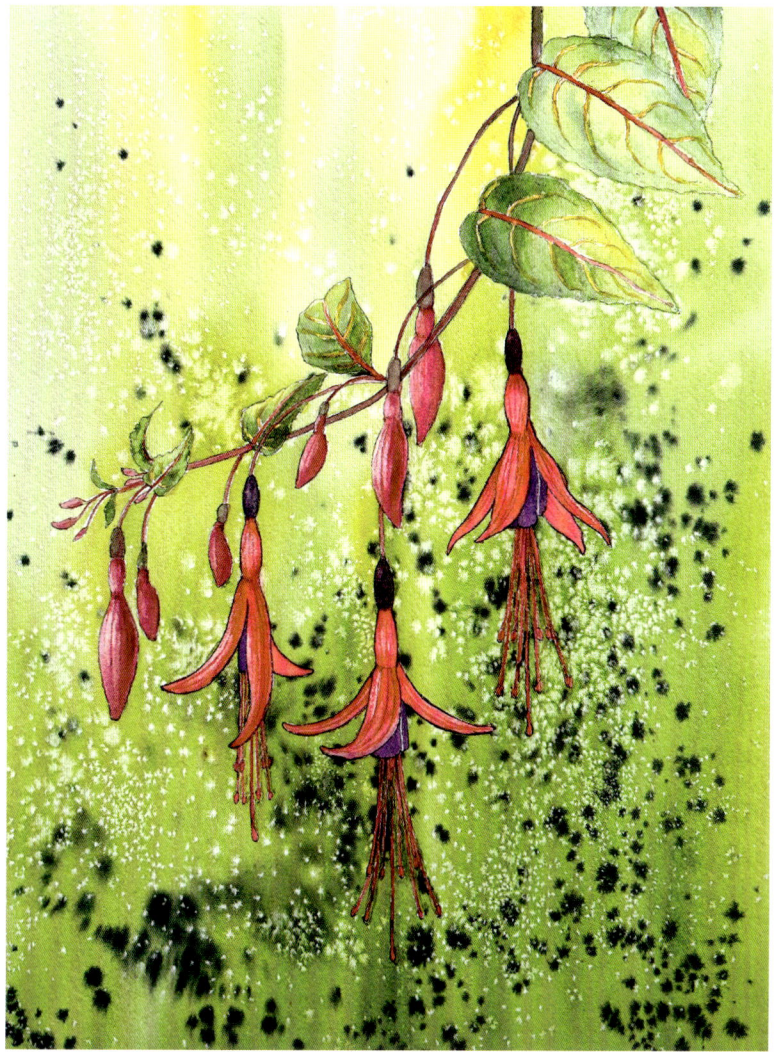

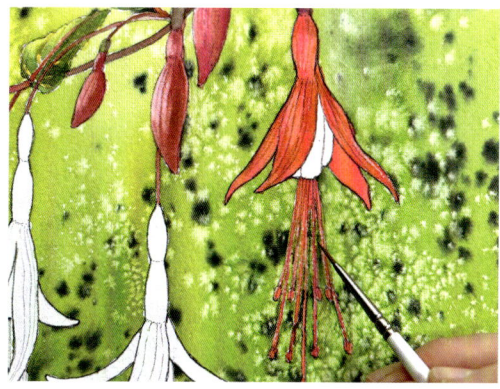

Tidy up between the stamens and other small details if necessary using the detail brush and a mix of Sap Green and Transparent Yellow that is similar to the background.

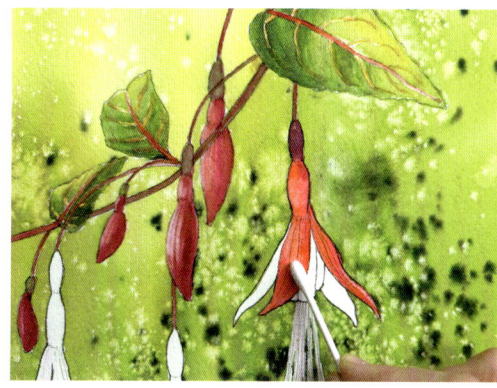

STAGE 4

Mix three wells: light-value Sap Green and light and mid-value Permanent Alizarin Crimson. Use the detail brush to paint the buds with light crimson. Add a little green at the top of the larger buds with the detail brush. Let this dry and dampen the buds with clean water. Use a variegated wash of both crimson mixes to paint light and shadow sides. Lift out a highlight with a cotton bud while still damp. Allow to dry then add a few fine veins.

Mix four wells: mid-value violet from French Ultramarine and Pyrrole Red, light-value Pyrrole Red, mid-value Pyrrole Red, and a mid-value violet from French Ultramarine and Quinacridone Magenta. Paint each flower in the same way: colour the top part with the first violet mix and let dry. Dampen the flower with clean water using the size 3 round brush and drop in light and mid-value Pyrrole Red, adding a highlight with a cotton bud. Once dry, paint the inner petals with the second violet mix, and the slender central flower parts with mid-value red.

Using a cotton bud (or swab) to dab out highlights allows for greater control and precision than using absorbent kitchen paper.

FOCUS ON
Painting White Flowers

Painting white flowers using watercolour is a unique challenge. It may seem at first that they are a relatively simple prospect: for a judicious painter, the white of the paper will do the lion's share of the hard work. However, aspects such tone and contrast should not be neglected: these are what will make your white blooms positively glow.

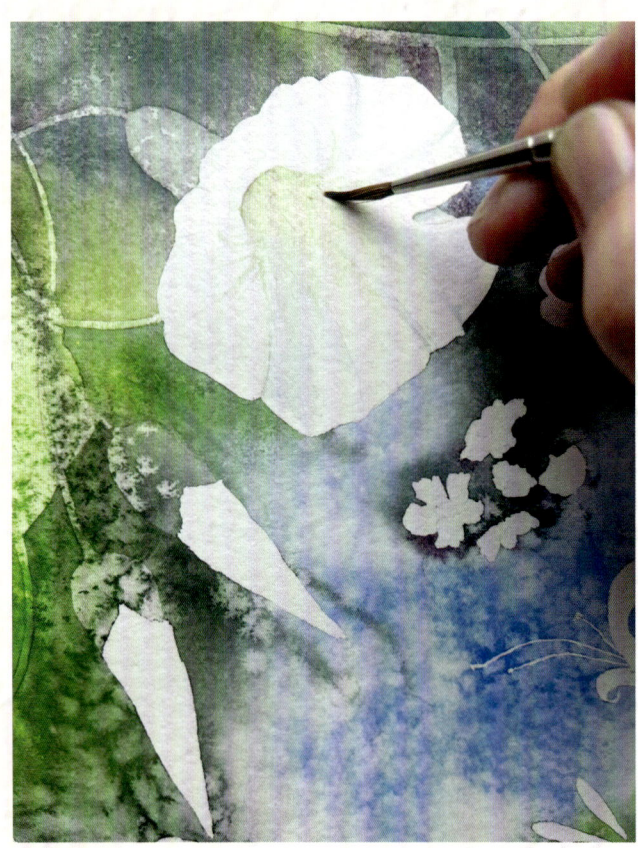

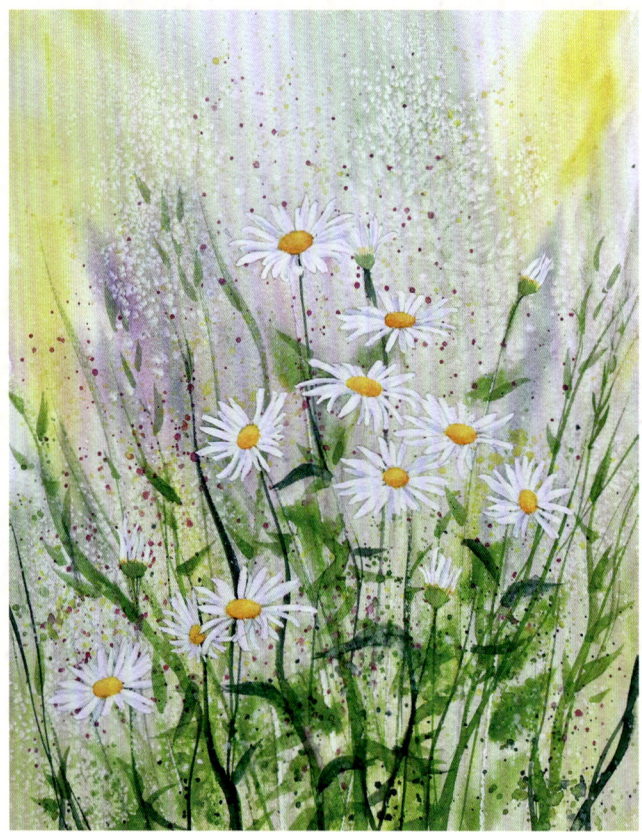

Colour placement

The sparsity of colour seen in white or pale flowers means that when adding paint, the *where* and the *what* of this hue is doubly important. Get your shading wrong, and your bloom will appear lumpy and misshapen, no matter how carefully you outlined the silhouette in pencil.

Most flowers have a variety of natural curves to them. They can sometimes be pronounced, as in tulips or fuchsias, or something more subtle, like the flatter faces of anemones or geraniums. Some, like hedge bindweed (see pages 86–91), have a deep trumpet shape with pronounced curves, which provide an obvious placement for shadows. Others, such as the ox-eye daises (see pages 26–31), only require a touch of shading. Careful observation and sketchbook practice is your friend here.

It is also vitally important to consider where the light source is coming from within your composition, as this will help you, naturally, to determine the shadow placement, too.

Tip

When planning pale flowers, try to keep your pencil marks light. Any heavy lines will show clearly through pale, soft washes. While having some visible pencil marks can be useful (e.g. to provide guidance for folds in petals that require painted shadows), it's worth trying to keep your lines faint to achieve a pale, ethereal quality in the finished painting.

Shadow colours

In the most general terms, blue and mauve tones are ideal for shading white flowers, as most shadows have a naturally cool hue. Paints such as French Ultramarine, Cobalt Blue and Dioxazine Purple, are excellent starting points, although these must be used with care when applying them as shadow tones, as all these colours are very richly pigmented.

It can also be useful to examine whether a white flower has other hints of colour in it. For example, the angelic white of the calla lily shades into yellowish green hues where the bloom meets the stem. This can be a useful guide to choosing your shadow colours, as choosing a similar warm to cool tone to your plant's foliage helps create pleasing tonal harmony.

For example, if you are painting a plant that has blue-green foliage, using a blue colour to add shadows (such as French Ultramarine) is ideal. In contrast, for a warm white flower that tends more towards cream, using a warmer-toned blend, such as Raw Sienna with a touch of Cobalt Blue or Cerulean can be very effective.

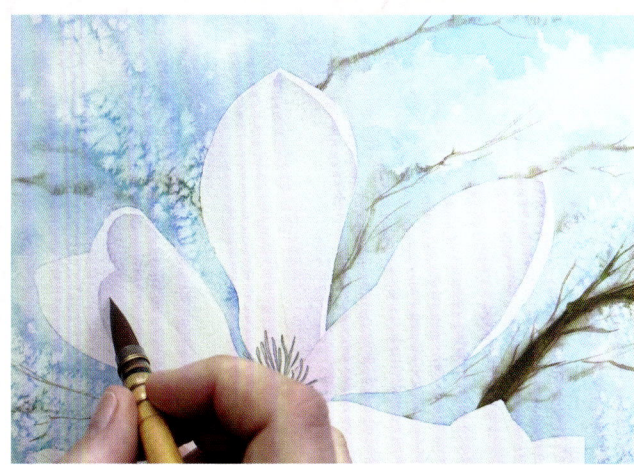

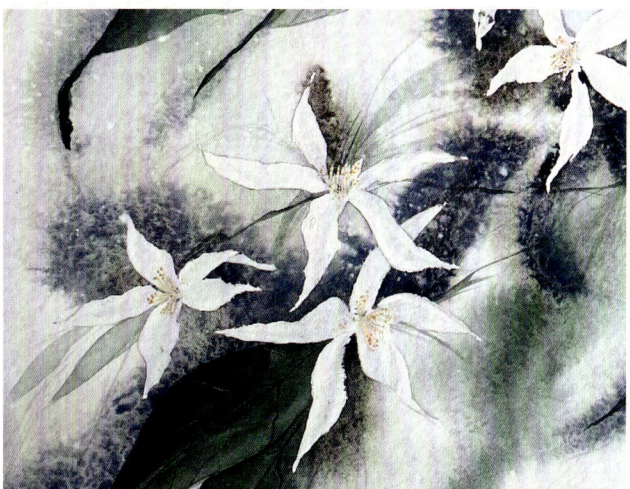

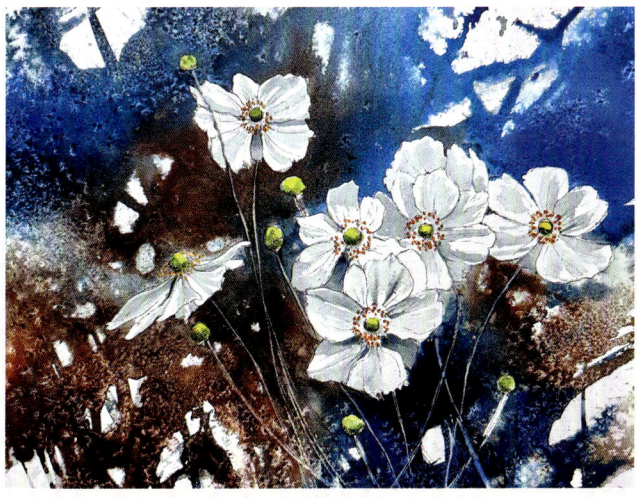

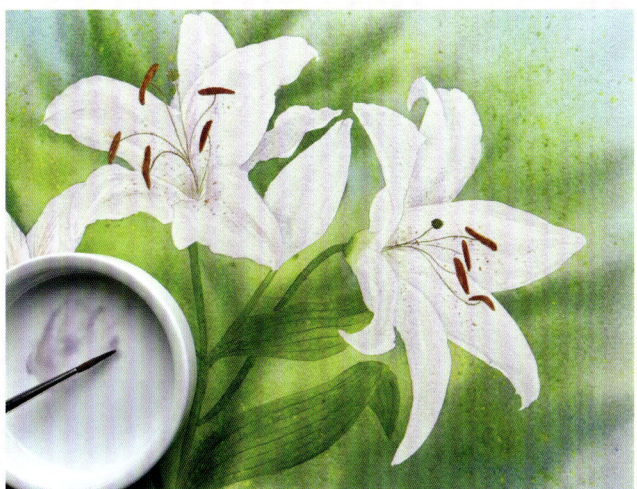

Tone and contrast

Just because a flower is white, doesn't mean we can neglect tone; this is a trap that's all too easy to fall into. There is a temptation to assume that we must only use very watery, light-value paint for pale-coloured blooms; and while this is true in some respects, it is important to remember that white flowers, like all painted flowers, need a variety of tonal values and areas of contrast to help them shine.

One way to approach this in your work is to use the plant's own foliage as a backdrop when setting up your initial composition. Try placing darker leaves behind your white flowers to emphasize the contrast of tone and colour. This is particularly useful for botanical-style paintings or illustrations that lack a colourful background.

Consider, too, that the central anatomy of a flower (the stigma, stamen, etc.) will often benefit from being painted in a dark-value colour, which can help white-petalled blooms to shine. Consider, for example, plants such as poppies, anemones and daisies, with colourful centres that can provide useful contrast to the pale, fragile beauty of the surrounding petals.

Signs of Spring

Flowering blossoms of magnolia trees are regularly one of the first harbingers of springtime. With their clusters of large, pale petals tilting upwards, they always make me think of cupped hands filled with light.

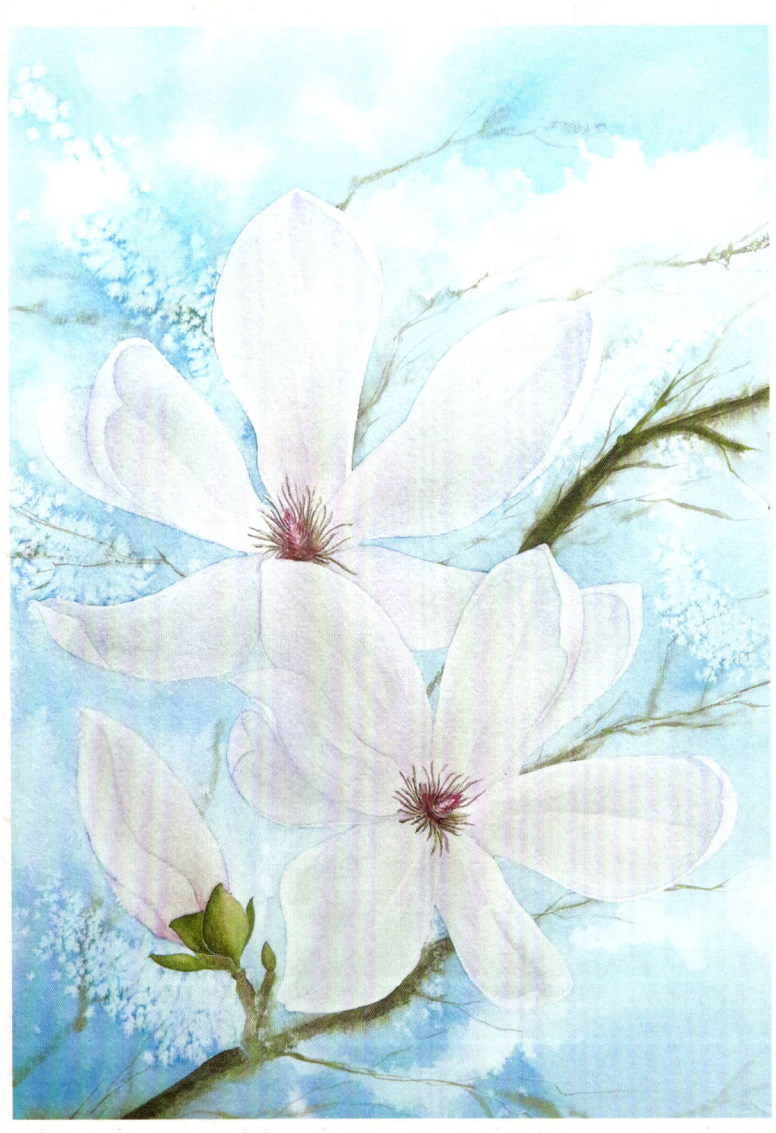

COLOURS NEEDED

Winsor Blue	Raw Umber	Burnt Sienna	Olive Green	Dioxazine Purple	French Ultramarine	Quinacridone Magenta
		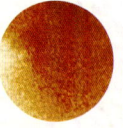				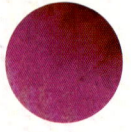

Sometimes, the simplest compositions can be the most rewarding to paint. Placed against the soft blue of a fresh spring sky, these large-scale magnolia flowers offer the opportunity to master the art of shading white petals. With their simple, cup-like shape and gentle, undulating curves, these are great flowers to get to grips with, especially as their larger size means they don't require too much fiddly detail.

Painting white petals can be a tricky business – technically, we're using blue and mauve hues to paint the shadows cast upon the petals, and leaving the white of the paper to do the rest. Take time to look at the direction that each petal curves, and consider where the darker patches would naturally fall. For more guidance, refer to the Focus On: Painting White Flowers (see pages 78–79) as necessary.

Setting up

To avoid using an excess of masking fluid, this painting is prepared by adding a line of masking fluid around the edge of each petal, to protect them from the sky blue background wash. While it's certainly possible to cover the entirety of the magnolia flowers with masking fluid if you prefer, strictly speaking, it's not necessary.

Begin by transferring the outline from the template onto hot-pressed watercolour paper, using the method described on page 21. Add a line of masking fluid around the edges of the magnolia flowers using the old, small pointed brush (see page 13). Once the mask has set, tape your pencil outline onto a board and lay it flat, ready to begin.

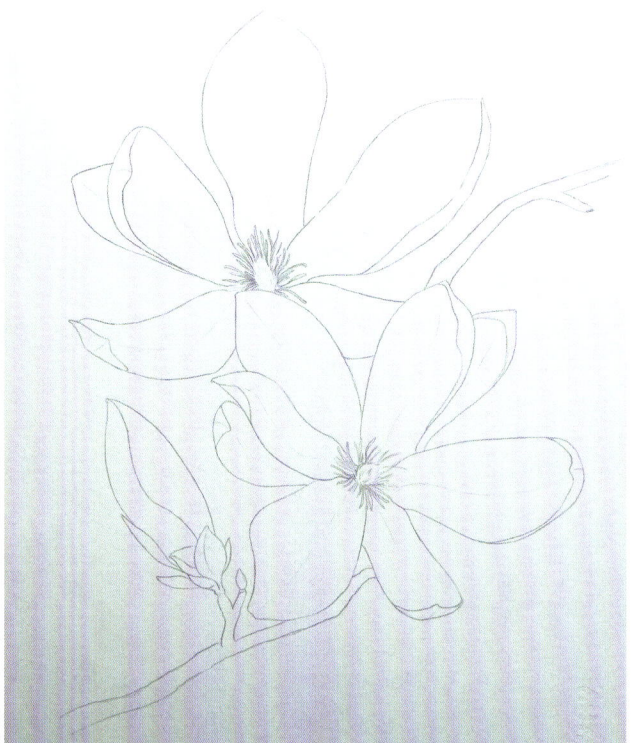

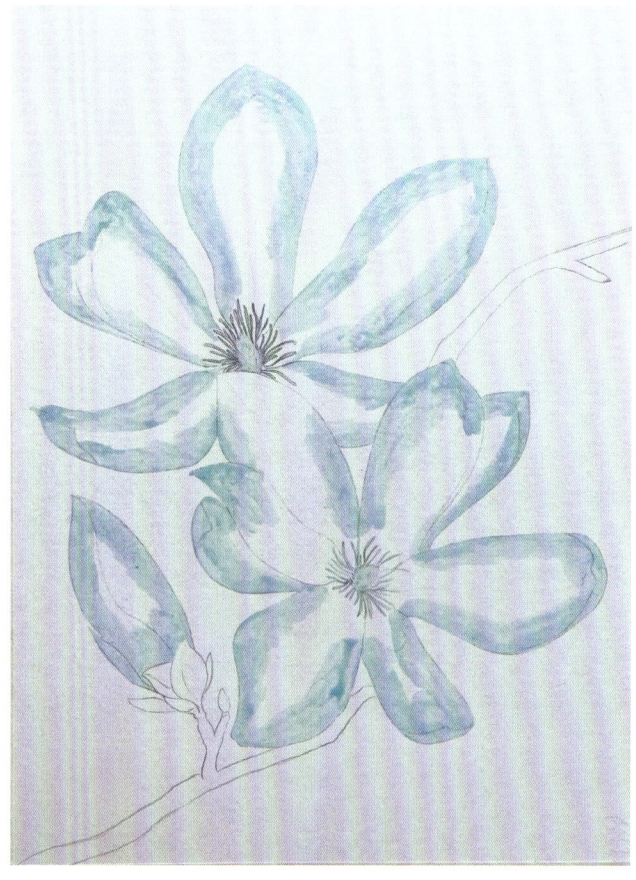

YOU WILL NEED

- *140lb (300gsm) hot-pressed watercolour paper*
- *Sketchbook or sketching paper and tracing paper*
- *Masking fluid and old, small pointed brush*
- *Adhesive eraser*
- *HB pencil and eraser*
- *Painting board and decorator's masking tape*
- *Sponge and absorbent kitchen paper*
- *Palette with several mixing wells*
- *Fine table salt*
- *Size 20 mop brush*
- *Size Small sword liner brush*
- *Size 2 synthetic quill brush*
- *Size 3 round brush*
- *Size 0 round detail brush*

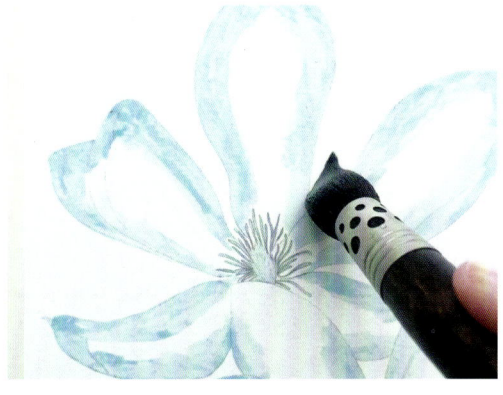

Use the delicate tip of the mop to work clean water in between the masked-out edges of the petals, making sure the whole area has been wetted before adding colour.

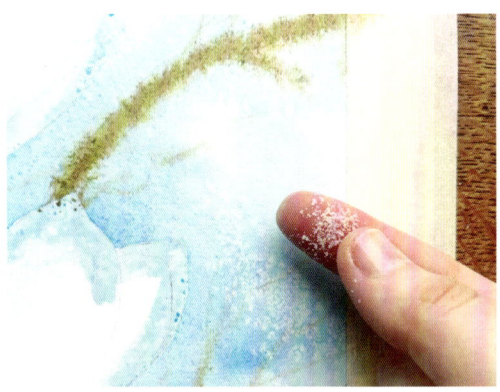

Sprinkle the salt in small clusters to create delicate pockets of interest in the wash; try to avoid throwing it over the entire background.

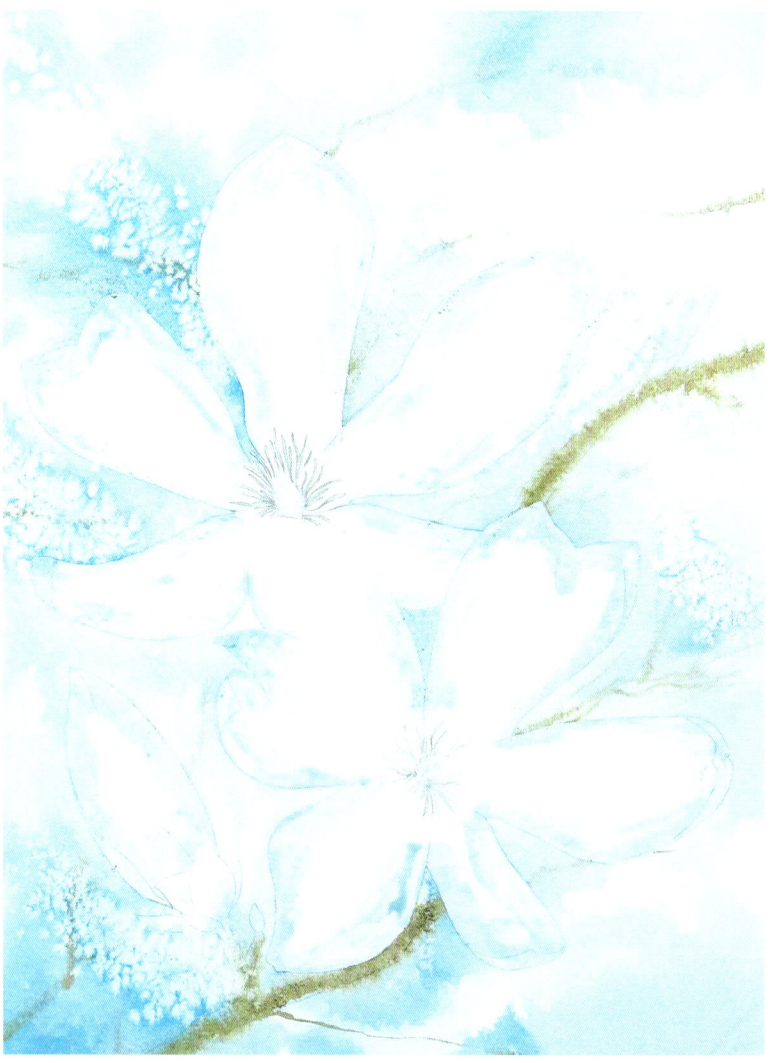

STAGE 1

Wet the paper around the masked-out flower shapes with clean water and allow to soak in for 30 seconds. Mix a large, mid-value well of Winsor Blue and use the size 20 mop brush to dab in a soft wash of colour across the entire background. Leave a little space between dabs for the wet paint to find its way, creating hints of cloud. Use clean, crumpled kitchen paper to lift away colour in some parts, creating stronger patches of pale cloud drifting between the blooms.

Mix up a well of mid-value Raw Umber, and using the sword liner brush, add this wet-in-wet, following the pencil lines of the stems. Next, use the tip of the sword liner to add some loose, whippy marks across the background, creating the impression of soft-focus background twigs. Sprinkle in a little salt and leave to dry.

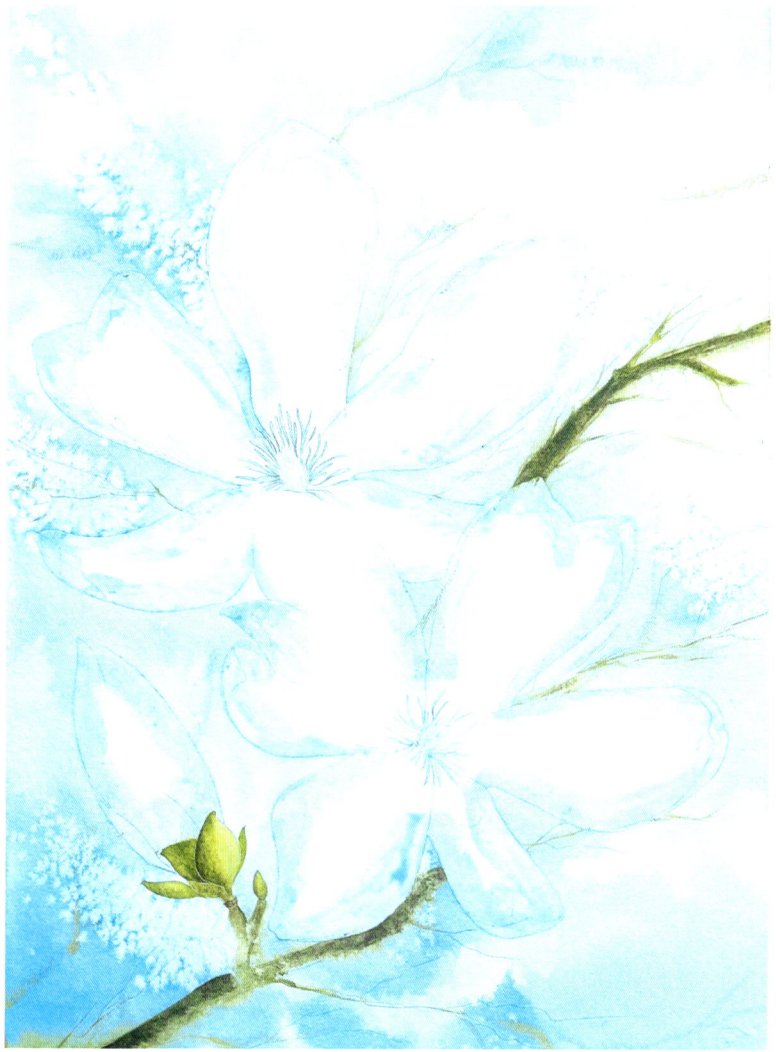

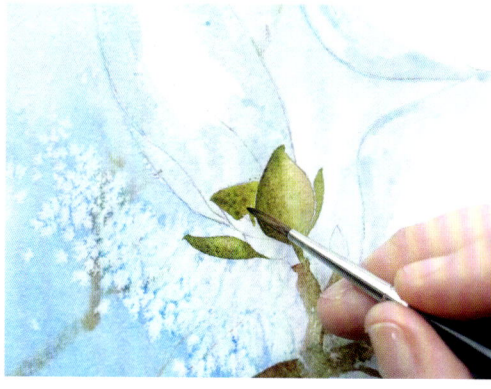

Vary the colour within an area, allowing it to be darker in tone on one side, and adding a little more water to your paint mix to create a paler hue on the side that is turned towards the light.

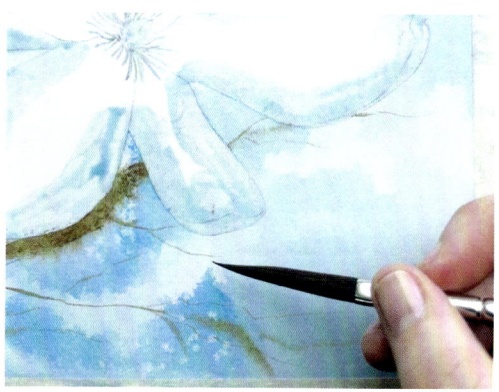

STAGE 2

Once dry, brush away any remaining salt with a clean brush. Mix two wells of mid-value Raw Umber. Add a touch of Burnt Sienna to one of these, creating a reddish brown. Use these colours and the size 3 round brush to add some hard-edged lines and details into the branches. Next, use the sword liner to add a handful more thin, twiggy marks. Allow to dry.

Now use the size 3 round and a blend of Olive Green and Burnt Sienna to paint the lower part of the magnolia bud. Add some touches of green among the branches, then leave to dry fully.

Layer some of the hard-edged lines across the soft-focus ones to create the illusion of criss-crossing twigs and branches.

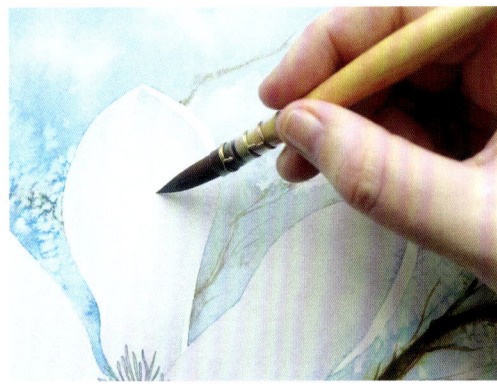

Follow the flower's natural curve, and allow some white paper to peek through in parts.

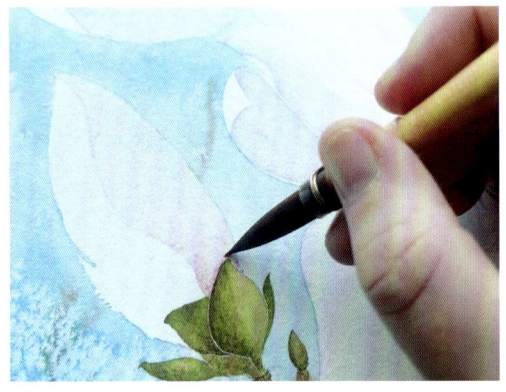

Add slightly stronger magenta to the lower part of the magnolia bud, as the outside of the petal tends to have slightly richer colour.

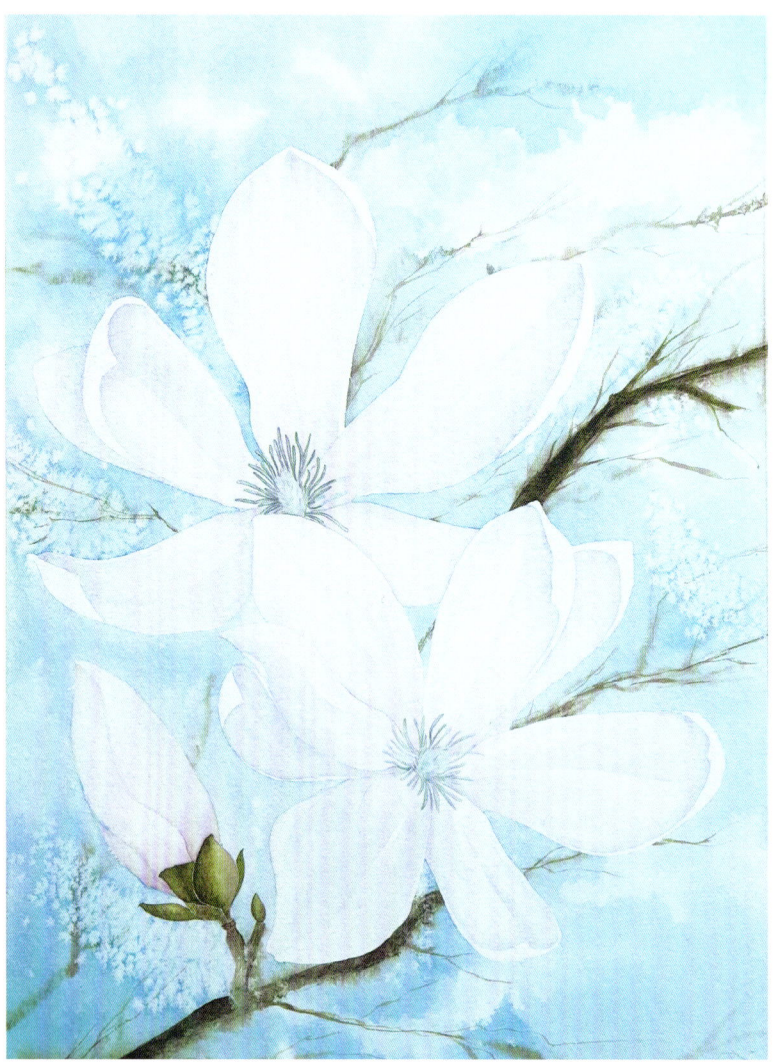

STAGE 3

Once dry, remove the mask from the magnolia petals using the adhesive eraser. Mix up three wells of very light-value colour: French Ultramarine, Dioxazine Purple and Quinacridone Magenta.

Using the size 2 quill brush, paint each petal one at a time, using the purple and the ultramarine to add patches of shadow around the edge of each petal. Tint the lower quarter of each petal (the area closest to the centre) with a little magenta. Leave to fully dry.

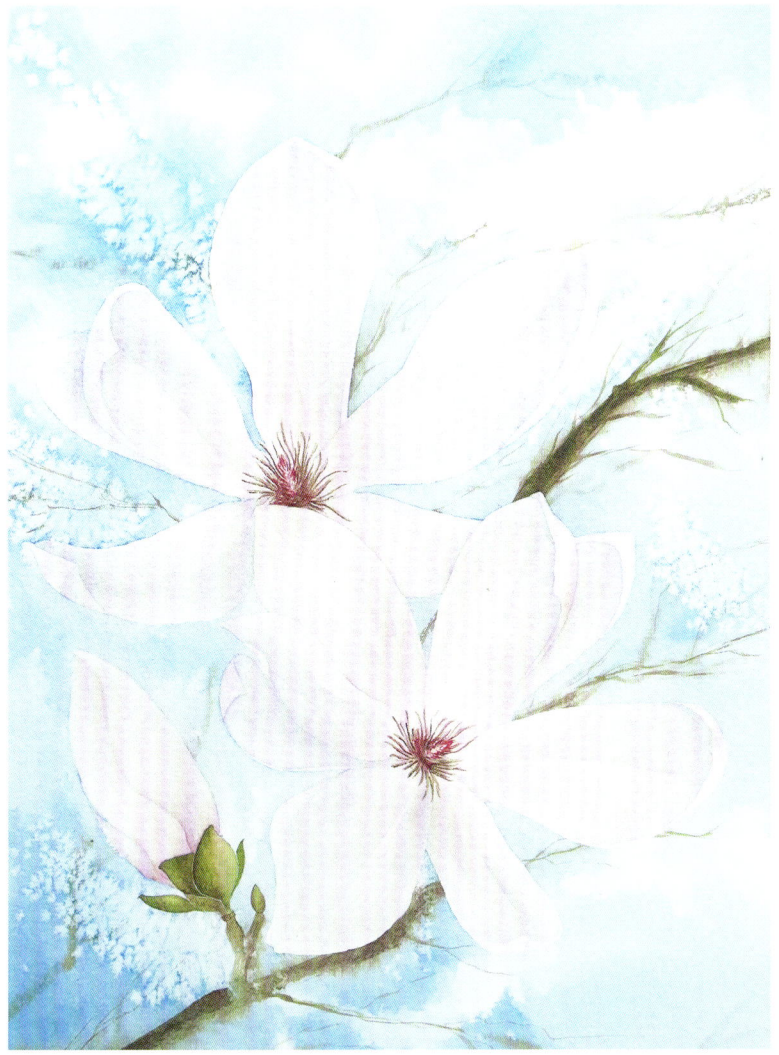

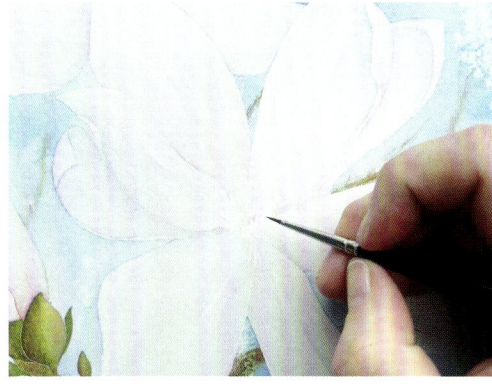

Slowly build layers of diagonal brush marks, following the natural shape and angle of the flower centre.

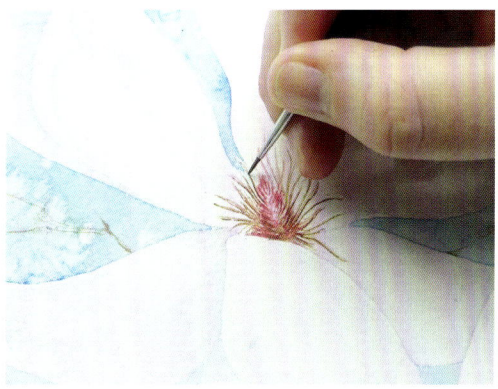

Laying a very fine line of green along the shaded side of the filaments will help them pop out beautifully.

STAGE 4

Remove the mask from the central stamens. Using the light-value Quinacridone Magenta and the size 0 detail brush, add hints of pink to the furled edges of the magnolia petals.

Now mix up a dark-value well of Quinacridone Magenta, alongside some more dark-value Olive Green and Burnt Sienna. Use these colours to build up the pattern of the central stamens by layering up a series of short, angled brushstrokes. Use the same colours to tint the delicate filaments around the flower centres, laying a thin line of rich green beneath each one to add a hint of shadow.

Bramble Ramble

This painting is a celebration of wild and wayward things! Hedge bindweed is a stubborn and tenacious climber that is often seen among dense clumps of bramble, turning its snowy white flowers towards the sun. In this painting, the contrast between richly coloured blackberries, the delicate honeysuckle and the eye-catching bindweed flowers creates a lively and enticing composition.

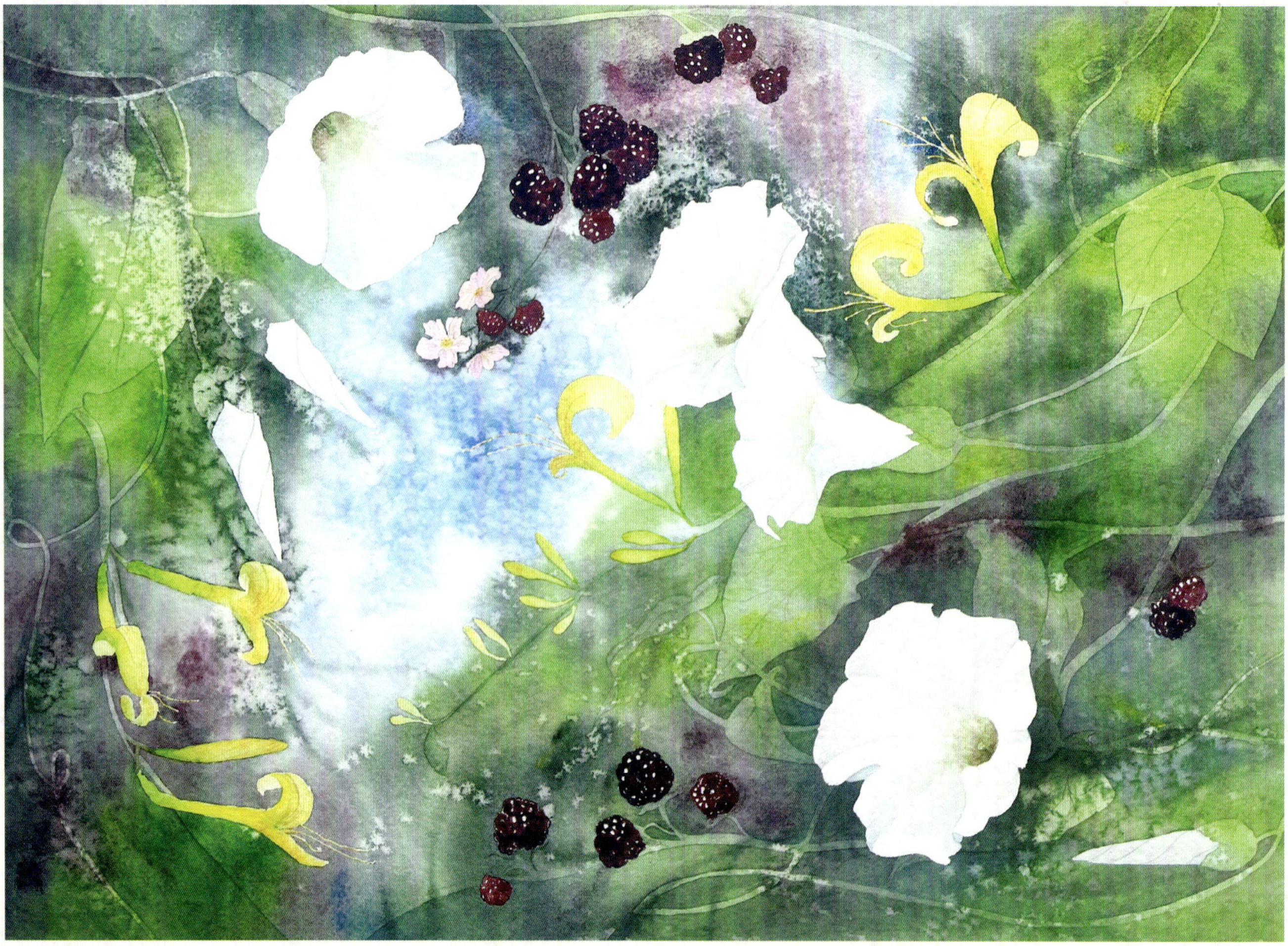

COLOURS NEEDED

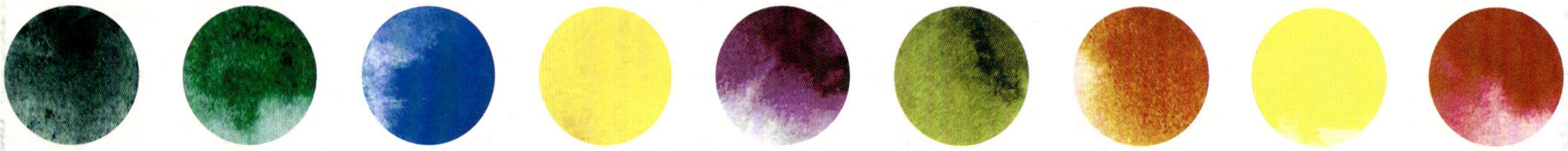

Perylene Green	Hooker's Green	French Ultramarine	Transparent Yellow	Permanent Magenta	Olive Green	Burnt Sienna	Lemon Yellow	Permanent Alizarin Crimson
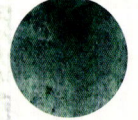	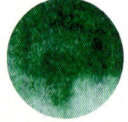			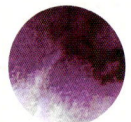		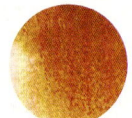		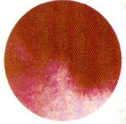

While unwelcome in most gardens, there is no denying that the luminous white trumpets of hedge bindweed are a thing of astonishing beauty. This plant can be regularly spotted tangling through untended hedgerows or as glittering patches in wasteland.

The bramble, too, is often viewed as an unwelcome garden interloper; so, this composition is a quiet celebration of the unloved beauty of wild things. Thin strands of honeysuckle trailing across the painting add delicacy and additional colour contrast when placed beside the rich dark hues of the ripening berries.

This painting uses the combination of a busy, soft-focus background wash and negative painting technique to pull the shapes of bud, bloom and stem out of the painting's background colours. Prior planning is essential when using negative painting, so take your time with this one, and refer to the section on negative painting (see page 25).

Setting up

Begin by transferring the outline from the template onto hot-pressed watercolour paper, using the method described on page 21. Mask out the flowers, buds and berries using masking fluid and the old, small pointed brush (see page 13). Once the mask has set, tape your pencil outline onto a board and lay it flat, ready to begin.

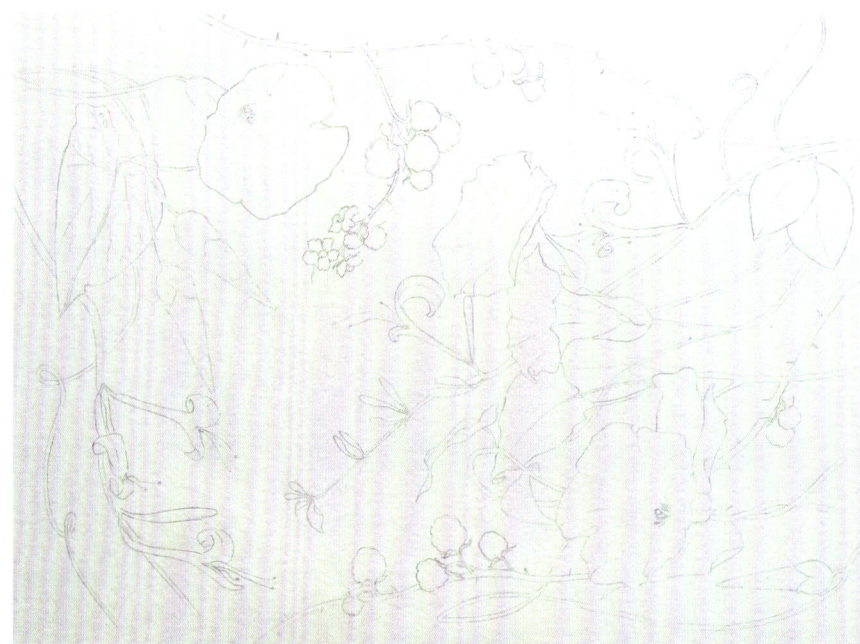

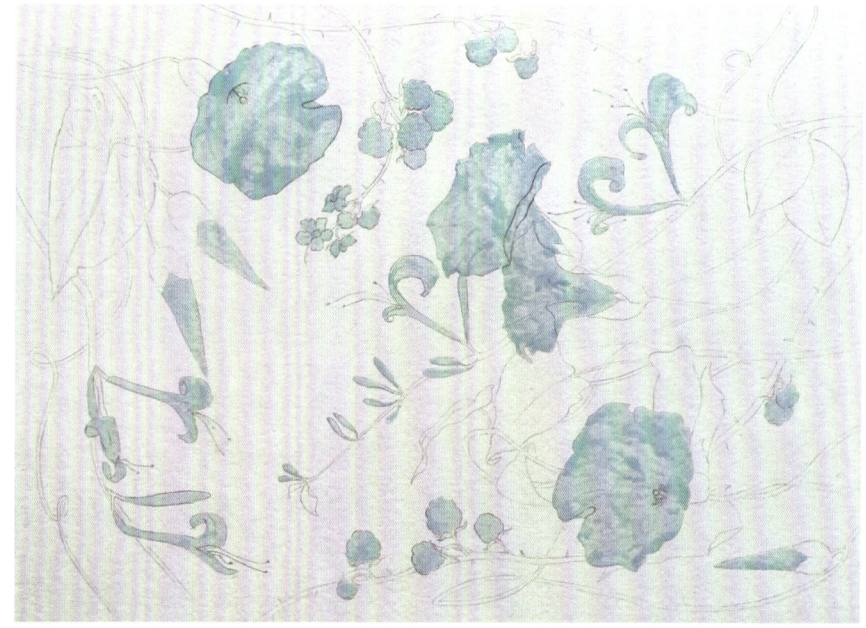

YOU WILL NEED

- 140lb (300gsm) hot-pressed watercolour paper
- Sketchbook or sketching paper and tracing paper
- Masking fluid and old, small pointed brush
- Adhesive eraser
- HB pencil and eraser
- Painting board and decorator's masking tape
- Sponge and absorbent kitchen paper

- Palette with several mixing wells
- Fine table salt
- Size 20 mop brush
- ½in (1.25cm) oval wash brush
- Size 2 synthetic quill brush
- Size 3 round brush
- Size 0 round detail brush

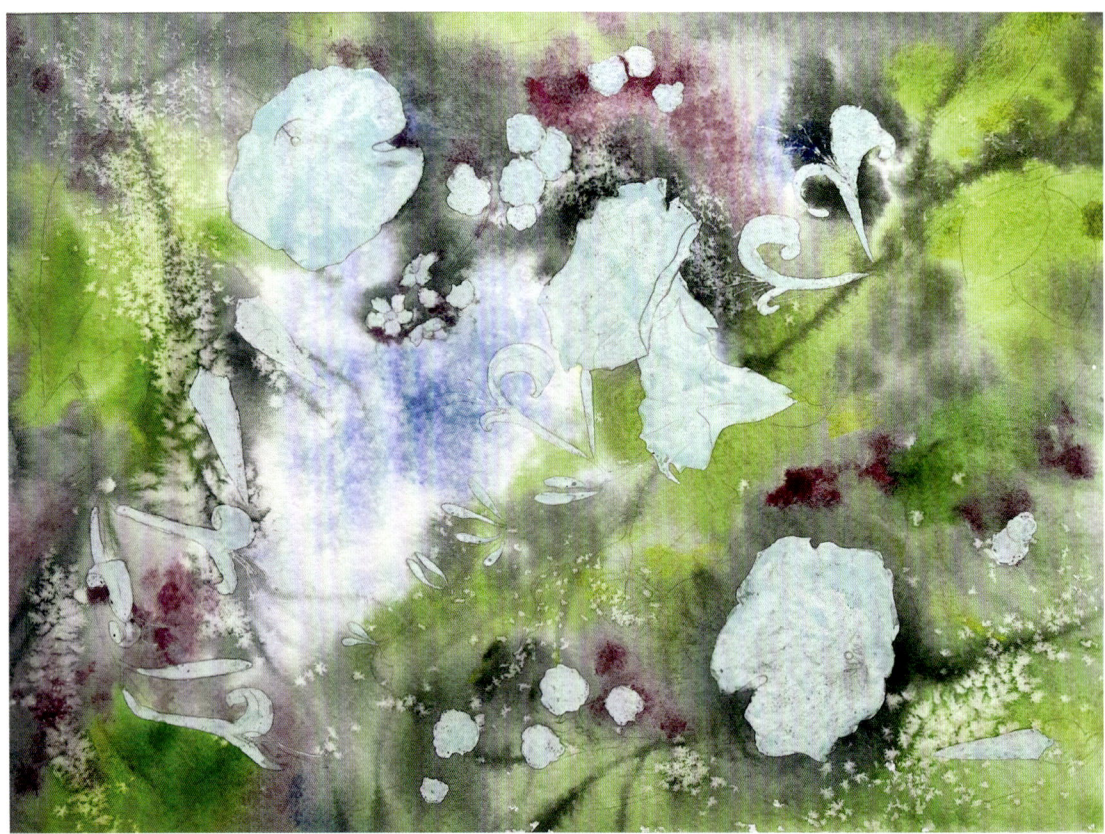

STAGE 1

Prepare five wells of rich colour, enough to cover the entire background: you will need Perylene Green, Hooker's Green, French Ultramarine, Transparent Yellow and Permanent Magenta. Wet the paper all over using the size 20 mop brush and allow the water to sink in for 30 seconds.

Use the mop and all five colours to create a patchy, soft-focus wash, using the technique described on page 23. Into this, using the oval wash brush, add some stronger dabs of magenta to mimic clusters of berries.

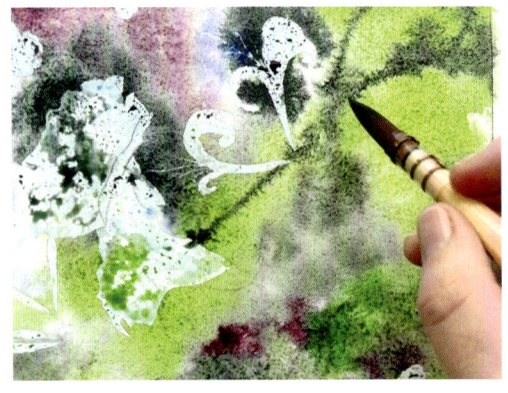

The fine point and springy bristles of the synthetic quill brush make it ideal for adding lines of stronger colour into a wet wash.

While the wash is still wet, use the size 2 quill brush to draw sympathetic lines across areas of colour to mimic the tangled bindweed stems already pencilled in. Add a sprinkle of salt and leave to dry.

Tip

Leave some areas of blue clear when creating the soft-focus wash to create the impression of a bright sky peeking through a patch of tangled bramble.

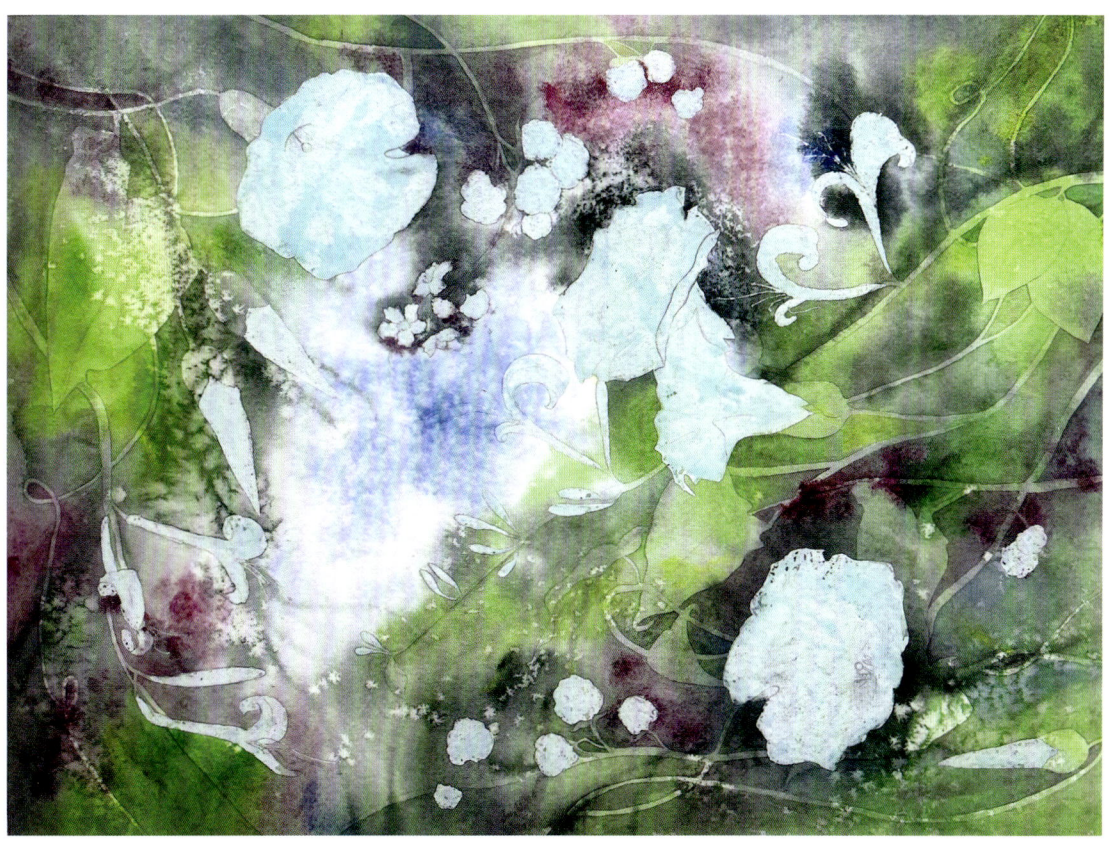

STAGE 2

Once dry, brush away any remaining salt with a clean brush. Mix light-value, watery glazes of the same five paints used in the previous stage: Perylene Green, Hooker's Green, French Ultramarine, Transparent Yellow and Permanent Magenta.

Now use the negative painting technique (page 25) to pull the stem and leaf details out of the colour wash, using the size 3 round brush and the size 0 detail brush. Negatively paint around the bindweed and honeysuckle, concentrating on the areas at the edges of the painting. Leave this to dry fully.

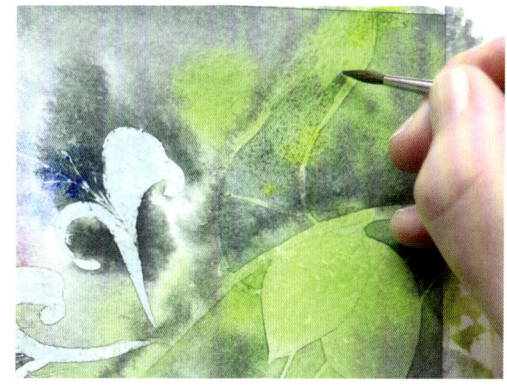

Use the detail brush to create crisp, sharp edges when pulling the shapes of leaves and stems out of the wash using negative painting.

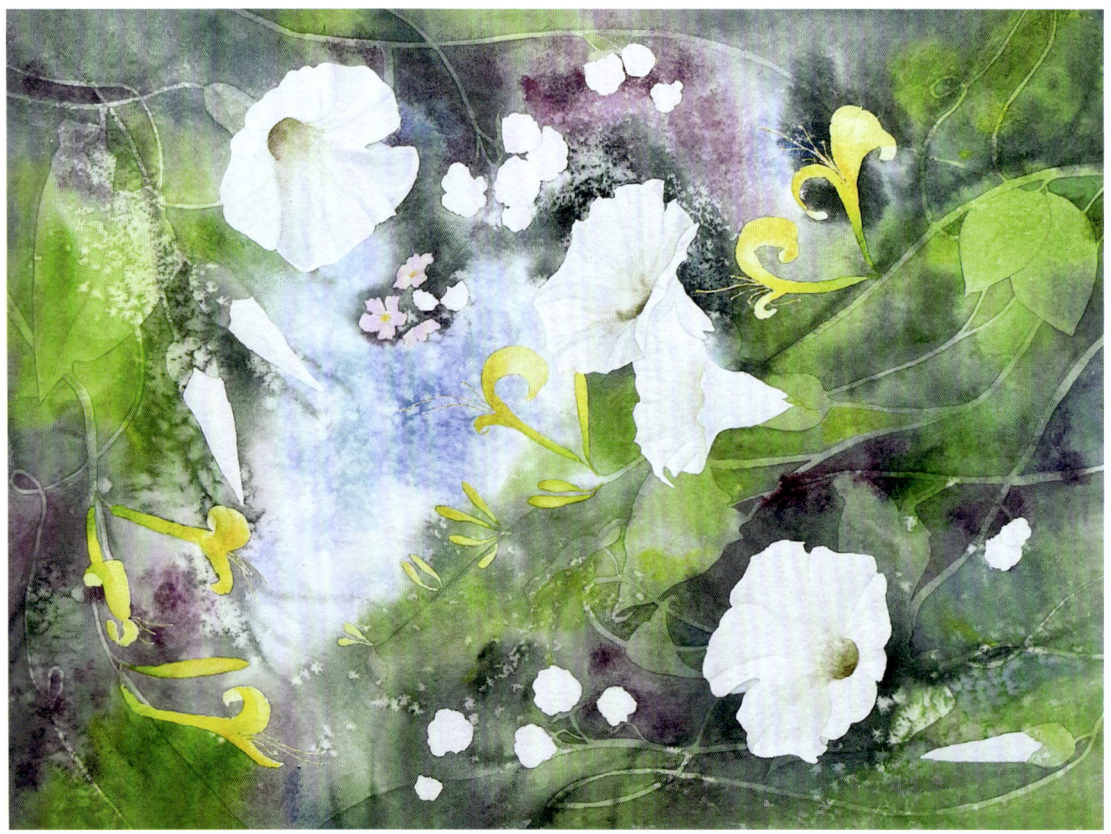

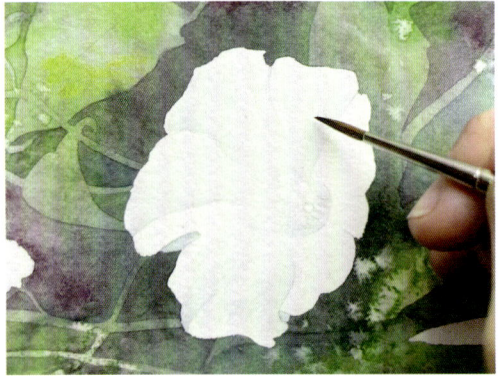

Using the palest wash of colour to lightly tint the bindweed flowers will help to maintain that characteristic glowing white appearance against the surrounding rich tones.

STAGE 3

Once dry, remove the masking fluid using the adhesive eraser. Now add colour to the blooms using the size 3 and size 0 round brushes. For the bindweed flowers, tint the white of the paper with light patches of French Ultramarine and Perylene Green to indicate shadows, and use dark-value Olive Green and a touch of Burnt Sienna to add colour to the flower's inner hollow.

For the honeysuckle, mix a little Hooker's Green with Lemon Yellow to create a vibrant mid-green, and use this alongside Lemon Yellow and Transparent Yellow to paint the honeysuckle blooms.

Use a little dilute Permanent Magenta to add a hint of pink blush to the small bramble flowers, and Transparent Yellow to tint the centres.

Tip

Don't forget to think about shadows for the narrow sections of the hedge bindweed buds and honeysuckle flowers, keeping the lighter areas towards the source of light.

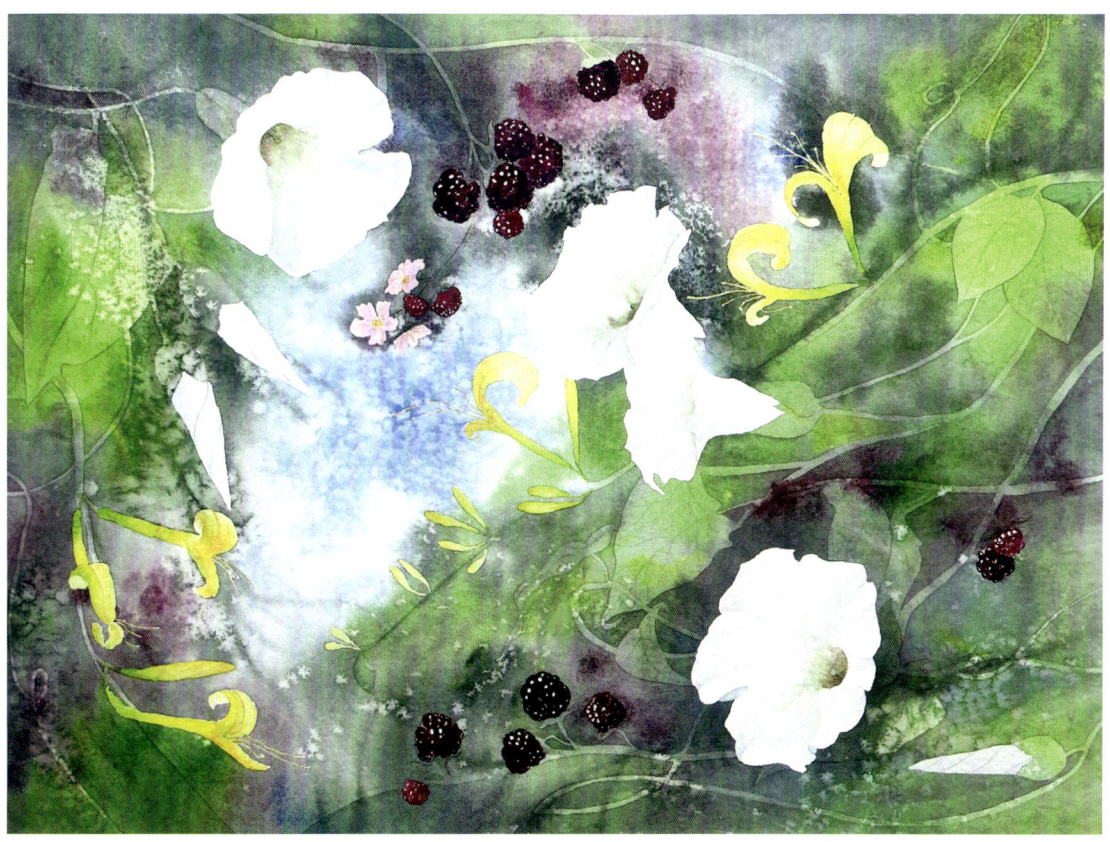

STAGE 4

Mix three mid-value wells of Permanent Magenta. Tint one with French Ultramarine to create a deep blueish-purple hue, and tint another with Permanent Alizarin Crimson to create a reddish colour.

Use these and the size 0 detail brush to add colour to the bramble berries. Use the darker colour for the larger, riper berries, and the redder tone for the smaller, unripe ones.

Next, use the detail brush to paint the final details: use a little more Olive Green to add a hint of the inner stamens to the bindweed flowers, as well as to paint a few subtle veins on the leaves. Finally, use Transparent Yellow to add fine directional lines to the honeysuckle.

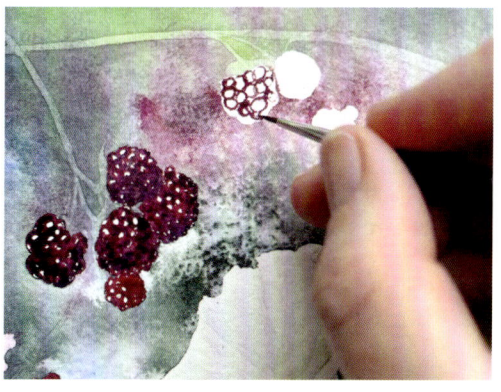

Leave some small flecks of white unpainted paper to show the light glinting off the rounded, glossy surfaces of the berries.

Tip
When adding directional lines to the honeysuckle make them of different lengths, following the curve of the petal's edges to help emphasize its shape.

Glossary

ARTISTIC LICENCE Minor changes or deliberate deviations from the standard form or realism for artistic purposes.

BLEND To smoothly merge together marks or colours.

COLOUR TEMPERATURE A way to describe the relative warmth or coolness of a colour.

COLOUR PALETTE A set of colours chosen to create a particular painting.

COLOUR WHEEL A circular depiction of primary and secondary colours organized via their relationship with one another.

COMPLEMENTARY COLOURS Pairs of colours that contrast or 'complement' one another. Traditionally, the pairing of one primary colour and one secondary colour, the latter mixed from the other two primaries (for example blue and orange, which is mixed from yellow and red)

COMPOSITION The way in which key elements of a painting are arranged in a particular way to be artistically pleasing.

GLAZE A transparent layer of paint that is brushed over other paint that has already dried.

GOUACHE An opaque style of watercolour paint.

HARD EDGES Paint applied in such a way that the edge of the brushstroke remains crisp, usually occurring when painting wet-on-dry.

HIGHLIGHTS The lightest part of the painting, often shown by preserving the white of the paper.

LIFTING OUT A technique whereby paint can be removed to correct mistakes or to lighten certain areas using a brush or paper towel.

LINE WORK The preliminary pencil or ink outlines drawn in preparation for a painting.

LOOSE PAINTING An expressive style of painting that aims more to capture the 'feel' of the subject, rather than focusing on detail.

MASKING A technique to preserve either the white of the paper or a layer of paint from subsequent additions of colour.

NEGATIVE PAINTING A method of defining a shape by painting the surrounding space to reveal the shape, rather than painting the shape itself.

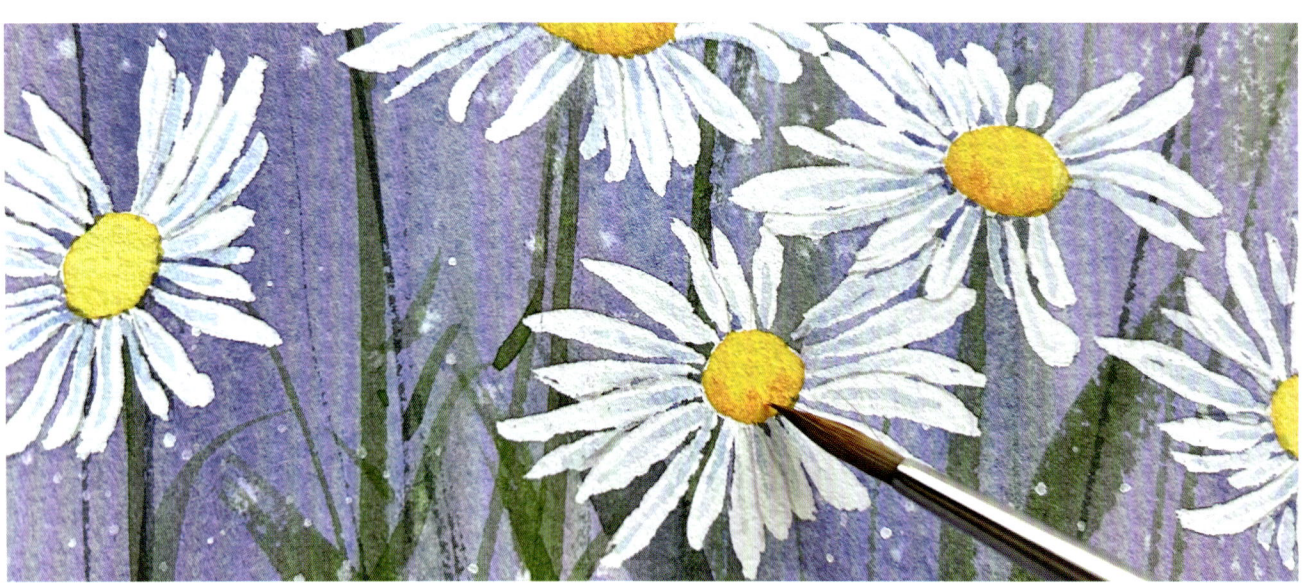

PRIMARY COLOURS Colours that cannot be created through mixing other colours: red, yellow, and blue.

RULE OF ODDS A compositional principle that suggests that an odd number of elements in a composition is more visually appealing than an even number.

RULE OF THIRDS A common guideline designed to aid composition by positioning points of interest in the upper or lower thirds of the painting to help them appear more visually pleasing.

SECONDARY COLOURS Colours which can be created by mixing two primary colours, for example mixing yellow and blue to create green.

SKETCH A rough drawing or painting created to work through preliminary ideas for a painting, and used to assist in creating a more polished finished picture.

SOFT EDGES Paint applied in such a way that the edge of the brushstroke softens and sometimes disappears, usually occurring when painting wet-in-wet.

SPATTER A pattern of dots and spots randomly created by tapping a loaded paintbrush over part of the painting.

STILL LIFE An art genre where everyday objects (including flowers) are arranged together into pleasing compositions for painting.

TEMPLATE A pre-designed pattern used for making copies.

TEXTURE The surface quality of a painting.

THUMBNAIL SKETCHES A series of small preliminary sketches used to test out compositional ideas.

TONAL VALUE The lightness or darkness of tones or colours, e.g., how dark or pale a colour is.

WASH A thin layer of colour often applied to a larger area than a single brushstroke can cover, e.g., a sky.

WET-IN-WET A technique of painting directly into a wet surface, allowing the watercolour paint to soften, blend and diffuse on the paper.

WET-ON-DRY A technique of painting directly onto dry paper without pre-wetting it, or painting onto a wash that has already dried.

Suppliers

UNITED KINGDOM

Lawrence Art Shop
www.lawrence.co.uk

Jackson's Art
www.jacksonsart.com

Bromleys Art Supplies
www.artsupplies.co.uk

Cass Art
www.cassart.co.uk

Curtisward Art Supplies
www.curtisward.com

SAA Art
www.saa.co.uk

UNITED STATES

Blick Art Materials
www.dickblick.com

Jerry's Artarama
www.jerrysartarama.com

Cheap Joe's
www.cheapjoes.com

About the Authors

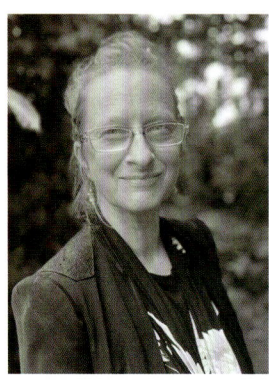

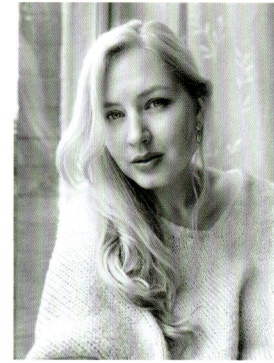

Lois Davidson is an English watercolour artist with over 40 years of experience. Her first book, *Landscapes in Watercolour*, was published by GMC in 2024, and is both an instructional guide for fledgeling painters and a celebration of the natural, rugged beauty of the world around us. She has been painting professionally since 2020, and was shortlisted for the Jackson's Painting Prize in 2021. She offers painting tutorials, watercolour workshops, and runs a popular online art community on Patreon. She sells her paintings across the world and exhibits her work locally and online.

Morgaine Davidson is an avid creative with a passion for art and wildlife. Since graduating from university with a master's degree in English & Creative Writing, she has worked in a variety of different media, experimenting with combining art and the written word. She has penned articles for Jackson's Art Blog, and her fiction has been shortlisted for a number of prizes, including the Mslexia Best Women's Short Fiction 2023. She currently teaches watercolour painting online via YouTube and Patreon, specializing in capturing the liminal beauty of the natural world.

Together, mother-daughter team Lois and Morgaine run a successful YouTube channel which has over 123,000 subscribers and demonstrates traditional and experimental watercolour techniques.

Acknowledgements

We would like to take this opportunity to thank the people who helped us make this book possible: Many thanks to Jonathan Bailey for inviting us to write this book, and to Tom, Robin and Ellie, the wonderful team at GMC Publishing, whose expertise and support have helped turn this vision into a reality. We also are indebted to the many students of watercolour and fellow artists, who have followed our artistic journeys online and offered endless encouragement.

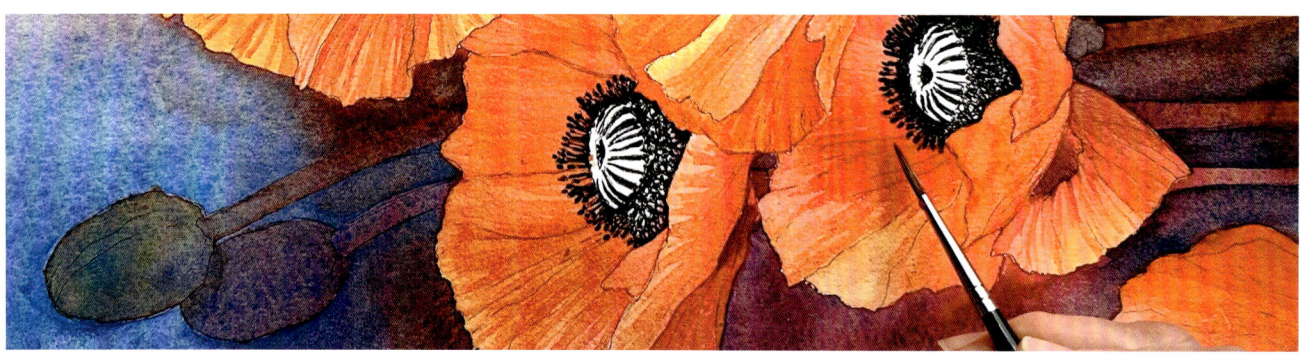

Index

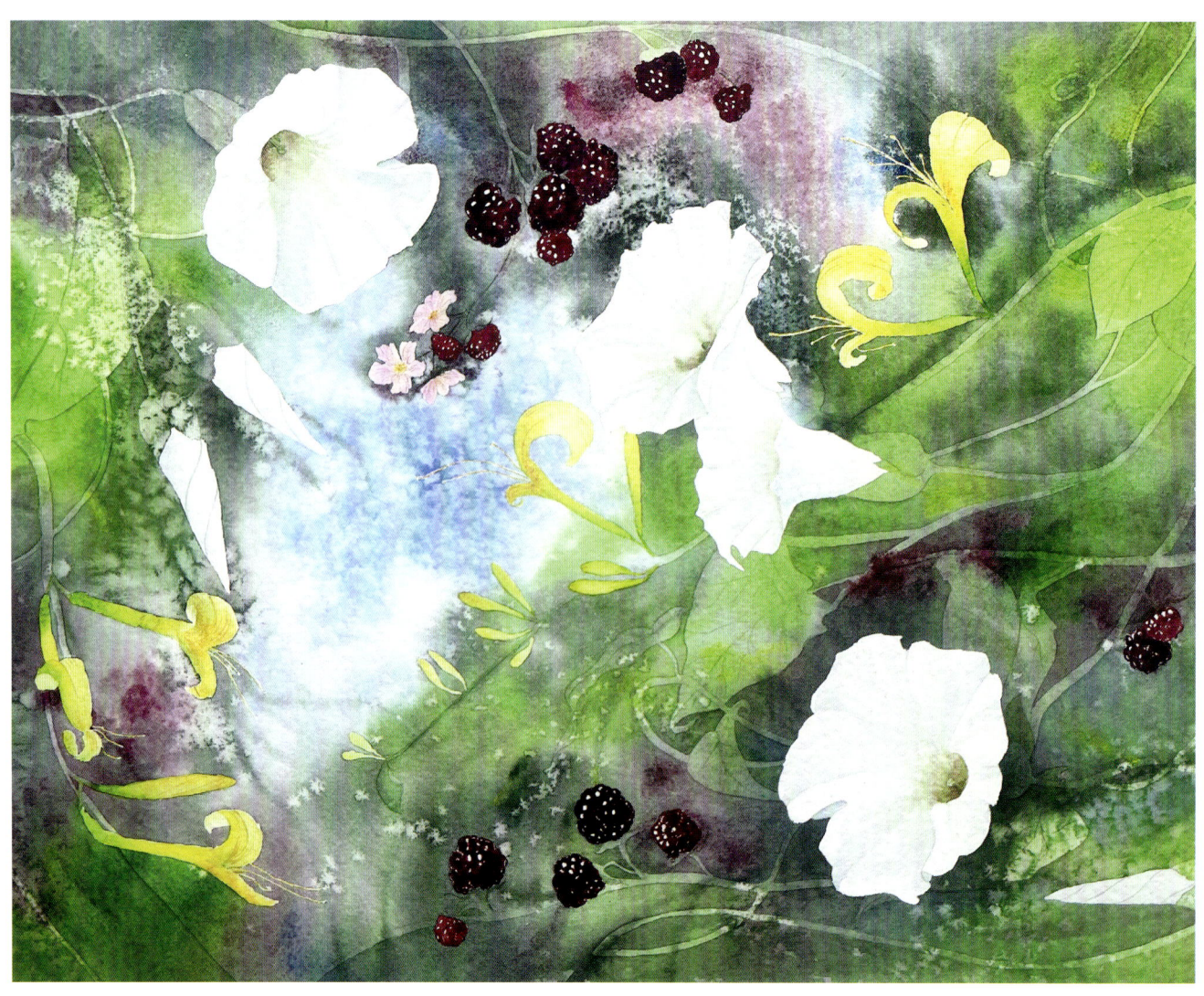

To order a book, contact:

GMC Publications Ltd

Castle Place, 166 High Street, Lewes, East Sussex, BN7 1XU

United Kingdom

Tel: +44 (0)1273 488005

www.gmcbooks.com